# So You Want to Write a Book

An Informational Guide to Planning, Writing, Editing, Publishing, and Marketing You Book

Douglas Owen

Tumbleweed Books
*Tumble through the pages of our books*

SO YOU WANT TO WRITE A BOOK
DOUGLAS OWEN

Tumbleweed Books
*Tumble through the pages of our books*

Tumbleweed Books
HTTP://TUMBLEWEEDBOOKS.CA
An imprint of DAOwen Publications

So You Want to Write a Book / Douglas Owen

ISBN 978-1-998029-27-3
EISBN 978-1-998029-28-0

This work is a non-fiction instructional guide. Names, examples, and incidents are the product of the author's memory and process of writing. The examples used have worked well for the writer of this book and all businesses, companies, steps and processes were researched and up to date at the time of the writing.

Cover art by MMT Productions

10 9 8 7 6 5 4 3 2 1

# Foreword

A Writer is someone for whom writing is more difficult than it is for other people.

–Thomas Mann 1875-1955

There are plenty of reasons why you might be holding this book right now.

- Maybe you want to write a book and don't know where to start.
- Maybe you've tried to write a book before, but things didn't exactly go according to plan.
- Or maybe a friend gave you this book because they think you've got "author" written all over you, and hey, it makes for a thoughtful gift.

Whatever the reason, here you are. And if someone gave this book to you, it's a sign they believe in you. Or they think you need a little nudge—or maybe both. Either way, congratulations! You've already taken the first step: preparing yourself for the wild ride of writing a book.

Now, let's be honest. Writing isn't easy. It takes self-discipline, a good chunk of your free time, and a willingness to sit alone with your thoughts—sometimes for hours. You'll have to wave goodbye to your loved ones when the muse strikes, lock the door, and dive headfirst into your story. But the payoff? Oh, it's worth it. Watching your ideas take shape on the page feels like magic. Plus, when you're done, you'll have something tangible to show for all that effort—a legacy in print.

Take Ron Schulz, for example. (Yes, that's his real name.) He decided to write about his life during the tumultuous 1960s and '70s—a way to capture his experiences and preserve them for future generations. Then there's S.A. Baker, who spins urban fantasy horror tales about a fictional town called Winterbourne. He's already got four books and a short story set there. Oh, and he also wrote a memoir about raising his daughter.

What drives writers like Ron and S.A.? The need to create, to share stories, and to put their thoughts into words. I'd recommend checking out works by small press authors like them. You might find inspiration, and maybe even see a bit of yourself in their creative drive.

So, do you fit into that category? If you're holding this book, there's a good chance you do. Let's find out together.

## *The Purpose of This Book*

Let's start with a truth bomb: writing a book is hard. It's exciting, sure. Romantic, even—if you picture yourself typing furiously in a dimly lit coffee shop, sipping something overpriced and organic. But it's also terrifying. You stare at the blank page, and it stares back, daring you to fill it with something worth reading. If you've ever had the thought, "How hard can it be?"—don't worry. By the end of this book, you'll have the answer. Spoiler: it's not as easy as it looks, but it's not impossible either.

So, why am I writing this book? For starters, because the world needs more books. Not just any books, but *your* book. Whether you want to share a gripping mystery, your grandmother's amazing pierogi recipe, or the secrets to surviving 20 Canadian winters without turning into a human icicle, you have something worth saying.

This book exists to help you say it.

### Who Is This For?

Are you a seasoned writer who's stuck in a rut? Great—you'll find something here to shake things up. Are you a complete beginner with zero clue where to start? Perfect, because that's where we'll begin. Are you someone who's Googled, "Can AI write my book for me?" Nice try, but let's put in some effort, eh?

This book is for anyone who's ever dreamed of writing a book and hasn't quite figured out how to get from "idea" to "finished manuscript." Whether you want to write the next great Canadian novel or a non-fiction guide to ice fishing strategies (which, by the way, I've read), this book will guide you through the process step-by-step.

## Why Write a Book?

Let's get real: writing a book isn't about fame or fortune. Sure, it *could* lead to those things, but if you're in it for money, you'd be better off investing in a Tim Hortons franchise. Writing a book is about something bigger. It's about:

1. **Sharing Your Story or Knowledge**
   - Everyone has something unique to share. Maybe you've lived through an experience that could help someone else. Maybe you've spent years mastering a skill and want to pass it on. Or maybe you've got an incredible imagination, and the world needs your stories.

Think of your book as a conversation starter—a way to connect with readers who might otherwise never hear what you have to say.

2. **Preserving Ideas and Memories**
   - Writing a book is like creating a time capsule. Long after we're gone, our words can stick around. That might sound a bit morbid, but it's also beautiful. Think about the books that have shaped your life. Your book could do that for someone else, decades—or even centuries—from now.
3. **Challenging Yourself**
   - Writing a book is the literary equivalent of running a marathon. It's long, tiring, and occasionally painful, but crossing the finish line is one of the

most rewarding experiences you'll ever have. Plus, it gives you bragging rights at parties.

4. **Learning About Yourself**
   o Writing forces you to dig deep—into your creativity, your patience, and your ability to handle rejection. (Pro tip: Keep chocolate nearby). Along the way, you might discover a lot about yourself that you didn't know before.

5. **Connecting with Others**
   o Books build bridges. Whether you're entertaining, educating, or inspiring your readers, you're creating a bond. And let's be honest: we could all use more connection these days.

### What Will This Book Teach You?

This isn't a book about sitting under a tree, waiting for inspiration to strike (although, if that works for you, go for it). It's about practical advice, useful tips, and a healthy dose of encouragement.

We'll cover everything from finding your idea to getting your book out into the world. Here's a sneak peek of what's ahead:

- **How to Find Your Big Idea:**
  o Don't worry if you haven't figured out what to write about yet. We'll explore ways to brainstorm and narrow down ideas that excite you.
- **Planning and Outlining:**
  o Some writers fly by the seat of their pants while others plan every detail like they're building a house. We'll help you figure out what works best for you.

- **Writing with Confidence:**
  - Struggling with imposter syndrome? You're not alone. We'll talk about how to silence that inner critic and get words on the page.
- **Editing Like a Pro:**
  - Writing is rewriting. We'll dive into how to polish your draft until it shines—and when to let go and call it done.
- **Publishing and Sharing Your Work:**
  - Whether you dream of seeing your book on a bookstore shelf or want to self-publish on Amazon, we'll break down the options.

### But I'm Not a "Real" Writer

Here's the thing: if you write, you're a writer. Full stop. You don't need a fancy degree, a book deal, or 100,000 Twitter followers to earn the title. You only need the courage to start, the discipline to keep going, and the willingness to learn.

I get it—putting yourself out there is scary. You're handing over a piece of yourself to strangers and hoping they'll be kind. But here's a little secret: the writing community is one of the most supportive, encouraging groups you'll ever find. We want you to succeed.

### What Makes This Book Different?

There are plenty of books about writing out there, and some of them are excellent (I see you, Stephen King's *On Writing*). But this one is different because it's not about rules or formulas. It's about figuring out what works for *you*.

Think of me as your guide—not your boss. I'm here to walk you through the process, cheer you on, and share a few laughs along the way. Writing a book should be challenging, but it should also be fun (see my work called *Broken World,* a zombie Apocalypse in Canada - gun control and all).

**Let's Get Started**

By the time you've finished this book, you'll have the tools, knowledge, and confidence to write your own. And who knows? Maybe a few years from now, someone will pick up your book and think, "Wow, this changed my life."

So, grab a coffee, find a comfy chair, and let's get to work. Your story is waiting to be told—and I can't wait to help you tell it.

## *My Connection to Writing*

You might be wondering, "Why should I trust this person to help me write a book?" Fair question. Here's where I tell you a bit about myself so you know I'm not just winging it.

I was born right at the tail end of the Baby Boomer generation, when bell bottoms were all the rage and the idea of a "home computer" was something out of Star Trek. My parents were supportive, loving, and made sure our home was as stable as they could manage—pretty lucky, really.

From the time I was a kid, I was always reading. I devoured *The Hardy Boys* and *Gun Smoke.* But the real game-changer? My grandmother on my dad's side. Her basement was a treasure trove of "Adult Fantasy" novels—think classic sci-fi and fantasy, not what you're imagining! She was a Science

Fiction superfan and spent most of her time with her nose buried in a book. That rubbed off on me in a big way.

When I wasn't reading, I was telling stories. Then, along came *Dungeons & Dragons*, and it was like the storytelling gods handed me a golden ticket. That game became my creative outlet for years, and it taught me how to craft worlds, build characters, and keep people hooked on a narrative.

Sports were another outlet, but then I discovered music, and it was all over. By the early '70s, I was playing in a marching band called The Sparkies. Between that and spending time in Cubs and Scouts, my schedule was packed. Then came Air Cadets in the late '70s, and since I could already play music, their band scooped me up. The discipline didn't hurt, either. That's where I found my love of sharpshooting and flying.

So there you have it—school, music, military stuff, and flying all rolled into one childhood.

As I entered the corporate world, I joined The Toronto Signals Trumpet Band. Turns out, my knack for training people was pretty useful. Over the years, I climbed the management ladder, writing training manuals and making sense of complicated processes. At one point, while I was knee-deep in rewriting ISO documents for the department, the thought hit me: "Hey, maybe I should try writing fiction."

Fast forward a few years, and I'd completed seven novels, all written during NaNoWriMo. Those months of frantic writing taught me a lot about perseverance and creativity. Inspired, I founded DAOwen Publications and opened four imprints to focus on different genres. I haven't looked back since.

In terms of formal training, I've studied writing through programs at Duke University and Mt. St. Joseph. During that time, I also got into writing for magazines. I created a writer's column called *The Written View* for *Self-Publisher Magazine*, which later transitioned to *IndyFest Magazine*, where I also handled distribution. After that, I spent two years contributing to *InD'tale Magazine*. Somewhere along the way, publishing took over my life. Editing, creating, managing—my days became a whirlwind of words.

Now, I run DAOwen Publications while managing several small companies that help writers. There's MMT Productions, where we handle cover art and editing services, and Arc Reviewers, which helps authors get reviews for their books. My latest project is Scriptophobia, a writers' community and workshop site designed to bring authors together.

In short? Writing, publishing, and helping other writers tell their stories has become my passion. It's been a journey, but it's one I wouldn't trade for anything. Now, I'm here to help you start your journey, too.

## *Your Courage and Goals*

First off, let's take a moment to give you a well-deserved round of applause. No, seriously—deciding to write a book is a big deal. It takes guts to put your thoughts, ideas, and maybe even your heart out there for the world to see. Not everyone has the courage to take that step, but here you are. That's huge.

Let's be real—writing a book isn't like assembling Ikea furniture. There's no clear instruction sheet (and if there was, it'd probably be missing a page). It's more like venturing into the great unknown with only a vague map, a leaky canteen, and a questionable sense of direction. Yet, here you are, ready to take on the challenge. That says something about your determination.

Now, I won't sugar-coat it: the road ahead has its share of potholes. There will be doubts, distractions, and moments where you'll question if your book idea is even worth pursuing (spoiler: it is). You might second-guess yourself so much that you consider giving up altogether. But don't worry—this book is your guide to navigating all that. Think of it as a flashlight to cut through the fog, a toolkit for fixing story problems, and maybe even a cup of coffee on those late nights when you're wondering if the words will ever come.

Your goals, whether they're big or small, matter. Maybe you're dreaming of bestseller lists, or maybe you just want to write something that makes your family proud. Whatever the case, this book will help you get there. It's packed with practical advice, encouragement, and a few laughs along the way to keep things from getting too serious.

So, keep that courage handy—it's going to come in handy. And remember: the fact you're even trying to write a book already puts you in a league of your own. You've got this. Let's get started!

## Closing the Foreword

So, here we are at the end of the foreword, and I hope you're feeling a little more excited (and maybe a little less intimidated) about starting your writing journey. If you're still feeling a bit wobbly, don't worry—it's completely normal. Every writer starts somewhere, and the fact that you're even holding this book is proof you've already begun. That's the hardest part for most people: deciding to take the leap. You? You're already in the air.

Now, let's talk about what's ahead. This book is designed to be your companion on the road to becoming an author. Think of it like a road trip: I'll be the chatty navigator in the passenger seat, pointing out landmarks, giving you directions, and occasionally asking if we can stop for snacks. There's a lot to explore, but we'll take it one chapter at a time so it's never overwhelming.

We'll start with the basics, like finding your big idea and figuring out what kind of book you want to write. Whether it's a sweeping epic fantasy, a heartwarming memoir, or a guide to growing the perfect tomatoes in Canadian soil, every great book begins with a clear idea and a dash of enthusiasm (okay, maybe more than a dash—but don't worry, I'll help with that).

From there, we'll dive into outlining and planning. Don't panic if you're not much of a planner in real life; there's no one-size-fits-all method to this. Whether you're the type to colour-code every detail or you prefer to dive in headfirst and see where the story takes you, we'll figure out a strategy that works for you.

Next, we'll tackle the writing itself—the nitty-gritty of getting words on the page, even when the words seem stubbornly elusive. I'll share tips on how to stay motivated, how to silence that little voice in your head saying, "This isn't good enough," and how to keep going even when you hit a creative wall. Spoiler alert: chocolate helps.

Once we've got a solid draft, we'll move on to editing and revision. Yes, this is where the magic happens—but also where things can get messy. Cutting scenes you love, reworking awkward sentences, and making sure your story or argument flows like a dream? It's all part of the process. The good news? By this point, you'll have something amazing to work with, and editing will help you polish it until it shines.

Finally, we'll cover what happens after the writing is done. Publishing, marketing, sharing your work with the world—it's all in there. Whether you dream of holding a printed copy of your book in your hands or sharing it digitally with a global audience, I'll guide you through the options and help you figure out what's right for you.

Here's the thing: writing a book is a lot like building a house. It's a process, and it takes time, patience, and effort. There's no magical shortcut that'll make it easy, but the steps are clear, and I'll be right here to walk you through them. By the time you've finished this book, you'll have the tools, the confidence, and the know-how to make your dream of writing a book a reality.

But before we dive into all that, let me leave you with this: writing a book is worth it. Not just because of the finished product (though that's a pretty great reward), but because of what you'll discover about yourself along the way. You'll learn how to push through self-doubt, how to think creatively, and how to persevere when things get tough. You'll gain a deeper appreciation for the stories and ideas that make up your world —and maybe even find a few new ones of your own.

So, here's my advice: take a deep breath, grab your favourite notebook or keyboard, and get ready. You don't have to be perfect; you don't even have to know exactly what you're doing yet. You just have to start. Writing a book is a journey, and it's okay to stumble a bit along the way. Trust me, the destination is worth it.

Keep a stash of highlighters, post-it notes, and bookmarks so you can add references!

Now, let's get going. Your story is waiting to be told, and I can't wait to help you tell it. Let's write something amazing together.

# Part 1
# **Preparation**

# Chapter 1

# Finding Your Idea

**Exploring Genres**

**Understanding Writing Genres: Finding Your Perfect Fit**

Let's dive into genres, shall we? Think of a genre as the "big umbrella" that your book fits under—fiction, non-fiction, romance, fantasy, etc. These are the main categories readers use to find books they'll love. But before we get too far, let's address something upfront: you might notice a few sub-genres missing from the main list.

What about *urban fantasy*, *steampunk*, or *cyberpunk*? Or *cosy mysteries* and *space operas*? While these are all fantastic (and fun!) sub-genres, they live under the broader genre umbrellas. For example, urban fantasy is part of fantasy, steampunk could fall under both fantasy and sci-fi, and cosy mysteries live happily in the mystery family. Don't worry; we'll tackle these in a separate list below.

For now, let's focus on the big categories to give you a solid foundation. Once you've chosen your primary genre, we can dig into sub-genres to help fine-tune your idea.

**Main Writing Genres**

**Fiction Genres**

1. **Mystery**
   - Whodunit! Mysteries revolve around solving a crime or uncovering secrets. Whether it's a grizzled detective hunting down a killer or an amateur sleuth uncovering family scandals, the goal is to keep readers guessing until the very end.
2. **Thriller/Suspense**
   - Think of thrillers as mystery's high-octane cousin. The stakes are higher, the pacing faster, and there's a constant sense of danger. Whether it's a psychological thriller or a political conspiracy, readers expect edge-of-your-seat tension.
3. **Romance**
   - Romance is all about relationships and emotional connections. From swooning regency romances to contemporary rom-coms, these stories focus on love and always leave readers with a sense of hope —and always a happy ending.
4. Love Stories
   - Love stories are all about relationships and emotional connections, but unlike romance, they don't have a happy ending.
5. **Fantasy**
   - Magic, dragons, epic quests—fantasy takes readers to worlds where the impossible becomes possible.

Whether you're writing high fantasy like *The Lord of the Rings* or modern takes like *Harry Potter*, fantasy unleashes imagination.

6. **Science Fiction (Sci-Fi)**
   - Sci-fi blends imagination with logic. It's where futuristic tech, space exploration, and "what if" scenarios come to life. Whether you're writing about alien civilizations or AI revolutions, sci-fi asks big questions about humanity.

7. **Historical Fiction**
   - Set in the past, historical fiction blends real events and fictional stories. Whether it's a romance set in the Victorian era or a soldier's tale in World War II, research is key to making the time period feel authentic.

8. **Horror**
   - Horror thrives on fear, suspense, and the macabre. From psychological scares to full-on gore, this genre taps into our deepest anxieties and gives readers a thrilling sense of dread.

9. **Literary Fiction**
   - This genre is all about emotional depth and thought-provoking themes. Literary fiction often focuses on character development, complex relationships, and big questions about life. It's like the "art film" of books.

## Nonfiction Genres

1. **Memoir**
   - Memoirs are personal, focusing on your life experiences. They zoom in on specific themes or

events, whether it's overcoming challenges, discovering passions, or reflecting on a meaningful journey.

2. **Self-Help**
   - Got wisdom to share? Self-help books offer readers advice, tools, and encouragement to improve their lives. From mental health to career advice, the key is actionable tips and relatable examples.

3. **Biography/Autobiography**
   - Like memoirs, but with a broader lens. Biographies explore someone else's life, diving deep into their achievements and struggles. Autobiographies tell your whole story, from start to finish.

4. **History**
   - History books focus on real events and eras, weaving facts into compelling narratives. Whether it's about the rise and fall of empires or cultural shifts in the 20th century, history books bring the past to life.

5. **How-To/Guidebooks**
   - These books teach readers how to do something— whether it's baking sourdough, building furniture, or starting a business. Clear steps and expert advice make them practical and accessible.

6. **Travel Writing**
   - Travel books take readers on a journey, sharing adventures, insights, and practical advice. Whether it's a cultural deep dive or a personal exploration, these stories inspire wanderlust.

**Sub-Genres: Adding Flavour to Your Story**

Sub-genres are like the toppings on your pizza—they add specific flavours and make your story unique. Here's a look at some popular sub-genres and where they fit:

**Fiction Sub-Genres**

1. **Urban Fantasy** (Fantasy)
   - Magic meets modern life. Urban fantasy takes fantastical elements—like wizards or werewolves—and drops them into contemporary settings, often with gritty or noir vibes.
2. **Steampunk** (Fantasy/Sci-Fi)
   - Imagine Victorian-era technology powered by steam, with a splash of goggles and gears. Steampunk blends historical aesthetics with speculative tech.
3. **Cosy Mystery** (Mystery)
   - A lighter take on mysteries, often set in quaint small towns with amateur sleuths solving crimes over tea. Think less gore, more charm.
4. **Space Opera** (Sci-Fi)
   - Big, sweeping stories in space. Space operas focus on epic battles, intergalactic politics, and larger-than-life characters (*Star Wars*, anyone?).
5. **Psychological Thriller** (Thriller)
   - Less action, more mind games. Psychological thrillers dive into manipulation, unreliable narrators, and characters that'll leave readers questioning everyone's motives.

6. **Paranormal Romance** (Romance)
   - Think love stories with vampires, ghosts, or other supernatural beings. It's all about love with a touch of the extraordinary.
7. **Dark Fantasy** (Fantasy)
   - A grittier, more shadowy version of traditional fantasy. Dark fantasy often blurs the lines between good and evil and adds a horror twist.

## Nonfiction Sub-Genres

1. **Creative Nonfiction** (Memoir/History)
   - Nonfiction that reads like fiction, using storytelling techniques to explore true events. Great for essays, personal stories, or narrative histories.
2. **Inspirational Memoir** (Memoir)
   - A personal story designed to motivate or inspire readers, often focusing on overcoming adversity or achieving great things.
3. **Pop Science** (How-To/Sci-Fi Adjacent)
   - Science explained in an accessible, entertaining way—perfect for anyone who wants to explore topics like space, biology, or AI without needing a PhD.

## Why Genres and Sub-Genres Matter

Genres help readers find your book, but sub-genres are what make it stand out. They're the details that attract specific audiences and let you carve out your unique niche. Picking a genre is step one; diving into sub-genres is where the real fun begins.

So, start broad, then drill down into what excites you most. Love fantasy but hate dragons? Try urban fantasy or steampunk. Obsessed with history but want a little drama? Historical fiction might be your thing. Let your interests guide you, and you'll find the perfect fit for your story

**How to Choose Your Genre**

If you're still not sure where your idea fits, here are some tips to help you decide:

1. **What Do You Love to Read?**
   - The books on your shelf probably say a lot about the genre you'll enjoy writing. If you're obsessed with fantasy series, you'll likely have a blast creating your own magical worlds.
2. **What Are You Passionate About?**
   - If you're constantly reading about personal growth, historical events, or alien lifeforms, lean into those interests. Passion translates into great writing.
3. **Experiment and Brainstorm:**
   - If you're torn between genres, try brainstorming ideas for a few different ones. Write a short synopsis or outline for each idea and see which one excites you most.

**Exercise: Your Top Three Genres**

Here's your homework:

1. Write down your top three favourite genres.
2. For each genre, list two or three potential ideas that come to mind.

3. Reflect on which genre (and idea) feels the most exciting or natural for you to write.

Once you've got that figured out, you'll be ready to dive into your book with confidence—and maybe even a little swagger.

**Homework Help: Getting Stuck? Expert Help Section**

We get it—choosing a genre and narrowing down sub-genres can feel a bit like picking the perfect donut at Timmies. There are so many options, and they all look good! If you're spinning your wheels, here's some extra guidance to help you find your path:

**Go Back to What You Love**

Still stuck? Take a moment to think about the books, movies, and shows you can't get enough of. Ask yourself:

- What stories or themes do I enjoy most?
- Epic battles? Slow-burn romances? Spine-chilling mysteries?
- What books have I re-read or recommended to friends?
- What kind of books would I love to see more of in the world?

Your favourite genres as a consumer are a great starting point for deciding what you might enjoy writing.

**Ask Yourself "What If?"**

The magic of storytelling often starts with a simple question: "What if...?"

- What if vampires lived in small-town Saskatchewan?
- What if a farmer in the 1800s invented steam-powered tech?
- What if a corporate climber's "self-help" journey turned into chaos?

Let your imagination wander. Jot down ideas—even the silly ones. You might discover the seed of your perfect genre in the process.

## Break it Down into Smaller Steps

If deciding a genre feels overwhelming, try this approach:

1. **Start broad:** Fiction or nonfiction?
2. **Narrow down:** What speaks to you more—romance, fantasy, thrillers, or something else?
3. **Get specific:** Explore sub-genres that add flavour to your story idea (like urban fantasy or cosy mystery).

Instead of forcing the decision all at once, take it step by step.

## Phone a Friend (or Book Nerd)

Sometimes you just need a second opinion. Share your ideas with a friend, family member, or fellow book lover. Describe your favourite types of books and see if they notice patterns you might've missed. Bonus: their excitement can help you feel more confident in your choice.

## Do a Quick Genre Mash-Up

Still feeling indecisive? Try this trick:

- Pick two or three genres you like.
- Smash them together and brainstorm an idea that blends them.

For example:

- Romance + Science Fiction = A love story set on a spaceship.
- Mystery + Fantasy = A detective solving crimes in a magical world.
- Self-Help + Memoir = A guide to life lessons told through your own journey.

You might discover that combining genres helps you find your unique angle.

**Study the Masters**

Dive into your chosen genre by reading some of the top books in it. Not sure where to start? Look up bestseller lists or award winners (e.g., Hugo Awards for sci-fi, RITA Awards for romance). As you read, take notes on what works, what excites you, and how you can bring your own twist to the genre.

**Permission to Change Your Mind**

Here's a little secret: you don't have to stick with one genre forever—or even for this project! If you choose a genre and realize partway through that it's not working, it's okay to pivot. Writing is a process, not a one-shot deal.

**Expert Help Tip**

Struggling with doubts? Here's a mantra for you:

- Every great author started somewhere.
- No idea is "too small" or "too weird."
- Your unique voice and perspective are what will make your story shine.

Take a deep breath, grab your pen (or keyboard), and remind yourself that this is your creative journey. You've got this!

## Who Are You Writing For?

Let's talk about your audience. Not the people politely nodding at your dinner party story or the ones scrolling past your social media posts (although they *might* be your readers too). We're talking about the specific group of people you're writing your book for—the ones who will pick it up, crack it open, and say, "This was written just for me."

Knowing your audience is like having a GPS for your writing journey. Without it, you're driving blind, hoping you'll end up somewhere good. With it, you can tailor your tone, style, and content to create a book that connects with your readers and keeps them coming back for more.

## Why Knowing Your Audience Matters

Imagine reading a kids' book that uses university-level vocabulary or a romance novel where the characters sound like robots. Doesn't quite work, does it? That's because the author missed the mark on who they were writing for.

Understanding your audience means your book will resonate. It's about speaking their language, addressing their interests, and meeting their expectations.

For example:

- If you're writing a *middle-grade fantasy novel*, your tone should be fun and adventurous, and your vocabulary should match what a 10-year-old can handle.
- If you're crafting *adult literary fiction*, readers expect thought-provoking themes, emotional depth, and complex characters.

The better you know your audience, the more likely you are to create a book they'll love—and recommend to their friends.

**How to Identify Your Audience**

Start by asking yourself these key questions:

**Who Is Most Likely to Enjoy or Benefit from This Book?**

- Is your book meant for kids, teens, or adults?
- Are you writing for a specific demographic, like single parents, retirees, or history buffs?
- Does your story appeal to a niche audience, like steampunk enthusiasts or lovers of cosy mysteries?

Knowing *who* you're writing for helps you refine every part of your book, from the tone to the types of jokes you include.

**What Does Your Audience Want to Feel, Learn, or Experience?**

- Fiction: Do you want readers to laugh, cry, or stay up all night turning pages?
- Nonfiction: Are you teaching them something new, solving a problem, or inspiring them to take action?

Think about how you want readers to feel when they close the book. Inspired? Entertained? A little smarter than when they started?

## What Problems Does Your Book Solve, or How Does It Entertain?

- For nonfiction: Consider what issues your readers might be facing. Are they trying to get healthier, become better parents, or learn a new skill?
- For fiction: Think about how your story transports readers. Does it provide a thrilling escape? A romantic getaway? A laugh-out-loud distraction from daily life?

Answering these questions helps you focus on what your book delivers, making it easier to keep your readers hooked.

### Adapting to Your Audience's Needs

Once you've got a clear idea of who you're writing for, the next step is making sure your book fits their needs. Let's break it down by fiction and nonfiction:

### For Fiction Writers

Your audience's age and interests should influence the key elements of your story:

- **Pacing:**
- Younger readers prefer faster-paced stories with lots of action and dialogue.
- Adult readers may enjoy a more leisurely pace with deeper character development and subplots.

- **Emotional Depth:**
- For middle-grade readers, keep emotions simple and relatable (like friendship challenges or family dynamics).
- For adults, you can explore more complex themes like loss, redemption, or identity.
- **Language and Style:**
- Teen readers (YA) appreciate snappy, modern dialogue.
- Adults might love rich, descriptive prose.

Example: Writing a mystery for teens? Keep the language accessible, focus on a relatable protagonist, and build suspense without being too graphic. Writing a mystery for adults? You can add more intricate twists, deeper character backstories, and darker themes.

### For Nonfiction Writers

Your audience's needs should shape how you present your information:

1. **Clarity:**
   - If you're writing for beginners, avoid jargon and explain terms clearly.
   - Writing for experts? Dive deeper into the subject matter and avoid oversimplifying.
2. **Relatability:**
   - Use anecdotes or examples that your audience can connect with. A guide for new parents might include funny, real-life moments, while a business book could use relatable workplace scenarios.
3. **Tone:**

- Self-help books often have an encouraging, conversational tone.
- Historical nonfiction might lean towards a formal, academic tone.

Example: Writing a how-to guide for gardeners? If your audience is beginners, focus on easy-to-follow tips and avoid overwhelming them with Latin plant names. For experienced gardeners, offer advanced techniques and deeper insights.

**Homework: Creating a Reader Profile**

To really nail your audience, it's helpful to create a profile of your ideal reader. Think of it like creating a character for your book—but this time, it's a character who'll pick up and love what you've written.

**Here's What to Include in Your Reader Profile:**

1. **Demographics**
   - Age range: Is your reader a curious 12-year-old, a 35-year-old career-climber, or a retired traveller?
   - Gender: Is your book geared toward women, men, or a broader audience?
2. **Interests and Hobbies**
   - What does your ideal reader love? If they're into fantasy, they might enjoy worldbuilding and magical creatures. If they're nonfiction readers, maybe they love self-improvement or history.
3. **Why They're Picking Up Your Book**
   - What's drawing them to your book? Entertainment? Education? Escapism?
4. **What They're Looking For**

- Are they looking for practical advice? A laugh? A heartwarming story? Think about the payoff your reader expects.

## Getting to Know Your Audience: A Little Extra Help

Still scratching your head about who your audience is? Here are some ways to figure it out:

- **Look at Similar Books:**
  - Research books in your genre and see who's reading them. Check reviews or join discussions online to see what readers love (or hate) about those books.
- **Ask Around:**
  - Share your book idea with friends or family and ask who they think would enjoy it. Their perspective can be surprisingly helpful.
- **Use Social Media or Communities:**
  - Platforms like Goodreads, Reddit, and Facebook groups can give you insight into what people in your genre are looking for.

## Wrapping It Up

Figuring out your audience isn't just a box to tick off—it's a tool that'll guide your entire writing process. Once you know who you're writing for, you can tailor every aspect of your book to speak directly to them. Your readers will feel like you wrote the book just for them—and that's how you create a loyal fanbase.

So, take your time with this exercise. Your ideal reader is out there, waiting for your book. You just need to figure out who they are, what they need, and how you can give it to them. Once you've done that, you'll be ready to start crafting a story or message that truly resonates

**Homework: Who Is Your Audience?**

Finding your audience is like figuring out who you're writing a love letter to—it shapes every word, tone, and idea. This homework assignment will help you nail down exactly who you're writing for, so you can create a book that truly connects with your readers. Grab a notebook, a snack, and let's dive in!

**Step 1: Imagine Your Ideal Reader**

Close your eyes (or keep them open if writing blind isn't your thing) and picture the person who would *love* your book. Answer these questions to flesh them out:

- **How old are they?**
  - Are they a kid, teen, young adult, or someone reminiscing about the good ol' days?
- **What's their life like?**
  - Are they juggling a career and kids? Studying for exams? Retired with time to binge-read?
- **What are their hobbies and interests?**
  - Do they love puzzles, cooking, or hunting for the perfect chai latte?

Write a paragraph describing your reader. The more detailed, the better.

**Step 2: Think About What They Want**

Now, get into their heads. What is your ideal reader looking for in a book?

- **For fiction writers:**
    - Do they want to escape reality for a while?
    - Do they crave romance, adrenaline-pumping action, or laugh-out-loud humour?
    - Do they want characters they can relate to or be inspired by?
- **For nonfiction writers:**
    - What problem are they hoping your book will solve?
    - What knowledge or skills are they looking to gain?
    - Do they want something light and motivational or detailed and technical?

Jot down at least three things your reader is hoping to get from your book.

**Step 3: The Bookstore Test**

Imagine your ideal reader is standing in a bookstore or scrolling through an online shop. They come across your book. What makes them pick it up?

Answer these questions:

- **What does your book's cover say to them?**
    - Fun and quirky? Dark and mysterious? Bright and educational?
- **What kind of title grabs their attention?**
    - A clever pun? A dramatic phrase? A question that intrigues them?

- **Why would they flip to the first page?**
  - Think about what your book offers that makes it irresistible—whether it's the promise of an epic journey, practical advice, or pure entertainment.

Write a short pitch for your book that would make your ideal reader say, "I need this!"

## Step 4: Create Your Reader Profile

Combine your answers from the previous steps to create a detailed profile of your ideal reader. Include:

- **Basic Info:**
  - Age, gender, life stage (e.g., student, parent, professional, retiree).
- **Personality and Interests:**
  - Hobbies, favourite genres, quirks (e.g., "loves dark humour" or "cannot resist books about time travel").
- **What They Want from Your Book:**
  - Escape, knowledge, inspiration, entertainment, or something else?
- **How You'll Deliver It:**
  - The tone, pacing, and unique elements of your book that will make it perfect for them.

Example Profile:

*My ideal reader is a 35-year-old parent who loves fantasy novels with strong female protagonists. They read to escape the chaos of family life and enjoy fast-paced, adventurous stories with a touch of humour. They'd pick up my book because it promises a thrilling quest with relatable characters and a good dose of banter.*

## Step 5: Share and Refine

Once you've created your profile, share it with a friend, family member, or writing group. Ask them if your description feels clear and relatable. They might even help you see something you missed!

## Bonus Challenge: Create a Reader "Mood Board"

If you're a visual person, take your reader profile to the next level. Gather images, quotes, and even book covers that remind you of your ideal audience and what they love. Use Pinterest, Google, or a good ol' collage to keep your audience front and centre as you write.

By the end of this homework, you should have a clear picture of who your audience is and what they're looking for in a book. Keep this profile handy—it'll guide you through every stage of your writing process. Happy brainstorming!

## Pro-Tips for Finding Your Audience

Feeling a bit stuck? No worries! These pro-tips will help you nail down your audience and keep the process fun and stress-free:

## Think About Your Reader's Biggest "Why"

Ask yourself: *Why* would someone pick up your book?

- Fiction: Do they want to laugh, cry, be inspired, or escape reality?

- Nonfiction: Are they solving a problem, learning a skill, or gaining insight?

Focusing on the reader's "why" makes it easier to picture who they are and what they want.

### Don't Overthink It

You're not writing for *every single person*. Narrowing down your audience doesn't limit you—it helps you write a book that feels personal and specific. Start small: think of one ideal reader. Picture them, write for them, and trust that others like them will find your work too.

### Be Specific, but Not Too Specific

Sure, you could imagine your reader as "Jordan, a 32-year-old dog groomer who loves black coffee, rainy days, and space operas." But your audience doesn't need to be *that* specific. Focus on broader traits like age range, hobbies, and why your book appeals to them.

### Mine Your Own Interests

The best books come from passion. If you love thrillers, self-help, or quirky humour, there's a good chance your audience does too. Think about what *you'd* want to read—that's often a great indicator of who your readers are.

### Think Like a Bookseller

Imagine your book on a shelf or in an online store. Where does it fit? Which readers would stop and take notice? Browse the categories, sub-genres, and book covers of similar works to get a clearer sense of your audience.

**Use Your Life as a Clue**

Your personal experiences can often point you to your audience. Are you writing for:

- People who've faced challenges similar to yours?
- Readers who share your quirky sense of humour?
- Folks who love diving into the same topics you do?

Draw from your life to connect with your ideal readers—it's like having a built-in audience.

**If You're Really Stuck, Imagine a Single Reader**

Sometimes it helps to think of a real person. Is it your best friend who loves epic fantasy? Your neighbour who's obsessed with historical dramas? Your coworker who swears by productivity hacks? Write with that person in mind—they're your prototype reader.

**Stay Open to Surprises**

While having a clear audience in mind is essential, don't stress about getting it *perfect*. You might find that your book appeals to people you didn't expect. That's okay! Start with a target audience, but let the story or message evolve naturally.

**Keep Your Reader Profile Visible**

Once you've completed the homework, keep your ideal reader profile somewhere you'll see it. Pin it on your bulletin board or save it on your desktop. It'll remind you who you're writing for when you hit those tricky moments.

With these tips in your back pocket, you're ready to tackle the homework and get one step closer to crafting a book your audience will adore. You've got this!

## Finding Your Unique Angle

Let's face it—there are *a lot* of books out there. From epic fantasies to how-to guides on raising pet ducks, the market is packed with all kinds of stories and ideas. So, how do you make sure your book stands out? That's where your unique angle comes in.

Having a unique angle is like adding secret sauce to your story—it's what makes your book memorable. Even if your idea isn't groundbreaking (spoiler alert: most ideas aren't), your voice, approach, or setting can make it feel fresh and new.

## Why Uniqueness Matters

Readers want something they haven't seen a hundred times before, and publishers are on the lookout for ideas that surprise them. But here's the thing: being unique doesn't mean reinventing the wheel. It means finding *your* take on a familiar concept.

Take *Harry Potter*, for example. A magic school? That's been done. But a magic school with houses, talking hats, and the looming threat of a nose-less villain? That's unique.

Or look at nonfiction. There are loads of books about parenting, but a guide that mixes practical advice with laugh-out-loud stories about cleaning crayon off the dog? Now we're talking.

Your uniqueness is the hook that gets people interested, so embrace what makes your book *yours*.

## How to Find Your Unique Angle

Not sure what makes your book special? Let's break it down:

### Draw from Your Life

Your experiences, passions, and knowledge are your best tools for creating something fresh.

- **What's personal to you?**
  - Maybe you've lived through something unusual, like growing up on a remote island or working in a haunted bakery. Your life offers a treasure trove of inspiration.
- **What do you love?**
  - Writing about something you're passionate about will naturally make your book more interesting. Readers can tell when you're genuinely excited about your topic or story.

Example: If you're writing a thriller and you're a botanist, maybe your killer uses rare plants as weapons. Creepy, but intriguing!

### Combine the Unexpected

Sometimes the best ideas come from mashing together things that don't seem to go together at first glance.

### What happens when you mix genres?

- A romance comady set during a zombie apocalypse (see my *Broken World* series).
- A science fiction novel written as a memoir (see *The Moon Is A Hard Mistress* by Robert A. Heinlein).

- A murder mystery set in the world of competitive dog grooming (yes, it's worth mentioning again).
- **What themes can you blend?**
  - Maybe your book is a fantasy story *and* a coming-of-age tale (my *Spear* series). Or a parenting guide *and* a comedy. Mixing elements can create something truly unique.

## Research the Market

Before you dive in, it's a good idea to scope out what's already out there.

- **What's popular in your genre?**
  - Read some recent books and notice trends. What are readers loving right now?
- **What's missing?**
- Is there a topic or theme that hasn't been explored? Maybe you notice a lot of fantasy novels focus on battles, but none explore what happens *after* the war. That's your opening.
- **What's overdone?**
- Avoid falling into cliché territory. For instance, do we really need another vampire romance where they meet in biology class? Probably not.

## Examples of Unique Angles

Need some inspiration? Here are a few ideas to spark your creativity:

**Fiction Examples:**

- A fantasy novel where magic comes from baking (movie *Simply Irresistible*). Wizards duel using enchanted pies and spellbound soufflés.
- A sci-fi adventure told from the perspective of the ship's onboard AI, who's having an existential crisis.
- A murder mystery set in a retirement community where a 78-year-old knitting enthusiast turns sleuth.

**Nonfiction Examples:**

- A self-help book about productivity, written for people who can't function before their second cup of coffee.
- A parenting guide by a comedian who tells it like it is —messy, chaotic, and full of hilarious life lessons (book *Wisdom from the Fuzzy Blue Chair* by S. A. Baker), .
- A history book exploring famous rebellions, written like a how-to guide for aspiring troublemakers.

**Homework: Craft Your Unique Hook**

It's time to take your idea and give it that special twist. Here's how:

1. **Write down your book idea in one sentence.**
   - Keep it simple—just the basic concept.
   - Example: *A young woman discovers she can speak to ghosts.*
2. **Now, ask yourself: What makes this idea special?**
   - Is it the setting? The characters? The tone?
   - How is your take on this different from other books with similar concepts?

Example: *The ghosts are all famous historical figures who need help finishing their unfinished business.*

3. **Combine your idea and unique angle into a "hook" sentence.**
   - A hook is a one-liner that shows off your book's special flair.
   - Example: *A young woman who speaks to ghosts helps famous historical spirits finish their unfinished business—with plenty of hilarious and heartwarming chaos along the way.*
4. **Polish your hook until it shines.**
   - Think of your hook as the pitch you'd use to grab a reader's attention. It should be clear, intriguing, and a little irresistible.\

**Pro Tip: Test Your Hook**

Once you've written your hook, share it with a few friends or fellow writers. If they say, "I'd read that!"—you're on the right track. If they look confused, tweak it until it clicks.

Finding your unique angle isn't about reinventing the wheel—it's about putting your spin on it. Whether it's your voice, your perspective, or an unexpected twist, your book already has the potential to stand out. You just need to dig a little to find the gold. So, go ahead and unleash your creative spark. The world hasn't seen your story yet—and that's exactly why it needs to. It also helps you focus on the theme of your book.

**Refining Your Big Idea**

Congratulations! You've got the spark of an idea for your book—maybe even a few sparks. Now it's time to fan those sparks into a flame and turn your general concept into a focused, polished idea. Think of this process like carving a block of marble into a sculpture: you start with something big and clunky, and chip away until the masterpiece underneath comes into view.

This step is all about clarity. You'll take the work you've done on your genre, audience, and unique angle and combine them into a single cohesive idea. Don't worry—it's easier than it sounds.

## Why Simplicity Matters

A great book idea should be clear and focused. If you can't explain your concept in one or two sentences, it probably needs a bit more refining. Why? Because readers (and publishers, if you're going that route) need to understand quickly what your book is about and why it's worth picking up.

Think about your favourite books or movies. Their concepts can often be boiled down to a single, intriguing sentence:

- *"A young wizard discovers he's the key to defeating an evil sorcerer bent on world domination."* (*Harry Potter*)
- *"A self-help book for people who love procrastinating but still want to get things done."* (*The Procrastinator's Guide to Productivity*)
- *"A comedy about a group of retirees who solve murders in their luxury retirement village."* (*The Thursday Murder Club*)

See how simple and clear those pitches are? That's the goal.

## How to Focus Your Idea

Let's break the process down step by step.

## Step 1: Start Broad

Begin with your general concept. Don't overthink it—just write down the first thing that comes to mind. For example:

- *"I want to write a novel about adventure."*
- *"I want to help people learn how to be more confident."*
- *"I want to write a fantasy story about dragons."*

At this stage, it's okay if your idea feels vague. The goal is to get it down on paper.

## Step 2: Narrow It Down

Now, start adding details based on what you've already figured out about your genre, audience, and unique angle. Ask yourself:

- Who is this book for?
- What makes my idea stand out?
- What's the central conflict or focus?

Let's refine the examples:

- *"A middle-grade fantasy about a kid who accidentally unlocks an ancient treasure map hidden in their school."*
- *"A self-help book for introverts who want to build confidence without feeling like they're faking it."*
- *"An epic fantasy where dragons aren't creatures—*

> *they're elemental forces controlled by rival wizards fighting for dominance."*

Notice how each idea is starting to sound more specific and exciting? That's the magic of narrowing things down.

## Step 3: Combine the Pieces

Once you've refined your idea, it's time to bring all the pieces together into a single, clear sentence or two. Here's a handy formula:

**[Genre] about [main character or subject] who/that [unique angle or central conflict].**

Examples:

- *"A middle-grade fantasy about a lonely kid who accidentally unlocks an ancient treasure map hidden in their school and must outsmart rival treasure hunters."*
- *"A self-help book for introverts, offering practical strategies for building confidence while staying true to their authentic selves."*
- *"An epic fantasy where rival wizards control elemental dragons and battle for dominance, threatening to destroy the fragile peace of their kingdom."*

This formula works because it's short, specific, and highlights what makes your book unique.

## Exercise: Summarize Your Book Idea

It's your turn! Grab a notebook or open a blank document and follow these steps:

1. **Write down your broad idea.**
   - Example: *"I want to write a mystery."*
2. **Add details about your genre, audience, and unique angle.**
   - Example: *"A cosy mystery for dog lovers about a veterinarian who solves crimes in her small town."*
3. **Craft a one- or two-sentence summary.**
   - Example: *"A cosy mystery about a veterinarian who becomes an amateur sleuth when a client's dog leads her to a murder victim. Perfect for dog lovers who enjoy lighthearted crime-solving."*
4. **Fine-tune it until it feels clear and exciting.**

**Tips for Success**

- **Stay Flexible:**
  - It's okay if your idea evolves as you write. This exercise is about getting started, not locking yourself into every detail.
- **Test It Out:**
  - Share your summary with a friend or writing buddy. If they say, "Ooh, I'd read that!" you're on the right track. If they look confused, tweak it until it clicks.
- **Keep It Short:**
  - Remember, you're aiming for one or two sentences. If your summary starts to feel like a paragraph, trim it down until it's concise.

**When to Stop Refining**

Here's the good news: your idea doesn't need to be perfect before you start writing. The point of this exercise is to give you a clear direction so you can dive into the writing process with confidence. If your summary feels focused and gets you excited, you're ready to move on.

So, grab your refined idea, take a deep breath, and get ready to start building your story or message. Your masterpiece is one step closer to becoming a reality!

**Overcoming Doubts: You've Got This!**

Every writer faces doubts at some point. The little voice in your head that asks, *"What if my idea isn't good enough?"* or *"What if someone else has already written this?"* It's completely normal to feel that way, but it's important to remember that every writer has been there. The trick is not letting those doubts stop you from moving forward.

In this section, we'll tackle those common fears head-on so you can move past them and keep your momentum going. Trust us—your idea has the potential to be amazing!

**"What If My Idea Isn't Good Enough?"**

Ah, the classic fear. You're staring at your idea, wondering if it's worth pursuing, or if it's just a "meh" concept. First, let me tell you: **every idea has potential**. Even the most basic idea can turn into something incredible with the right execution. It's not just about the concept, but how you tell the story, the characters you create, and the unique spin you bring to the table.

Take a look at some of the most famous stories:

- *Harry Potter*: A boy discovers he's a wizard. Simple concept. But the world-building, the characters, and the magical details made it one of the most beloved stories of all time.

- *The Hunger Games*: A dystopian world where kids are forced to fight in an arena. Again, the concept isn't new, but the way the story is told—the emotional stakes, the character arcs—set it apart.

So, don't worry if your idea feels small or simple right now. The key is in how you bring it to life. **Your voice, your perspective, and your creativity are what will make it shine.**

**"I Have Too Many Ideas!"**

This is a great problem to have, right? But it can also be overwhelming. If you've got a dozen ideas bouncing around in your head, how do you choose which one to focus on?

The first step is to **prioritize**. Ask yourself:

- Which idea excites me the most?
- Which one do I feel the most passionate about?
- Which idea can I see myself writing for months (or years)?

If you're still torn, here's a trick: Pick the idea that fits best with your current skills and interests. If you're new to writing, maybe pick an idea that's simpler to execute, and save the more complex ideas for later. Don't feel like you have to write your magnum opus on the first try—start with the idea that excites you most right now.

**Pro Tip:** You can always circle back to the other ideas later. Write them down and keep them for future projects. They won't go anywhere, and you can revisit them once your current project is done.

**"What If Someone Else Has Already Done It?"**

Ah, the fear of "unoriginality." Let's get this out of the way: **every story has been told in some form**. Whether you're writing a romance, a fantasy, or even a memoir, chances are, someone else has tackled similar themes. But here's the thing: **it's not about the idea itself—it's about how you tell it.**

Your unique perspective, voice, and style will make the story feel fresh. Two people could write the same idea, but their stories will be wildly different based on their life experiences, writing style, and approach. Think of it this way:

- *Cinderella* has been retold hundreds of times, but each version brings something new to the table, whether it's a modern twist, a different cultural take, or a deeper dive into the characters' motivations.
- *The Great Gatsby* isn't the only novel about the American Dream, but it's a classic because of how it's written, the setting, and the characters it portrays.

So, don't worry about whether someone else has already done it. Instead, focus on how you can bring your own unique perspective to the story. **Your voice is what will make it stand out.**

**Exercise: Tackling Your Fears and Doubts**

Let's tackle those fears head-on and turn them into opportunities. Grab a notebook or open up a blank document and write down the doubts or fears you have about your book idea. Then, for each one, write down **one way to overcome it**. Here's an example to get you started:

**Fear 1:** *What if my idea isn't good enough?*

- **Overcome it:** I will focus on bringing my unique voice to the story. Even the simplest idea can shine with the right perspective. Plus, I'll write the best version of it that I can and refine it later.

**Fear 2:** *I have too many ideas!*

- **Overcome it:** I'll choose the one that excites me most right now, and I can always revisit the others later. I'll start with a smaller, more manageable project to build my confidence. Believe me, this works. I have dozens of novel ideas floating through my head at any one time.

**Fear 3:** *What if someone else has already done it?*

- **Overcome it:** I'll focus on how I tell the story, not just the idea itself. Every story is unique based on the author's voice, style, and perspective. My story will be one-of-a-kind because I'm the one writing it. My unique voice will make a BIG difference.

**Pro Tip: Talk it Out**

Sometimes the best way to overcome doubt is to talk it through. Share your fears with a fellow writer, a friend, or even a family member who's supportive of your creative journey. Getting an outside perspective can help you see your ideas in a new light and remind you of why you started writing in the first place.

## Wrapping It Up

Remember, **every writer has doubts**. It's part of the process. The key is not letting those doubts stop you from moving forward. Your idea has potential. You have the talent. And with a little patience and persistence, you'll bring your story to life. So, take a deep breath, put those doubts aside, and get back to writing! Your book is waiting to be written.

## Committing to Your Idea

You've done the brainstorming, the refining, and the tackling of doubts. Now comes the big moment: committing to your idea. Don't worry—you don't have to carve it into stone or get a tattoo of it (though hey, no judgement if you do). This step is simply about saying, "Yes, this is the idea I'm going to work on."

Committing doesn't mean you're locked in forever. Your idea can grow and evolve as you write—that's part of the magic of the creative process. But by planting your flag now, you're giving yourself a solid starting point. And let's face it, starting is often the hardest part.

## It's Okay to Tweak Your Idea Later

First, let's bust a myth: committing to your idea doesn't mean you can't change it. Writing is messy, and your idea will probably shift as you get deeper into the story. Maybe a side character steals the spotlight, or you discover a better plot twist halfway through. That's all part of the journey.

Think of your idea as the blueprint for a house. You can add a porch, knock down a wall, or even slap a new coat of paint on it as you go. The key is to start building. You can't remodel a house that doesn't exist yet.

**Why You Should Start Now (Even If It's Not Perfect)**

Let's be honest: waiting for the "perfect" idea is just a fancy way of procrastinating. No idea starts out perfect—it's in the writing and revising that your book takes shape. The important thing is to get those first words down on the page.

Think of it like cooking. You don't wait for the ingredients to magically turn into a meal—you chop, mix, and experiment until you've got something delicious. Writing works the same way. You've got your idea, so roll up your sleeves and start making it into something great.

**The First Step is the Biggest**

Starting is scary, no doubt about it. But it's also exciting. By committing to your idea, you're taking the first big step toward making your book a reality. You're saying, "I'm doing this," and that's a huge deal.

Remember, even the most celebrated authors had to start somewhere. J.K. Rowling didn't know *Harry Potter* would become a global phenomenon when she started scribbling ideas on napkins. She just knew she had to write it.

**Exercise: Make It Official**

It's time to make your commitment real. Here's a simple exercise to help you get started:

1. **Write Down Your Idea in Bold Letters**
   - Keep it short and focused. One sentence is enough to capture the heart of your book.
   - Example: *"A cosy mystery about a retired chef solving crimes with her trusty dachshund."*
2. **Pin It Somewhere Visible**
   - Stick it to your fridge, pin it on your bulletin board, or set it as your phone background. Somewhere you'll see it every day.
3. **Say It Out Loud**
   - Yes, really. Say, "This is my idea, and I'm going to write it." It feels a little silly, but trust me—it works.
4. **Celebrate!**
   - Treat yourself to something small but special. A fancy coffee, your favourite dessert, or an uninterrupted hour to binge-watch your favourite show. Committing to your idea is a big step, and it deserves a little celebration.

**Pro Tip: Build a Support System**

Share your idea with someone you trust. It could be a friend, a family member, or even a writing group. Letting someone in on your plan can make it feel more real—and they can cheer you on when you need a boost.

**The Journey Starts Now**

You've done the hard part: choosing your idea and committing to it. The road ahead might be a bit bumpy, but it's also full of discovery and creativity. Whether your idea stays exactly as it is or morphs into something completely different, you're on your way to writing a book. And that's pretty amazing.

So, take a deep breath, look at your idea pinned proudly on the wall, and get ready to start writing. You've got this!

**Pro Tip: Personal Experience**

Back in the day, a salesman asked me how I am so focused on selling (in the car industry). I commented that, on my desk, I keep an image of my goal (at that time, a 18 foot bass boat). It reminded me of what my end goal is. Something that I was shooting to achieve. Do the same, and you'll find a focus for your efforts.

# Chapter 2

# **Research and Inspiration**

## **The Twin Engines of Writing**

Research and inspiration are the dynamic duo of writing. One grounds your ideas in reality, while the other lets your creativity take flight. Whether you're crafting a sweeping fantasy epic or a practical self-help guide, research and inspiration work together to give your writing depth, clarity, and that all-important "wow" factor.

This section is here to help you figure out how to gather the materials you need, stay inspired, and organize everything without spiralling into chaos (we've all been there). But first, let's talk about why research is such a big deal.

## **Why Research Matters**

## **Adding Authenticity**

Nothing pulls a reader out of a story faster than a detail that doesn't ring true. Imagine reading a thriller where the hero calls 9-1-1... in the 1800s. Oops. Whether you're writing about dragons, detectives, or dinner parties, research helps make your work believable.

This is especially true for settings, professions, or cultural details that aren't part of your personal experience. If your protagonist is a firefighter, for example, understanding their day-to-day life can make your scenes feel more authentic. Similarly, even in fantasy, grounding your world in relatable details—like the economics of dragon feed—can help readers immerse themselves in the story.

Pro Tip: You don't need to include every fact you learn. Readers don't want a dissertation—they want authenticity. Use research to enhance your story, not overwhelm it.

### Filling Knowledge Gaps

Here's a secret: no writer knows everything. Shocking, I know. But that's where research comes in—it fills in the blanks.

Writing a medical drama? You don't need a degree in medicine, but you should know enough to make the dialogue between doctors sound plausible. Writing a historical novel? You'll want to avoid putting smartphones in Victorian hands (unless time travel is involved).

Even nonfiction writers aren't off the hook. Readers expect facts, so if you're writing about, say, sustainable farming, you'd better know your free-range chickens from your pasture-raised ones. Research bridges the gap between what you know and what your readers expect.

**Pro Tip:** Start with the basics, and don't be afraid to consult experts or reliable resources for deeper dives. (Yes, you can email that professor or call up your neighbour who's a retired beekeeper. Most people love sharing their expertise!)

**Inspiring Creativity**

Research isn't just about getting the facts right—it can also light your creative spark. Sometimes, the details you stumble across while researching are the very things that make your book shine.

For instance:

- You're reading about medieval trade routes and discover a fascinating fact about how they transported salt. Suddenly, you've got an idea for a fantasy subplot involving smuggled magical minerals.
- You're researching for a parenting book and come across a hilarious quote from a sleep-deprived parent. Boom—your introduction practically writes itself.
- You're researching for a medical drama and find out when a person flat lines, they do not shock them, but do CPR until the heart starts beating again.

The facts you uncover can open doors to unexpected plot twists, quirky characters, or fresh angles for your nonfiction. The key is to stay curious and let your research guide you to new and exciting places.

Pro Tip: Keep a "research inspirations" file where you jot down random tidbits that might not fit your current project but could spark ideas for future ones. That fun fact about 17th-century cheese taxes? Save it for later—you never know.

**Wrapping It Up**

Research is the backbone of good writing. It adds authenticity, fills in the gaps, and can even surprise you with fresh inspiration. But remember, research isn't about perfection—it's about giving your work the details and depth it needs to stand out.

Now that you know why research matters, it's time to roll up your sleeves and dive in. Don't be afraid to explore, experiment, and embrace the process. After all, the best stories often start with a simple question: *"What if...?"*

## Where to Find Research Material

So, you've got your big idea and you're ready to dig into some research. But where do you start? Don't worry, there's no shortage of places to find material for your book—whether it's inspiration for a fictional world or facts for a how-to guide. Here are some top sources to help you gather the information you need, all without falling into an endless research rabbit hole (well, maybe just a little).

## Books and Articles

When it comes to research, good ol' books and articles are a goldmine. Libraries, bookstores, and even online resources like Google Scholar are perfect for finding credible, detailed information.

- **Libraries:** A library card is like a free pass to endless knowledge. Librarians can help you track down books, articles, and archives on just about any subject. Plus, there's something inspiring about working in a place surrounded by books—like a quiet little nudge saying, *"You can do this too!"*

- **Online Resources:** From journal articles to blog posts, the internet has something for every topic under the sun. For nonfiction, make sure you're using reputable sources—Wikipedia is a decent starting point, but don't let it be your final stop.

**Pro Tip:** Keep an eye out for source lists in the back of books or footnotes in articles—they often point you to other great material. It's like finding a treasure map hidden in plain sight!

### Documentaries and Interviews

If flipping through pages isn't your thing, try visual and conversational sources like documentaries and interviews. They're engaging, informative, and sometimes even entertaining.

- **Documentaries:** Watching a well-made documentary can be both enlightening and creatively inspiring. Whether it's a nature doc about migratory birds or a historical deep dive on ancient civilizations, you're bound to find nuggets of information you can use.
- **Interviews:** Talking to people who know their stuff can bring a whole new level of depth to your work. For example, if you're writing about life as a paramedic, an actual paramedic can tell you what the textbooks miss—the humour, the exhaustion, and the weird things people do when they've had one too many drinks.

**Pro Tip:** If you're planning to quote or paraphrase someone directly, get their permission first—it's polite *and* keeps things above board.

**First-Hand Experience**

Sometimes the best way to understand something is to roll up your sleeves and try it yourself. First-hand experience not only adds authenticity but can also give you insights you won't find in any book or article.

- **Hands-On Research:** Writing about rock climbing? Hit up a climbing gym and try it out (or at least watch and take notes while pretending you're not intimidated by the pros). Writing a novel set in a bakery? Spend an afternoon learning to make sourdough—you'll be amazed at how many details you can use.
- **Observational Research:** If direct participation isn't an option, observing is the next best thing. Sit in on a pottery class, shadow a friend at work, or spend some time people-watching in a coffee shop.

**Pro Tip:** Bring a notebook to jot down sensory details—sights, sounds, smells, and feelings. You never know when that random observation might inspire the perfect scene.

**Online Communities**

The internet can be an amazing resource for connecting with people who share your interests—or who know way more about a topic than you do.

- **Reddit and Forums:** Niche online communities are a treasure trove of knowledge. Whether you're learning about Victorian fashion or quantum physics, there's probably a subreddit or forum for it.

- **Social Media Groups:** Facebook, Discord, and other platforms have groups dedicated to everything from medieval swordplay to mushroom foraging. Ask questions, lurk, or just soak up the conversations for ideas.

**But Beware:** The internet is a double-edged sword. It's full of great information—but also plenty of misinformation. Cross-check anything you find, especially for nonfiction. If it sounds too wild to be true, it probably is (but hey, it might inspire a great plot twist!).

### Wrapping It Up

Research doesn't have to be boring or overwhelming. By mixing and matching these sources, you can gather everything you need while keeping the process fun and engaging. Whether you're reading, watching, doing, or chatting, you'll discover details that enrich your writing and make your work stand out.

Now grab your library card, fire up Google, or head to your local climbing wall—it's time to dig into the fascinating world of research. Who knows? You might even enjoy it more than you expected.

### Staying Inspired: Keep the Creativity Flowing

Writing is a marathon, not a sprint, and even the most dedicated writer needs a little spark of inspiration now and then. The good news? Inspiration is everywhere—you just need to know where to look. This section is all about keeping your creative juices flowing by thinking outside the box and embracing the unexpected.

## Read Widely

We all have our go-to genres and topics, but staying in that comfort zone can limit your creativity. Inspiration often comes from the least expected places, so mix it up and read beyond your usual interests.

- **Step Outside Your Genre:**
- If you're writing a romance novel, try picking up a sci-fi thriller or a memoir. If you're crafting a gritty crime story, take a detour into historical fiction or poetry. You'd be amazed how reading outside your genre can spark fresh ideas for your own work.

*Example:* A sci-fi author might borrow the emotional depth of a literary novel, while a fantasy writer could find a brilliant subplot idea in a biography about a trailblazing explorer.

- **Learn From the Masters:**
- The classics, modern hits, or even niche cult favourites, can all teach you something—whether it's clever wordplay, pacing, or how to keep readers hooked.

**Pro Tip:** Keep a reading journal where you jot down interesting ideas, quotes, or story structures that resonate with you. You never know when those notes might come in handy.

## Creative Cross-Pollination

Sometimes the best ideas come when you step away from

words entirely. Art, music, and other forms of storytelling can breathe new life into your creative process.

- **Explore Art:**
- A painting can do more than just look pretty. The colours, the mood, or even the scene depicted might inspire a setting or a character in your book.

*Example:* A stormy seascape might lead to a dramatic shipwreck scene in your adventure novel.

- **Dive Into Music:**
- Lyrics can offer snippets of dialogue or themes, while melodies can set the tone for a scene. Put together a playlist for your project—it might surprise you how much it helps.
- **Watch Performances:**
- Plays, films, or even a well-crafted TV series can show you how to pace a story, develop characters, or build tension.

**Pro Tip:** If something moves you—whether it's a song, a sculpture, or even a graffiti mural—ask yourself *why*. Digging into that emotional reaction can reveal ideas you can weave into your writing.

### Embrace Curiosity

Ever fall down a rabbit hole while Googling something? You start with "What did people eat in medieval times?" and two hours later, you're reading about the history of cheese taxation. Guess what? That's not wasted time—it's research with a side of inspiration.

- **Follow Your Interests:**
- Let your curiosity guide you. Even if a topic seems unrelated to your project, it might spark an idea for a subplot, a character quirk, or a clever twist.

*Example:* Researching the mating habits of penguins might lead to a hilarious metaphor for your rom-com or a unique dynamic for your fantasy kingdom.

- **Collect Interesting Tidbits:**
- Found a weird fact or a strange anecdote? Write it down! These random nuggets often become the seeds of memorable scenes or themes.

**Pro Tip:** Create a "Curiosity File" where you stash all the random, fascinating stuff you discover. Think of it as a treasure chest for future inspiration.

### Wrapping It Up

Staying inspired isn't about waiting for a lightning bolt of creativity—it's about keeping your eyes (and ears) open to the world around you. Read widely, explore different art forms, and embrace your natural curiosity. The more you engage with diverse ideas and experiences, the richer your writing will become.

So, take a detour, follow a rabbit hole, or pick up a book in a genre you've never explored before. Who knows? You might stumble upon your next brilliant idea. And if nothing else, you'll have some fun along the way!

### Organizing Your Research: Keep It Simple and Sanity-Saving

Research is a fantastic tool for making your book richer and more believable, but without a system, it can get out of hand fast. You don't want to end up buried under a pile of random notes, wondering where that brilliant fact about medieval cheese taxes disappeared to. (Yes, it always comes back to cheese, doesn't it?)

This section is all about keeping your research organized, relevant, and useful—so when you're deep in the writing process, you'll have everything you need at your fingertips.

**Keep It Simple**

First things first: don't overcomplicate it. Whether you're a tech wizard or a pen-and-paper purist, the goal is the same— keep all your research in one place.

- **Notebooks and Binders:**
  - Perfect for those who love the tactile joy of flipping pages and scribbling in margins. A few dividers or sticky tabs can help keep things neat and tidy. Bonus: There's zero risk of a low battery.
- **Digital Tools:**
  - Apps like Evernote, OneNote, or Google Docs are lifesavers for keeping everything searchable and easy to update. You can tag, colour-code, and even add links to your sources.
- **Hybrid Approach:**
  - Can't pick a favourite? Use both! Keep digital copies of articles but jot down thoughts and key points in a physical notebook. Sometimes, a handwritten note is the perfect way to make an idea stick.

**Pro Tip:** Name your files or sections clearly, so you can find what you need without scrolling endlessly. Nobody wants to click through "Document_47_FINAL_FINAL_EDIT" during crunch time.

## Highlight What's Relevant

Here's the truth: you're not going to use *all* your research. And that's okay! The key is figuring out which parts directly support your story or argument and letting the rest go.

- **Mark the Good Stuff:**
- Highlight, underline, or tag the information that really stands out. The parts that make you think, *"This will take my book to the next level."*
- **Let Go of the Extras:**
- It's tempting to cram in every interesting tidbit you find, but your readers don't need a five-page tangent about the history of spoons (unless you're writing *The Ultimate Spoon Compendium*, in which case, go for it).

**Pro Tip:** If you're reluctant to part with those fun but unnecessary facts, save them in a "Maybe Later" folder. Who knows? They might inspire a sequel.

## Create a System

An organized writer is a happy writer. Setting up a system for your research early on can save you hours of frustration later.

- **Categorize by Topic:**
- Group your notes into categories, like "Character Development," "World-Building," or "Chapter 5." This

makes it easier to find what you need when you need it.

- **Colour-Code or Tag:**
- Use highlighters, sticky tabs, or digital tags to mark your notes. For example:
- Blue for setting details.
- Yellow for plot ideas.
- Green for fun facts about penguins that *might* fit somewhere.

**Pro Tip:** If you're using a digital tool, take advantage of search functions. Being able to type "dragon lore" and instantly pull up all your notes on magical reptiles is a lifesaver.

### Avoid Overloading Your Draft

Research is there to support your story, not steal the show. It's easy to get carried away and dump too much information into your manuscript. (We see you, aspiring historians and trivia buffs!)

- **Focus on the Narrative:**
- Use research to enhance your story, not distract from it. For example, if your detective novel takes place in 1920s Toronto, sprinkle in details about streetcars and prohibition—but don't derail the plot to describe every building on Yonge Street.
- **Write First, Fact-Check Later:**
- When drafting, focus on the story and leave detailed research for the editing phase. You don't want to lose momentum chasing obscure facts mid-sentence.

**Pro Tip:** Trust your instincts. If a fact feels forced or unnecessary, leave it out. Your readers will thank you for keeping things engaging and streamlined.

## Wrapping It Up

Organizing your research doesn't have to be a chore. With the right tools and a little strategy, you can create a system that works for you—and actually makes writing easier. Keep it simple, highlight what matters, and remember: the goal is to write a compelling story or argument, not an encyclopedia.

So, grab your notebook, binder, or favourite app, and get your research in order. Future-you will be grateful when it's crunch time, and everything you need is right where it should be!

## Homework: Build Your Research Toolkit

It's time to take everything you've learned about research and put it into action. Think of this homework as setting up your writer's toolbox—gathering the tools and resources you'll need to bring your book to life. Whether you're writing fiction or nonfiction, this exercise will help you get organized, stay inspired, and keep your ideas flowing.

## Step 1: Make a List of Resources

Start by brainstorming all the resources you want to use for your book. This could include:

- **Books:** Titles related to your topic or genre. Check your local library, bookstore, or even that pile of unread books on your nightstand.
- **Websites:** Credible sources like academic sites, niche

blogs, or online archives. Remember to bookmark them for easy access.

- **People:** Experts you can interview, whether it's a historian, a beekeeper, or your great-aunt who swears she once met Elvis. Real-life stories can add richness to your work.
- **Media:** Documentaries, podcasts, or even YouTube videos on your subject.

**Example List:**

- *Books: The Anatomy of Story* by John Truby, *Salt: A World History* by Mark Kurlansky.
- *Websites:* Canadian Geographic for setting research, Reddit's r/Writing for writing tips.
- *People:* My neighbour who's a retired pilot, and my friend's grandma who grew up in the 1940s.
- *Media:* A podcast episode on the history of railways, and a YouTube video on the basics of fencing.

**Pro Tip:** Don't go overboard. Start with a manageable number of resources so you don't overwhelm yourself.

**Step 2: Decide How You'll Organize Your Notes**

Next, choose the system that works best for you. The goal is to keep your research in one place and make it easy to find later.

- **Physical Notebook:** Perfect for writers who love the feel of pen on paper. Use sticky tabs or coloured markers to keep things neat.
- **Digital App:** Evernote, OneNote, or Scrivener are great options for those who prefer searchable,

taggable notes. Plus, you'll always have your research handy if inspiration strikes while you're on the go.

- **Index Cards:** Old-school but effective. Use them for quick notes, quotes, or brainstorming sessions, and rearrange them as needed.

**Example Setup:**

- *Notebook:* For brainstorming and jotting down ideas on the fly.
- *Google Docs:* For saving links and long-form research notes.
- *Colour Coding:* Green tabs for character research, blue for plot, and yellow for random but fun facts.

**Pro Tip:** Stick with one system (at least for this project) to avoid scattering your notes across five different places. Trust me, it's easier to stay focused when everything's in one spot.

### Step 3: Write Three to Five "What If?" Questions

This is where the fun begins. Take what you've learned so far and let your imagination run wild. "What if?" questions are a great way to spark new ideas or add unexpected twists to your story.

- **For Fiction:**
- What if a historical event went differently?
- What if your character had a secret nobody knew about?
- What if the setting itself created the conflict?
- **For Nonfiction:**

- What if I included personal anecdotes to make my advice more relatable?
- What if I tackled a controversial angle on my topic?
- What if I broke my book into smaller, easy-to-digest sections?

**Examples:**

1. *What if a small-town librarian discovered a long-lost treasure map hidden in an old book?*
2. *What if a storm stranded the characters in a remote cabin, forcing them to confront their secrets?*
3. *What if my self-help book used humour to address tough subjects, like failure and rejection?*
4. *What if the villain in my story thought they were the hero?*
5. *What if I framed my nonfiction book around a series of personal challenges I took on while researching it?*

**Pro Tip:** Keep adding to your "What if?" list as you research and write. Sometimes the best ideas pop up when you least expect them.

**Wrapping It Up**

By the end of this exercise, you'll have a solid toolkit ready to fuel your writing process. With your resources lined up, your notes organized, and your imagination sparked, you're one step closer to turning your book idea into reality.

So, grab your notebook (or fire up your favourite app), start jotting down those "What if?" questions, and watch your story or message come to life. You're officially in research ninja mode now—go forth and conquer!

## Avoiding Research Pitfalls: Stop, Check, and Write

Ah, research—the endless ocean of fascinating facts and "just one more search" moments. I know, more about research, but while it's an essential part of writing, it's also where many writers get stuck. It's easy to fall into traps like over-researching, trusting dodgy sources, or cramming in too much information. But fear not! With a little planning (and a lot of willpower), you can sidestep these common pitfalls and keep your writing on track.

## Paralysis by Analysis

Research is important, but it can also be an excellent excuse to avoid actually writing. We've all been there: you're hunting for one little detail, and suddenly you're 47 tabs deep into obscure historical events, reading about the Great Molasses Flood of 1919 (which is *fascinating*, by the way).

Here's the thing: you'll never know *everything* about your topic, and you don't need to. At some point, you have to stop researching and start putting words on the page.

- **Set a Research Limit:** Decide in advance how much time you'll spend researching before you start writing. It could be a week, a month, or a specific number of sources. Once you hit your limit, it's time to move on.
- **Write First, Research Later:** If you're stuck on a detail, make a note to come back to it and keep writing. Don't let a missing fact derail your momentum.

**Pro Tip:** Remind yourself that your first draft doesn't need to be perfect. You can always refine and add more research in later drafts. For now, focus on getting your ideas down.

**Trusting Unreliable Sources**

The internet is a wonderful tool, but let's be real: not everything you find online is true. (Shocking, I know.) From Wikipedia entries to obscure blogs, there's plenty of misinformation out there, and it can sneak into your work if you're not careful.

- **Double-Check Your Facts:** If you find a juicy piece of information, verify it using multiple credible sources. If three reputable sites agree, you're probably on solid ground.
- **Use Reputable Sources:** For nonfiction, stick to well-known publications, scholarly articles, or interviews with experts. For fiction, seek out books or documentaries by reliable creators.
- **Beware of "Too Good to Be True" Stories:** If a fact sounds wildly dramatic or unbelievable, it might be exaggerated—or outright false.

**Pro Tip:** Treat Wikipedia as a starting point, not the final word. Use it to get an overview of your topic, then dig deeper into the references it provides.

**Pro Tip:** Pick up the book *Putting The Science in Fiction*. This book has expert advice for writing with authenticity in Science Fiction, Fantasy, and other genres.

**Overloading Your Book**

Once you've gathered a mountain of research, the temptation to use *all* of it can be strong. After all, you worked hard to find those fun facts about medieval shoe-making or penguin behaviour! But here's the truth: not everything belongs in your book.

- **Focus on Relevance:** Choose the details that directly support your story or argument. If a fact doesn't enhance your plot, characters, or message, leave it out.
- **Avoid Info Dumps:** Readers want to be entertained or informed, not overwhelmed. A well-placed detail is far more effective than a 10-page tangent.
- **Remember Your Audience:** Tailor your level of detail to what your readers need. A thriller audience doesn't need a forensic science lecture, and a self-help book shouldn't read like a textbook.

**Example:** If your book is about the history of chocolate, readers don't need the chemical composition of cocoa unless it directly supports your narrative. Keep it tasty, not technical.

**Pro Tip:** Save unused research in a separate file or notebook. It might not fit this project, but it could spark ideas for a future one.

### Wrapping It Up

Research is a vital part of writing, but it's easy to overthink, overload, or misstep along the way. By setting limits, trusting reliable sources, and staying focused on what's truly relevant, you can keep your research under control and your writing moving forward.

So, close those extra tabs, double-check your facts, and resist the urge to cram in every fun tidbit. Your book—and your readers—will thank you for it. Happy writing!

## Bonus: Pro Tips for Effective Research

Research is a crucial part of writing, but it's also where things can go hilariously off the rails. One minute you're looking up the history of lighthouses for your nautical adventure, and next, you're knee-deep in articles about why cats are afraid of cucumbers. It happens to the best of us!

Here are a few pro tips to help you stay on track, save time, and keep your research from taking over your life (or your book).

## Set Research Time Limits

If research was a buffet, you'd never stop filling your plate. There's always more to learn, but at some point, you've got to step away and start writing.

- **Set a Timer:** Give yourself a specific amount of time —say, two weeks or 10 hours—to focus on research. When the timer's up, it's pencils down (or browsers closed) and keyboards ready.
- **Chunk Your Time:** Break your research into smaller tasks, like "one hour on Victorian fashion" or "30 minutes finding penguin mating habits." This helps keep things manageable.

**Pro Tip:** Treat yourself for sticking to your limit! Reward your discipline with a coffee, a cookie, or a guilt-free YouTube binge.

**Use a Research Journal**

A research journal is like your best friend during the writing process—it keeps all your brilliant discoveries in one place, so you're not scrambling to remember which tab had that perfect fact about medieval shoe-making.

- **Choose Your Format:** It could be a physical notebook, a Word document, or a fancy digital app like Evernote. The key is consistency—stick to one place so you don't lose track of your notes.
- **What to Include:** Jot down quotes, stats, quick summaries, or links to useful sources. Bonus points if you add a note about *why* the information is important.

**Pro Tip:** Make your journal searchable. If it's digital, use tags or keywords. If it's physical, create a simple index or use sticky tabs to mark important sections. Your future self will thank you.

**Pro Tip:** Microsoft One Note is a great resource for keeping notes, and you can set it to save in your One Drive.

**Keep a Curiosity File**

Every writer knows the thrill of stumbling upon a completely unrelated but fascinating fact. Maybe you're researching ancient Greek festivals and come across a story about a goat that accidentally became a town mayor (yes, it happens). Instead of letting it derail your current project, stash it in a "Curiosity File."

- **What It Is:** A separate notebook, file, or folder where you collect those odd little gems that don't fit into your current book but are too good to forget.
- **Why It's Useful:** These tidbits might inspire future projects, add a quirky subplot to your next novel, or just give you a fun fact to share at parties.

**Pro Tip:** Review your curiosity file every now and then. It's like digging through a treasure chest—you never know what will spark your next big idea.

### Wrapping It Up

Effective research doesn't have to be overwhelming. By setting limits, staying organized, and keeping a place for those random nuggets of inspiration, you'll make the process more manageable—and maybe even fun.

So, grab your journal, set your timer, and start digging into your topic. Who knows what fascinating details you'll uncover? Just remember to save the cucumber-cat videos for later.

And congratulations - you made it through the long winded research section!

# Chapter 3

# **Planning and Outlining**

## **Planning and Outlining: Mapping Out Your Book**

Planning and outlining are like GPS for your book. Whether you're a meticulous planner or someone who prefers to wing it, having at least a rough idea of where you're headed can save you a lot of headaches later. Outlining helps you stay on track, avoid plot holes, and figure out what happens next when you inevitably hit that "middle-of-the-book" fog.

There's no one-size-fits-all approach to outlining, so let's explore some popular methods to find one that fits your style.

1. **The Snowflake Method**
2. **Chapter Summaries**
3. **The Three-Act Structure**
4. **Mind Mapping**
5. **The Beat Sheet**
6. **Post-It Notes**

7. **Freewriting Outline**
8. **The Index Card Method**
9. **The Hero's Journey**

Let's take a deep dive into each so you can pick which ones fit your style of writing.

**Pro Tip:** Don't get stuck by trying to pick just one. You can muddle around and morph two or three types together and come out with exactly what works for you.

## The Snowflake Method: Build Your Story, One Flake at a Time

The Snowflake Method is like creating your book the way nature makes snowflakes—starting small and building up layer by layer until you've got something intricate and unique. It's a structured yet flexible way to outline your story, perfect for writers who like to organize their ideas while leaving room for creativity.

Let's break it down and add a sprinkle of examples and tips to get you started.

### How the Snowflake Method Works

The Snowflake Method is a step-by-step process that expands your story idea, starting with a single sentence and growing into a detailed outline. Here's how it works:

### Step 1: The One-Sentence Summary

Boil your entire story down to one sentence. This is the core of your book—the big idea that captures what it's all about.

**Example:**

- *"A shy teenager discovers they have magical powers and must save their kingdom from an evil sorcerer."*

**Pro Tip:** Don't worry about making this perfect right away. It's just the seed of your story—you'll flesh it out later.

## Step 2: Expand to a Paragraph

Take that sentence and turn it into a short paragraph. Include the main character, their goal, the conflict, and the stakes.

**Example:**

- *"Sixteen-year-old Mira has always felt out of place in her small village, but when she discovers she's the heir to an ancient magical legacy, everything changes. With her kingdom under threat from the Dark Sorcerer, Mira must embrace her newfound powers, gather allies, and stop his reign of terror—or risk losing everything she loves."*

**Pro Tip:** This is your story's foundation. It should give you a clear sense of the beginning, middle, and end.

## Step 3: Flesh Out Your Characters

Create a one-paragraph summary for each major character. Include their role in the story, their goals, and their challenges.

**Example:**

- *Mira: The protagonist. Shy and uncertain, Mira must overcome her self-doubt to become the hero her kingdom needs.*
- *The Dark Sorcerer: The antagonist. Ambitious and power-hungry, he'll stop at nothing to rule the land.*
- *Liam: Mira's best friend. Loyal and brave, he serves as her moral compass and occasional comic relief.*

**Pro Tip:** Focus on what drives each character—what do they want, and what's standing in their way?

### Step 4: Expand to a One-Page Summary

Take your paragraph from Step 2 and expand it into a full page. Include more details about the plot, subplots, and key turning points.

**Example Highlights:**

- Introduce how Mira discovers her magical powers.
- Detail her first encounter with the Dark Sorcerer.
- Show how Mira grows stronger through training and forms a ragtag team of allies.
- Build up to the final showdown and her triumphant victory—or bittersweet sacrifice.

**Pro Tip:** Don't get bogged down in the tiny details just yet. Focus on the main events and how they connect.

### Step 5: Break It into Scenes

Now, turn your one-page summary into a scene-by-scene outline. Each scene should move the story forward—whether it's through action, character development, or world-building.

**Example Scenes:**

1. Mira discovers her magical powers while saving her brother from an accident.
2. The village elder reveals her lineage and sends her on a quest.
3. Mira meets Liam, who insists on joining her.
4. First clash with the Dark Sorcerer's minions—Mira's powers fail, and she barely escapes.

**Pro Tip:** Think of each scene as a building block. If one doesn't feel essential, it might not belong.

### Why the Snowflake Method Works

- **It's Flexible:** You can stop at any step or dive deeper if you need more detail.
- **It's Incremental:** You're building your story in manageable chunks instead of tackling it all at once.
- **It's Great for Clarity:** By the time you're done, you'll have a clear road map for your book.

### Tips for Using the Snowflake Method

1. **Don't Rush the Process:** Each step builds on the last, so take your time. Let your ideas grow naturally.
2. **Adapt It to Your Needs:** You don't have to follow every step to the letter. If you prefer a shorter outline, stop at Step 4.
3. **Use Visual Aids:** Write your steps out on sticky notes or index cards if you're a visual learner. Arrange them to see the bigger picture.

4. **Review and Refine:** Once you've finished, revisit your outline. Does the story flow? Are the stakes high enough? This is your chance to tweak things before you start writing.
5. **Have Fun With It:** The Snowflake Method is a tool, not a rulebook. Make it work for you, and don't be afraid to experiment.

**Wrapping It Up**

The Snowflake Method is a fantastic way to build a solid foundation for your book while still keeping the creative process enjoyable. Whether you're crafting an epic fantasy, a gripping thriller, or a heartfelt memoir, this step-by-step approach will help you stay organized and focused.

Now grab your pen, notebook, or laptop and start with that one perfect sentence. Who knows? By the end, you might just have a snowstorm of inspiration on your hands!

**The Chapter Summary Method: Your Story, One Chapter at a Time**

The Chapter Summary Method is like creating a map for your story, with each chapter serving as a clear marker along the way. It's simple, straightforward, and perfect for writers who like to see their story laid out in manageable chunks. Think of it as the "to-do list" of outlining methods—you know what needs to happen and where, but there's still room to make changes as you go.

Let's break it down, with some tips and examples to get you started!

**How the Chapter Summary Method Works**

This method involves writing a short summary for each chapter before you start drafting. It doesn't have to be super detailed—just a couple of sentences that outline what happens in each chapter and why it matters.

**What Goes Into a Chapter Summary?**

- **The Action:** What happens in this chapter?
- **The Purpose:** Why does it matter? How does it move the story forward or develop your characters?

You're essentially creating a mini blueprint for each part of your book. It's simple, flexible, and keeps you focused on the big picture.

**Example: A Fantasy Adventure**

Here's what a few chapter summaries might look like for a fantasy novel:

Mira discovers she can control fire when her emotions spiral out of control during a village festival. The townsfolk are terrified, and Mira is forced to flee.

Lost in the forest, Mira stumbles upon a mysterious traveller, Liam, who offers to help her learn more about her powers. He reveals he has secrets of his own.

Mira and Liam are ambushed by shadowy figures sent by the Dark Sorcerer. Mira's powers fail her in the heat of battle, leaving Liam to save the day.

Determined to grow stronger, Mira begins training under

Liam's guidance. She uncovers an ancient prophecy that suggests her powers are tied to the kingdom's survival.

**Why Use the Chapter Summary Method?**

This method works because it gives you a clear sense of direction without boxing you in. You can easily shuffle chapters around, expand scenes, or tweak the details as your story evolves.

**Benefits:**

- **Organized Progress:** You always know what comes next, which makes drafting easier.
- **Big Picture View:** It helps you spot pacing issues or gaps in the plot early on.
- **Room for Creativity:** The summaries give you structure but leave enough flexibility to make changes along the way.

**Tips for Using the Chapter Summary Method**

1. **Start With Key Moments:**
2. If writing every chapter summary feels daunting, start with the major turning points in your story—the beginning, the climax, and the resolution. Fill in the gaps later.
3. **Keep It Brief:**
4. Aim for 2-3 sentences per chapter. Focus on the essentials, and don't worry about including every little detail.

**Example:**

Instead of: *"Mira meets Liam, they argue about the weather, Mira eats a sandwich, and then they walk for two hours before stumbling on a mysterious cave,"* try: *"Mira meets Liam, and together they discover a mysterious cave with strange symbols carved into the walls."*

5. **Highlight Emotional Beats:**
6. A good story isn't just about what happens—it's about how your characters feel and grow. Make sure your summaries include important emotional shifts or decisions.
7. **Stay Flexible:**
8. Your outline is a guide, not a contract. If you come up with a brilliant twist halfway through writing, adjust your chapter summaries to reflect it.
9. **Check for Pacing:**
10. Once you've outlined all your chapters, step back and look at the flow. Are the stakes rising? Do the chapters build toward a satisfying climax? If the middle feels slow, consider adding tension or tightening the action.

**Pro Tip: Use Index Cards or Sticky Notes**

For a hands-on approach, write each chapter summary on an index card or sticky note. Lay them out on a table or board, and move them around to experiment with the order. It's a fun way to visualize your story and make adjustments on the fly.

**Wrapping It Up**

The Chapter Summary Method is a fantastic option for writers who want a clear, organized path through their story without getting bogged down in too much detail. It's flexible, efficient, and helps you keep track of the big picture while still allowing for creativity.

So, grab a notebook, some index cards, or a digital document, and start plotting out those chapters. Before you know it, you'll have a roadmap for your book—and a story that's ready to come to life!

## The Three-Act Structure: Your Story's Beginning, Middle, and End

The Three-Act Structure is one of the most classic storytelling methods out there. It's the foundation of many great books, movies, and plays, and for good reason—it works! Think of it as the storytelling equivalent of a three-course meal: an intriguing appetizer, a hearty main course, and a satisfying dessert. Each act serves a purpose, building the tension and excitement until you reach the big, juicy finale.

### What Is the Three-Act Structure?

At its core, the Three-Act Structure divides your story into three parts:

1. **Act One – Setup:** The introduction. You meet the characters, learn about their world, and discover the problem they're about to face.
2. **Act Two – Confrontation:** The middle. This is where the stakes get higher, the challenges get tougher, and your characters are pushed to their limits.

3. **Act Three – Resolution:** The grand finale. The conflicts reach their peak, everything comes to a head, and the story wraps up with (hopefully) a satisfying conclusion.

## Breaking Down the Three Acts

## Act One: The Setup

This is where your story begins. You introduce the main character, their everyday life, and the conflict that's about to turn their world upside down.

- **Key Elements:**
- Who is your protagonist, and what do they want?
- What's standing in their way? (This is the inciting incident—the event that kicks off the main story.)
- What's at stake? Why should the audience care?

**Example:**

In *The Hunger Games*:

- Katniss lives in a dystopian world where life is a daily struggle.
- The inciting incident? Her sister's name is drawn in the Reaping, and Katniss volunteers to take her place in the deadly Hunger Games.
- Stakes? Life or death—both for Katniss and her family.

**Pro Tip:** Don't over-explain. Act One should hook the reader and set the stage for the action, not drag on with too much backstory.

## Act Two: The Confrontation

Welcome to the middle of your story, where things get messy. Act Two is all about challenges, conflict, and growth. Your protagonist starts facing obstacles that force them to change, adapt, or grow stronger.

- **Key Elements:**
- Raise the stakes: Make things harder for your protagonist.
- Introduce twists and turns: Keep the reader guessing.
- Develop subplots: Add layers to your story with secondary characters or conflicts.

**Example:**

In *The Hunger Games*:

- Katniss navigates the brutal arena, forms alliances, and faces threats from other tributes, the environment, and the Capitol's manipulations.
- The stakes? Survival becomes even more complicated when she's forced to grapple with trust, strategy, and her growing feelings for Peeta.

**Pro Tip:** This act is often the longest, so pace yourself. Build tension gradually, keeping the reader hooked without overwhelming them with non-stop action.

## Act Three: The Resolution

This is the big finish, where everything comes together. The conflicts reach their climax, the loose ends are tied up (mostly), and the protagonist faces their ultimate challenge.

- **Key Elements:**
- The Climax: The make-or-break moment where the protagonist confronts their biggest obstacle.
- The Resolution: How does it all end? Did your protagonist achieve their goal? How have they changed?

**Example:**

In *The Hunger Games*:

- The climax? Katniss and Peeta outwit the Capitol by threatening to eat poisonous berries, forcing the Gamemakers to declare them co-winners.
- The resolution? Katniss returns home, but life has changed forever—both for her and her world.

**Pro Tip:** Stick the landing. A strong, satisfying ending can leave readers feeling fulfilled, even if everything doesn't wrap up with a neat little bow.

### Why Use the Three-Act Structure?

This structure works because it mirrors the natural flow of storytelling—introduce a problem, complicate it, and then resolve it. It's a straightforward framework that keeps your story focused and engaging.

- **For Planners:** It gives you a clear roadmap for your story.
- **For Pantsers:** Even if you write by the seat of your pants, this structure can help you shape your draft during revisions.

## Tips for Using the Three-Act Structure

1. **Start with the Big Moments:**
   - Outline your story's inciting incident, climax, and resolution first. These are the pillars of your plot.
2. **Build Bridges:**
   - Once you've nailed the big moments, fill in the gaps with smaller scenes and subplots that connect everything together.
3. **Keep Raising the Stakes:**
   - Each act should build on the tension and stakes of the previous one. Don't let your story plateau in the middle.
4. **Focus on Character Growth:**
   - Your protagonist should change in some way by the end of the story. Whether they've overcome a flaw, achieved their goal, or learned a hard truth, their journey is what makes the story compelling.

## Wrapping It Up

The Three-Act Structure is a tried-and-true method for crafting a well-paced, engaging story. It's flexible enough to suit any genre, and it helps you stay focused on the big picture while still leaving room for creativity.

So, grab your notebook, sketch out your acts, and start filling in the details. With this structure as your guide, you'll have a solid foundation for a story that readers won't want to put down!

## Mind Mapping: A Visual Brainstorming Adventure

If you're a visual thinker who loves watching ideas come to life, mind mapping might just be your perfect outlining method. It's like creating a spiderweb of your story or topic, with your central idea at the heart and all the connecting threads branching out in every direction. It's creative, flexible, and a little bit messy—in the best way possible!

**What Is Mind Mapping?**

Mind mapping is a brainstorming tool that helps you organize your ideas visually. You start with one central concept—like your book's title, theme, or main idea—and branch out with related topics, characters, settings, or scenes.

It's less about structure and more about exploring connections between your ideas. Plus, it's a great way to spot gaps or discover new angles you hadn't considered.

**How to Create a Mind Map**

1. **Start with the Big Idea:**
   - Write your main idea in the centre of a blank page. For example, if you're writing a mystery novel, your central idea might be *"Solve the Case!"*
2. **Branch Out:**
   - From the central idea, draw lines (or "branches") to related concepts. These could include:
     - Main characters
     - Possible suspects
     - Key settings
     - Plot points or twists
3. **Go Deeper:**
   - Add smaller branches to expand on each idea. For example, under "Main Characters," you might list:

- Detective Claire: Obsessed with coffee and justice.
- Sidekick Jamie: Comic relief but surprisingly good with puzzles.
4. **Keep Adding Until It Feels Complete:**
   - Let your ideas flow! There's no wrong way to do this—just follow where your creativity leads.

**Example: Mind Mapping a Mystery Novel**

Here's what part of a mind map for a mystery novel might look like:

**Central Idea:** *"Solve the Case!"*

- **Main Characters:**
  - Detective Claire: Grumpy but brilliant.
  - Jamie: Witty, slightly clumsy sidekick.
  - Chief Inspector Brooks: Claire's ex-boss with a secret.
- **Key Settings:**
  - The crime scene: A lavish mansion during a thunderstorm.
  - Detective Claire's office: Cluttered but full of clues.
  - The local café: Where Jamie gathers gossip.
- **Plot Points:**
  - The murder weapon is missing.
  - A coded letter is found in the library.
  - The butler has an alibi, but it doesn't check out.

**Why Mind Mapping Works**

Mind mapping is like a brainstorming session on paper (or screen). It's perfect for writers who:

- Want to explore ideas without worrying about structure.
- Think visually and prefer seeing their story laid out in a way that makes connections clear.
- Love the freedom to expand or revise ideas as they go.

It's also a great way to get unstuck when you're not sure where to take your story next.

**Tips for Using Mind Mapping**

- **Use Colour to Stay Organized:**
  - Assign different colours to categories. For example:
    - Red for characters.
    - Blue for settings.
    - Green for plot twists.

This makes your map easier to read and adds a bit of fun to the process.

5. **Start Simple:**
   - Don't worry about making your map look perfect. Start with the basics, and let it grow naturally.
6. **Go Digital if You Prefer:**
   - Digital tools like MindMeister, Miro, or Canva are great for creating polished, editable mind maps. Plus, you can move branches around without needing an eraser!
7. **Focus on Connections:**

- Look for unexpected links between ideas. Maybe your villain is tied to a key setting, or a subplot enriches your main theme.

8. **Keep It Visible:**
   - Pin your mind map near your writing space, or save it as your desktop background. Seeing your ideas laid out can keep you inspired and focused.

## Wrapping It Up

Mind mapping is a flexible, creative outlining method that's as fun as it is effective. Whether you're planning a sprawling epic or a concise how-to guide, this approach helps you explore your ideas and connect the dots in a way that's uniquely yours.

So grab some paper (or fire up a digital tool), start with your big idea, and let your imagination run wild. By the time you're done, you'll have a map of your story or topic that's ready to guide you through the writing process—and maybe even a few surprises along the way!

## The Beat Sheet: Hitting the High Notes of Your Story

If your story were a song, the beat sheet would be its rhythm. This outlining method helps you plan out the key "beats" or moments in your story—the turning points, emotional highs and lows, and all the juicy bits that keep readers turning pages. It's an excellent tool for pacing your story and making sure you're hitting all the right notes at the right time.

Let's break it down with examples and tips to help you master this simple yet powerful method.

## What Is a Beat Sheet?

A beat sheet is like a story blueprint. Instead of outlining every detail, it focuses on the key events or "beats" that make up your plot. These beats are the moments that move your story forward, build tension, and create emotional payoffs for the reader.

Think of it as a highlight reel of your book. You're sketching out the big moments first, so you'll have a clear path to follow when it's time to write.

### How to Create a Beat Sheet

1. **Start with the Basics:**
   - A typical beat sheet includes the major beats of your story:
     - **The Opening Image:** How does your story begin? What sets the tone?
     - **The Inciting Incident:** The event that kicks off the action.
     - **The Midpoint:** A major turning point where everything changes.
     - **The Climax:** The moment of highest tension— the big showdown.
     - **The Resolution:** How does your story wrap up?
2. **Fill in the Gaps:**
   - Once you've nailed down the major beats, add smaller ones in between. These could be moments of character growth, plot twists, or subplots that tie into the main story.
3. **Keep It Brief:**
   - Each beat should be a sentence or two—just enough to remind you what happens and why it's important.

**Example: Beat Sheet for a Mystery Novel**

**Title:** *The Case of the Missing Manuscript*

- **Opening Image:** Amateur sleuth Clara is stuck working in a dull library job, dreaming of adventure.
- **Inciting Incident:** A famous author's priceless manuscript goes missing during a library fundraiser. Clara is the prime suspect.
- **First Plot Point:** Clara discovers a cryptic clue hidden in the author's notes that points to a disgruntled rival.
- **Midpoint:** Clara confronts the rival, only to realise the clue was a red herring. The real thief is someone she trusted.
- **Dark Moment:** Clara is ready to give up, fearing she'll never clear her name.
- **Climax:** Clara pieces together the final clue and catches the thief red-handed during a high-stakes auction.
- **Resolution:** With her name cleared, Clara gets a promotion and decides to pursue her dream of becoming a detective.

**Why Use a Beat Sheet?**

The beauty of the beat sheet is its simplicity. It gives you just enough structure to guide your writing without boxing you in.

- **Great for Pacing:** It ensures your story keeps moving and doesn't sag in the middle.
- **Flexible:** You can adapt it to suit any genre or writing style.

- **Quick and Easy:** It's a fast way to outline your story without getting bogged down in details.

## Tips for Using the Beat Sheet

1. **Start with the Big Beats:**
   - Focus on the major turning points first. Once you have those in place, you can fill in the smaller beats later.
2. **Think in Scenes:**
   - Each beat should represent a key scene or moment in your story. Ask yourself: *What happens here, and why does it matter?*
3. **Keep the Stakes High:**
   - Every beat should move the story forward or raise the stakes. If a beat feels unnecessary, it might be time to cut or rethink it.
4. **Make It Personal:**
   - Don't just focus on plot. Include beats that show your character's growth, relationships, and struggles.
5. **Revise as You Go:**
   - Your beat sheet isn't set in stone. Feel free to tweak it as your story evolves—sometimes the best ideas come while you're writing.

## Wrapping It Up

The Beat Sheet is a fantastic outlining method for writers who like a clear roadmap without too much detail. It keeps your story focused, helps with pacing, and ensures you're hitting all the right emotional and plot beats.

So, grab a notebook or open a blank document and start jotting down your beats. Whether you're crafting a sweeping epic or a snappy rom-com, this method will keep your story marching to the perfect rhythm. And remember—every great story needs a strong beat to dance to!

## The Post-it Note Method: Plotting with Sticky Squares of Genius

The Post-it Note Method is a fun, flexible, and highly visual way to outline your book. Whether you're planning a novel, a memoir, or a how-to guide, this method lets you see your entire story at a glance and move things around as needed. Plus, who doesn't love the satisfying *plonk* of peeling a sticky note off the stack?

### What Is the Post-it Note Method?

At its core, this method is all about breaking your story into individual pieces—scenes, chapters, or ideas—and writing each one on a separate Post-it note. Then you arrange (and rearrange) them on a wall, board, or table until your story starts to take shape.

Think of it like building a puzzle, except you get to decide where all the pieces go. It's a great way to experiment with structure and make changes without having to rewrite your entire outline every time inspiration strikes.

### How to Use the Post-it Note Method

1. **Gather Your Supplies:**
   - You'll need a stack of Post-it notes (bonus points if they're colourful) and a surface to stick them on—

like a corkboard, whiteboard, or even the wall above your desk.

2. **Write Down Your Ideas:**
   - Each Post-it represents one element of your story, like a scene, chapter, or key moment.
   - Write a short description on each note. For example:
     - "Detective Jones finds the missing diary."
     - "Protagonist confesses their feelings at the big dance."
     - "Introduction to the three main suspects."

3. **Stick and Arrange:**
   - Place your notes on the board (or wall) in the order you think they'll appear in your story.
   - Move them around as needed. If a scene doesn't fit, it's easy to peel it off and stick it somewhere else—or toss it entirely.

4. **Colour-Code for Clarity:**
   - Use different colours for different elements, like plotlines, characters, or themes. For example:
     - Blue = Main plot.
     - Yellow = Subplots
     - Green = Character development

5. **Fill in the Gaps:**
   - Once your main scenes or ideas are laid out, look for gaps. Are there parts of the story that feel underdeveloped? Add more notes to fill them in.

**Example: Post-it Note Plotting for a Mystery Novel**

Here's what part of your board might look like:

- **Blue Notes (Main Plot):**
  - "Detective Jones is assigned the case."
  - "A clue is found at the crime scene—a torn theatre ticket."
  - "The villain is revealed in a dramatic confrontation backstage."
- **Yellow Notes (Subplot):**
  - "Jones deals with tension in her friendship with partner Riley."
  - "Riley's secret connection to the case is revealed."
- **Green Notes (Character Development):**
  - "Jones flashes back to her first unsolved case."
  - "Villain's motive is explained—revenge for a family tragedy."

As you stick and move notes around, you can see how the story flows and where things might need tweaking.

**Why Use the Post-it Note Method?**

This method is perfect for writers who:

- Love to see their story visually.
- Need the freedom to rearrange ideas without committing to anything too soon.
- Want a hands-on, interactive way to plot their book.

**Tips for Using the Post-it Note Method**

1. **Start Simple:**
   - Don't try to outline every single detail right away. Start with the big scenes or ideas and fill in the rest as your story takes shape.

2. **Keep It Flexible:**
   - Don't be afraid to experiment. Move notes around, try different orders, and see what works best.
3. **Use a Legend:**
   - If you're colour-coding, create a little legend so you don't forget which colour means what.
4. **Snap a Photo:**
   - Once you're happy with your arrangement, take a picture of your board or wall. That way, you'll have a backup if your notes fall off or get moved around.

5. **Reuse Notes for Revisions:**
   - When it's time to edit, use the same method to reorganize or refine your story. You can even swap out notes for new ideas.

**Wrapping It Up**

The Post-it Note Method is a fantastic way to outline your story while keeping things fun and flexible. Whether you're piecing together a thriller or mapping out a memoir, this hands-on approach lets you see the big picture while giving you the freedom to make changes as you go.

So grab your sticky notes, claim a wall, and start plotting! By the time you're done, you'll have a colourful, visual roadmap for your book—and maybe even a new appreciation for office supplies.

**The Free-Writing Outline: Let Your Ideas Run Wild**

If the word "outline" makes you feel boxed in, the Free-Writing Outline might be exactly what you need. This method lets you brainstorm your story in an open-ended, unstructured way.

Think of it as a no-rules writing sprint where you spill your ideas onto the page without worrying about order, grammar, or making sense.

Free-writing is about capturing the raw essence of your story —the characters, the plot twists, the juicy details—and figuring out how it all fits together later. It's messy, but it works!

**What Is a Free-Writing Outline?**

Unlike a traditional outline with bullet points and numbered chapters, a Free-Writing Outline is more like a stream of consciousness. You sit down, start typing (or scribbling), and let the ideas flow. You don't have to worry about structure or even complete sentences. The goal is to get your thoughts out of your head and onto the page.

It's brainstorming meets journaling, and it's perfect for writers who prefer to discover their story as they go.

**How to Create a Free-Writing Outline**

1. **Set the Mood:**
   - Grab your favourite pen, open a blank document, or pull out a notebook. If music or coffee helps get the creative juices flowing, go for it.
2. **Write Without Stopping:**
   - Start with what you know about your story. Maybe it's a vivid scene, a character idea, or the general premise. Whatever comes to mind, write it down. No editing, no second-guessing—just write.
3. **Follow Your Tangents:**
   - If one idea sparks another, go with it! Free-writing

is about exploring possibilities, so don't worry about staying on track.

4. **Embrace the Chaos:**
   - Your outline doesn't have to look pretty or make perfect sense. You're capturing ideas, not creating a polished draft.

### Example: Free-Writing for a Romance Novel

Here's what a Free-Writing Outline might look like:

"Okay, so the protagonist is a baker in a small town—let's call her Emma. She's got this big dream of opening her own bakery, but she's stuck working for her grumpy boss, Harold. One day, a charming stranger—Alex?—comes to town. Maybe he's a food critic, or he's opening a rival bakery? That could be fun—competition and chemistry. Oh, what if Harold tries to sabotage Emma when she decides to go out on her own? And Alex helps her... but there's a big misunderstanding about why he's really in town. Maybe he's hiding something? Hmm... need to figure out the climax—maybe a big bake-off?"

It's not polished, but it's full of potential!

### Why Use a Free-Writing Outline?

The Free-Writing Outline works because it:

- **Gets Ideas Flowing:** No pressure, no rules—just pure creativity.
- **Frees You From Perfectionism:** It's about ideas, not execution, so you can write without worrying about getting it "right."

- **Builds Momentum:** Once you start writing, the ideas will often come faster and easier.

**Tips for Using the Free-Writing Outline**

1. **Set a Timer:**
   - If staring at a blank page feels daunting, give yourself a time limit—say 10 or 15 minutes—and just write until the timer goes off.
2. **Focus on What Excites You:**
   - Write about the parts of your story that feel the most vivid or exciting right now. Don't worry about the boring bits—you can fill those in later.
3. **Revisit and Refine:**
   - Once you've captured a bunch of ideas, go back and highlight the ones that stand out. These will become the foundation for your more structured outline (if you want one).
4. **Don't Hold Back:**
   - Even if your ideas feel silly or outlandish, write them down. You never know when a random thought might spark something brilliant.
5. **Use It as a Starting Point:**
   - If your free-writing outline feels chaotic, that's okay! Think of it as the raw material for your story. You can sort, expand, and refine it into a more detailed outline later.

**Wrapping It Up**

The Free-Writing Outline is perfect for writers who want to dive into their story without getting bogged down by structure.

It's creative, flexible, and a great way to capture the essence of your idea before worrying about the finer details.

So grab your notebook or laptop, take a deep breath, and let the ideas flow. You might end up with a wild, wonderful mess —but that's the first step toward creating something amazing!

## The Index Card Method: Plotting One Card at a Time

The Index Card Method is a classic outlining technique that's as simple as it is effective. It's all about breaking your story into bite-sized chunks and giving each one its own little card. Whether you're plotting a novel, mapping out a nonfiction book, or even organizing a screenplay, this method lets you arrange (and rearrange) your ideas as easily as shuffling a deck of cards.

The best part? It's low-tech, portable, and oddly satisfying. Plus, who doesn't love a good excuse to raid the stationery aisle?

## What Is the Index Card Method?

At its core, this method is all about flexibility. Each index card represents one scene, chapter, or key idea in your book. You can spread them out, move them around, and experiment with the structure of your story until it feels just right. It's like having a puzzle where you get to decide what the picture looks like.

## How to Use the Index Card Method

1. **Grab Your Cards:**
    - You'll need a stack of blank index cards and a pen.

Bonus points if you colour-code them for extra flair (more on that later).

2. **Write One Idea per Card:**
    o Each card should represent one key element of your story, like a scene, plot twist, or character moment.
        ▪ Keep it brief. A few words or a short sentence is enough to capture the essence of the idea.

**Example:**

- "Detective finds a bloody glove at the crime scene."
- "Protagonist's secret is revealed during family dinner."
- "Villain's motive is hinted at in a cryptic letter."

3. **Arrange Your Cards:**
    o Lay your cards out on a flat surface, like a table or the floor, and start arranging them in order.
    o Play around with the sequence—move cards to test different story flows or experiment with pacing.

4. **Group and Colour-Code:**
    o Use colours to represent different aspects of your story, like subplots, character arcs, or themes.
    o For example:
    o Blue = Main plot
    o Green = Character development
    o Yellow = Subplots

5. **Review and Adjust:**
    o Step back and look at the big picture. Are there

gaps in your story? Do certain sections feel too slow? Add, remove, or rearrange cards as needed.

## Example: Index Card Method for a Mystery Novel

Here's what part of your stack might look like:

## Main Plot (Blue Cards):

- "Detective is assigned to investigate a missing art piece."
- "Clue found: a broken watch at the museum."
- "Chase scene through the city leads to suspect's hideout."

## Subplot (Yellow Cards):

- "Detective's strained relationship with her partner."
- "Partner hides a key piece of evidence."

## Character Development (Green Cards):

- "Detective recalls a failed case that still haunts her."
- "Villain reveals personal connection to the detective's past."

Once everything is laid out, you can start tweaking the order or adding new cards to flesh out your story.

## Why Use the Index Card Method?

This method works because it's both simple and flexible. You can easily rearrange scenes, add new ideas, or remove parts that don't work—without feeling locked into anything. It's also great for spotting gaps or pacing issues in your story before you start writing.

**Tips for Using the Index Card Method**

1. **Use Colours Wisely:**
   o Assign a different colour to each element of your story—plot, characters, themes, or even chapters. It'll make it easier to see the balance of your story at a glance.
2. **Keep It Portable:**
   o Store your cards in a small box or binder clip so you can work on your outline anywhere. Have a plot twist idea at the coffee shop? Whip out your cards and add it on the spot.
3. **Don't Overthink It:**
   o Your cards don't need to be perfect. This is about brainstorming and planning, not writing polished prose.
4. **Test Different Arrangements:**
   o Lay your cards out in different orders to see how it changes the flow of your story. It's much easier to experiment now than during the drafting phase!
5. **Snap a Picture:**
   o Once you've arranged your cards in an order you love, take a photo. This way, you'll have a backup if your cat decides the cards make a great toy.

**Wrapping It Up**

The Index Card Method is a hands-on, visual way to map out your story while staying flexible and creative. Whether you're crafting a tightly plotted thriller or a sprawling fantasy epic, this method lets you experiment with structure and pacing before committing to a single word on the page.

So grab a stack of cards, find a flat surface, and start plotting! By the time you're done, you'll have a colourful, organized roadmap for your book—and maybe even a newfound love for stationery.

## The Hero's Journey: Your Guide to Epic Storytelling

The Hero's Journey is a classic storytelling structure that's been captivating audiences for centuries. It's the blueprint for many of your favourite tales—think *Star Wars*, *The Lord of the Rings*, and *The Lion King*. This method is perfect for crafting stories of growth, transformation, and big adventures, where a hero faces challenges, learns lessons, and returns changed.

If your story needs a sense of adventure and emotional depth, the Hero's Journey is here to guide you. Let's dive into what it's all about, with examples and tips to make it your own.

### What Is the Hero's Journey?

The Hero's Journey is a storytelling structure popularized by Joseph Campbell in his book *The Hero with a Thousand Faces*. It breaks a story into 12 steps that follow a protagonist (your hero) as they embark on an adventure, face obstacles, and return transformed.

Think of it as a road map for your story, with twists, turns, and a satisfying destination.

### The 12 Steps of the Hero's Journey

Here's a quick breakdown of the steps, with examples from *The Lion King*:

1. **The Ordinary World:**
   - The hero starts in their normal life.
   - *Example:* Simba enjoys a carefree life as the future king of Pride Rock.
2. **The Call to Adventure:**
   - Something disrupts the hero's life and pulls them toward an adventure.
   - *Example:* Mufasa's death forces Simba to face the idea of becoming king.
3. **Refusal of the Call:**
   - The hero resists the adventure, doubting their ability to succeed.
   - *Example:* Simba runs away, blaming himself for Mufasa's death.
4. **Meeting the Mentor:**
   - A mentor appears to guide the hero.
   - *Example:* Rafiki helps Simba realise his potential and destiny.
5. **Crossing the Threshold:**
   - The hero leaves their comfort zone and steps into the unknown.
   - *Example:* Simba returns to the Pride Lands to confront Scar.
6. **Tests, Allies, and Enemies:**
   - The hero faces challenges, makes allies, and encounters foes.
   - *Example:* Simba teams up with Timon, Pumbaa, and Nala to overthrow Scar.
7. **Approach to the Inmost Cave:**

- The hero prepares for the biggest challenge.
- *Example:* Simba confronts Scar's reign and his own fears about his past.

8. **The Ordeal:**
   - The hero faces their greatest challenge or fear.
   - *Example:* Simba fights Scar, risking his life to save the Pride Lands.

9. **The Reward (Seizing the Sword):**
   - The hero achieves their goal or gains a reward.
   - *Example:* Simba reclaims his place as king, bringing balance back to Pride Rock.

10. **The Road Back:**
    - The hero returns to their ordinary world, changed by their journey.
    - *Example:* Simba takes his rightful place as king.

11. **The Resurrection:**
    - The hero faces a final test, proving their growth.
    - *Example:* Simba stands strong against Scar's accusations, showing he's no longer the scared cub who ran away.

12. **Return with the Elixir:**
    - The hero returns home with newfound wisdom or power, benefiting others.
    - *Example:* Simba leads the Pride Lands into a new era of peace.

**Why Use the Hero's Journey?**

This method works because it mirrors real-life struggles and triumphs. Readers connect with heroes who grow, change, and overcome challenges—it's inspiring, relatable, and oh-so-satisfying.

It's also flexible. While not every story needs all 12 steps, you can adapt the structure to suit your narrative.

**Tips for Using the Hero's Journey**

1. **Start with the Hero:**
   - Who is your protagonist, and what do they want? The best journeys are personal, so make sure the stakes matter to your hero.
2. **Focus on Transformation:**
   - Your hero should change in some way by the end of the story. Whether they gain wisdom, confidence, or a new perspective, the journey should leave them (and your readers) transformed.
3. **Add Your Twist:**
   - This structure is a classic for a reason, but that doesn't mean your story has to feel predictable. Add unexpected elements or subvert the steps to keep things fresh.
4. **Use the Structure as a Guide, Not a Rulebook:**
   - Don't feel pressured to hit every single step. If your story works with 8 steps instead of 12, that's totally fine!
5. **Create Compelling Challenges:**
   - Each step should bring your hero closer to their goal while raising the stakes. Think of the tests and trials as the backbone of your plot.

**Example: Hero's Journey in a Space Adventure**

**Ordinary World:** Captain Zara is a disgraced space pilot living on a remote asteroid.

**Call to Adventure:** She's asked to rescue a missing diplomat from a hostile alien planet.

**Refusal of the Call:** Zara refuses, haunted by a failed mission that cost her crew's lives.

**Meeting the Mentor:** A quirky AI guide convinces Zara she's the only one who can complete the mission.

**Crossing the Threshold:** Zara agrees and sets off, entering the alien territory.

**Tests, Allies, and Enemies:** She faces alien traps, earns the trust of a rebel fighter, and battles bounty hunters.

**Approach to the Inmost Cave:** Zara sneaks into the alien stronghold, confronting memories of her past failure.

**The Ordeal:** She must pilot a stolen ship through a deadly asteroid field to escape with the diplomat.

**The Reward:** Zara regains her confidence and earns the respect of her peers.

**The Road Back:** She returns home, bringing the diplomat to safety.

**The Resurrection:** Zara confronts the mission board, proving she's ready to lead again.

**Return with the Elixir:** She's reinstated as a captain and inspires a new generation of pilots.

### Wrapping It Up

The Hero's Journey is a timeless framework that's perfect for crafting stories filled with growth, adventure, and emotional depth. Whether you're writing epic fantasy, sci-fi, or even a heartfelt memoir, this structure can help you guide your hero through a meaningful transformation.

So grab your map, plot out your journey, and send your hero on an unforgettable adventure. Just remember: it's not about the destination—it's about how they grow along the way.

# Part 2
# **The Writing Process**

# Chapter 4
# **Creating a writing Routine**

## Why Writing Routines Matter

Writing isn't always about waiting for that magical lightning bolt of inspiration to strike. Let's be honest—if you rely on inspiration alone, you'll probably spend more time staring at your blank page than actually filling it. That's where a good writing routine comes in. By showing up regularly, you'll keep the words flowing, even on the days when you're not feeling particularly "inspired."

## Consistency Beats Inspiration

Sure, inspiration is great. When it hits, you feel like a literary genius. But let's be real—it's also unpredictable. Some days, the muse might be on vacation, and you can't afford to wait for her to send a postcard.

That's where consistency saves the day. By carving out regular time for writing, you train yourself to show up, no matter what.

Writing becomes a habit, like brushing your teeth (except way more creative). The more often you write, the easier it gets to tap into that creative part of your brain. And, funnily enough, the muse tends to visit more often when she knows you're already working.

**Habits Lead to Progress**

Think about it: even small, consistent efforts add up over time. Writing just 500 words a day might not sound like much, but guess what? In less than six months, you'll have a full novel draft.

Here's the math:

- 500 words x 30 days = 15,000 words a month
- 15,000 words x 4 months = 60,000 words—a solid draft!

It's all about momentum. By sticking to a routine, you'll build the kind of steady progress that turns a blank page into a finished manuscript. Even if some days feel like pulling teeth, the important thing is that you're writing—and that's what counts.

**Wrapping It Up**

A consistent writing routine is like your secret weapon. It beats waiting for inspiration, helps you build momentum, and turns your writing dreams into a regular habit. Remember: it's not about churning out perfection every day. It's about showing up, putting words on the page, and letting those small efforts snowball into something amazing. Now, go grab a notebook—or a keyboard—and get started!

## Setting Realistic Writing Goals

Goals are like a map for your writing journey—they give you direction and keep you motivated. But here's the catch: your goals need to be realistic. It's great to dream big, but if your plan involves writing a bestseller in a weekend, you might want to rethink things. Let's break it down into something more manageable.

## Long-Term Goals

First, figure out your endgame. What's the big goal you want to achieve? Maybe it's finishing your novel, completing a memoir, or drafting a screenplay. Whatever it is, make sure it's specific. Saying "I want to write a book" is nice, but saying "I want to write an 80,000-word fantasy novel" gives you a clear target.

## Short-Term Goals

Big goals can feel overwhelming, so the trick is to break them into smaller, bite-sized chunks. Think of it as tackling your book chapter by chapter or page by page.

Here are some examples:

- Write one chapter this week.
- Edit 5 pages today.
- Spend 30 minutes brainstorming character backstories.

Small goals make big ones feel doable, and every little milestone you hit brings you closer to the finish line.

## Measurable and Flexible

Goals work best when they're clear and measurable. Instead of saying, "I'll write a bit this week," try something like, "I'll write 2,000 words by Sunday." This gives you something concrete to aim for.

That said, life happens. Maybe your week doesn't go as planned (because when does it ever?). The key is flexibility. Adjust your goals when needed, and don't beat yourself up if you fall short. Progress is progress, even if it's slower than you'd hoped.

**Track Your Progress**

Keeping track of your goals can be surprisingly motivating. Use whatever tool works for you:

- A word count tracker to watch your numbers climb.
- A writing app that reminds you to stay on schedule.
- A good old-fashioned calendar to mark off your achievements.

There's something satisfying about seeing your progress laid out—and it might even inspire you to keep going when the going gets tough.

**Wrapping It Up**

Setting realistic writing goals is about finding the sweet spot between ambition and practicality. Aim high, but keep it manageable. Break it down, track your progress, and be kind to yourself when life throws you a curveball. Now go set those goals—you've got this!

**Managing Time Effectively**

Let's face it: life is busy, and finding time to write can feel like searching for your keys when you're already late. But here's the good news—you don't need hours of uninterrupted quiet to make progress on your book. With a little planning and a few clever strategies, you can carve out time for writing, even in the busiest of schedules.

## Finding Writing Time

The first step is figuring out where writing can fit into your day. Look for those sneaky pockets of time—early mornings, lunch breaks, or after the kids are in bed. Even a quick 15 minutes can add up if you're consistent.

**Tip:** Carry a notebook or keep a writing app on your phone. That way, if you find yourself waiting in line or stuck in traffic (not driving, obviously!), you can jot down a few ideas.

**Pro Tip:** Most people type at 15-35 word per minute. Five minutes will work out to 75 to 175 words. If you are lucky, like me, you can type 50-65 words a minute. That works out to 250-325 words in a five minute stint!

## The Myth of the Perfect Block of Time

Many people think they need hours of uninterrupted time to write. Spoiler alert: you don't. Sure, a whole afternoon at your desk would be lovely, but life rarely offers that luxury. The truth is, a focused 15-minute session can be surprisingly productive.

**Example:** Use a timer and challenge yourself to write as much as you can in 15 minutes. You might be amazed at how much you get done when the clock's ticking!

### Time-Blocking Techniques

Treat your writing time like an appointment you can't miss. Block off dedicated writing sessions on your calendar and stick to them. Whether it's a daily 30-minute session or a weekly 2-hour block, make it non-negotiable.

**Pro Tip:** If you're easily distracted, let people in your life know you're unavailable during your writing time. Yes, this includes ignoring your phone—texts and TikToks can wait!

### Multitasking Myths

Multitasking sounds productive, but it's usually the opposite. If you're trying to write while answering emails, folding laundry, and listening to a podcast, chances are you're not giving your best to any of them. Writing requires focus, so give it your undivided attention—at least for a little while.

**Pro Tip:** Create a writing environment where distractions are minimal. Turn off notifications, close unnecessary tabs, and let yourself sink into the work.

### Time Audit Exercise

Still not sure where writing fits in? Try a simple "time audit" exercise:

1. Spend a day or two logging how you spend your time. Include everything—work, commuting, scrolling social media, Netflix binges, etc.
2. Review your log to find hidden time. Maybe those 20 minutes spent doom-scrolling Instagram could be better spent on your book.
3. Block off those found moments for writing.

## Wrapping It Up

You don't need perfect conditions or endless hours to make progress on your writing. By finding hidden pockets of time, blocking out dedicated sessions, and focusing on one task at a time, you can make writing a regular part of your routine—even with a busy schedule. Now go grab your timer and get started—those 15 minutes aren't going to write themselves!

## Overcoming Procrastination

Procrastination is a writer's most persistent frenemy. It whispers sweet nothings like, *"You'll write better tomorrow,"* or, *"You deserve a quick TikTok break,"* until you've lost half the day and haven't written a single word. Sound familiar? Don't worry—you're not alone, and you're definitely not doomed.

Let's dig into why procrastination happens and, more importantly, how to kick it to the curb.

### Why Writers Procrastinate

Procrastination isn't laziness—it's often fuelled by deeper issues, like:

- **Fear of Failure:** Worrying your writing won't be good enough can make it hard to start at all.
- **Perfectionism:** Feeling like every sentence must be flawless before you move on.
- **Not Knowing Where to Start:** A blank page can feel overwhelming, especially if you're not sure what comes next.

**Pro Tip:** Remember, your first draft is supposed to be messy. Think of it as dumping out all the puzzle pieces—you can sort and perfect them later.

**Strategies to Beat Procrastination**

Sometimes, the best way to overcome procrastination is to outsmart it. Here's how:

1. **Start Small:**
   - Tell yourself you only need to write one sentence, or set a timer for just 5 minutes.
   - Once you start, momentum often takes over, and you'll find yourself writing more than you planned.

**Pro Tip:** Keep your expectations low. Writing even a little bit is better than not writing at all.

2. **Set Rewards:**
   - Promise yourself a treat after hitting a milestone— whether it's a square of chocolate, an episode of your favourite show, or a guilt-free scroll through social media.
   - Make the reward something you genuinely look forward to.

**Example:** Write 500 words and earn a fancy coffee or tea break.

3. **Eliminate Distractions:**
   - Turn off notifications on your phone or computer.
   - Clear your workspace of clutter.

- Use distraction-blocking apps like Freedom or Stay Focusd to keep social media temptations at bay.

**Pro Tip:** Create a dedicated "writing zone" if possible. Even a small corner with a comfy chair and good lighting can help you focus.

4. **The Power of Accountability:**
   - Join a writing group or find a buddy who's also working on a project. Share your goals and check in regularly.
   - Participate in online writing challenges like NaNoWriMo to stay motivated and connect with a community of writers.

**Pro Tip:** Deadlines are magical. Even if it's self-imposed or set by a friend, knowing someone is expecting your work can be a powerful motivator.

**Pro Tip:** I usually warm myself up before working on my work in progress. It could be creating a flash fiction piece, or also working on a short story. It works for me, but may not work for you. Experiment to see what helps you get in the zone!

**Procrastination-Busting Checklist**

If you're stuck, try these quick fixes:

- **Stop Mid-Sentence:** Deliberately leave off in the middle of a sentence or scene. It makes starting easier tomorrow because you already know where you're headed.

- **Use a Timer:** Set a timer for 10 minutes and write without stopping.
- **Break It Down:** Instead of "Write Chapter 5," aim for "Write the opening paragraph of Chapter 5."
- **Set a Deadline:** Even a fake one can create a sense of urgency.
- **Change Your Scenery:** Try writing in a different spot—a café, library, or even a different room in your house.

### Wrapping It Up

Procrastination might be sneaky, but it doesn't stand a chance against a determined writer armed with the right strategies. Start small, reward yourself, block out distractions, and lean on others for accountability when you need it.

Now, take that first step—even if it's just writing one sentence. The rest of your book is waiting!

### Building Writing-Friendly Habits

Writing is like any other habit—it gets easier when you make it part of your daily routine. By creating an environment and mindset that supports your writing, you'll set yourself up for success. Plus, adding a few rituals and rewards can make the process feel a little less like work and a lot more enjoyable.

### Create a Writing Ritual

Your brain loves routines, and a writing ritual can help signal that it's time to get serious (or at least semi-serious) about your work. Whether it's brewing a cup of tea, lighting a candle, or blasting your "Epic Writing Playlist," a ritual can ease you into the right mindset.

**Examples of Writing Rituals:**

- Start your session by jotting down one sentence about how your day is going.
- Play the same piece of instrumental music every time you sit down to write.
- Spend a couple of minutes stretching or meditating before you begin.

**Pro Tip:** Keep your ritual simple and repeatable, so it becomes second nature. Before you know it, your brain will associate that playlist or cup of tea with getting words on the page.

**Set a Dedicated Writing Space**

You don't need a fancy home office to get into the writing zone, but having a consistent spot for writing can make a huge difference. Your space doesn't need to be big—it just needs to be comfortable, distraction-free, and inspiring.

**What to Include in Your Writing Space:**

- A good chair and a clutter-free surface (your back will thank you).
- Items that inspire you, like a favourite book, a photo, or a plant.
- Whatever tools you need to write, whether it's a laptop, a notebook, or a pile of sticky notes.

**Pro Tip:** If your space doubles as something else (e.g., the kitchen table), try setting it up specifically for writing during your sessions. A small shift—like clearing the surface or adding a lamp—can help you switch gears.

## Celebrate Wins

Writing a book is a big undertaking, so it's important to celebrate your progress along the way. Finished a chapter? That's a win! Wrote 100 words on a day you didn't feel like writing? Another win! Recognizing these milestones helps keep you motivated and reminds you how far you've come.

### Ways to Celebrate:

- Treat yourself to your favourite snack or drink.
- Take a victory lap around the block (or your living room).
- Share your progress with a friend who's cheering you on.

**Pro Tip:** Don't wait for the "big wins" like finishing the whole book—small victories deserve recognition too.

## Use a Streak Tracker

A streak tracker is a simple but powerful tool for building momentum. Every time you write, mark it down on a calendar, app, or notebook. Seeing your streak grow can be incredibly motivating—and you won't want to break it!

### How to Use a Streak Tracker:

- Set a goal that works for you, like writing every day or five times a week.
- Track your streak with something visual, like coloured dots on a calendar or a digital tracker app.

- Celebrate when you hit a milestone, like a 10-day or 30-day streak.

**Pro Tip:** If you miss a day, don't let it derail you. Just start a new streak and keep going!

### Wrapping It Up

Building writing-friendly habits is all about creating a routine and environment that works for you. Whether it's lighting a candle, setting up a dedicated space, or celebrating small wins, these habits will make writing feel less like a chore and more like an enjoyable (or at least manageable) part of your day. Start small, stay consistent, and watch those streaks—and your book—grow!

### Staying Motivated Long-Term

Writing a book is a big commitment, and staying motivated over the long haul can feel like trying to keep a plant alive—you start with great intentions, but halfway through, things might wilt a little. The good news? With the right mindset and strategies, you can keep your writing energy alive and thriving. Let's dig into ways to stay on track, avoid burnout, and even enjoy the process (yes, it's possible!).

### Revisit Your 'Why'

When the excitement of starting a book wears off and the slog of the middle kicks in, it's time to remind yourself why you started this journey. Maybe you've always dreamed of seeing your name on a cover, or perhaps you want to share a story that's been living in your head for years.

Take a moment to reflect:

- **Why does this book matter to you?**
- **What's the end goal?**

Write down your answers and keep them somewhere visible—like on your desk or taped to your computer. When motivation dips, revisit these notes to reignite your spark.

**Pro Tip:** Remind yourself that even the most successful authors faced tough moments. J.K. Rowling started *Harry Potter* in a café, balancing life as a single mum. If she can do it, so can you!

## Avoid Burnout

Burnout is the kryptonite of motivation. Writing is important, but so is taking care of yourself.

- **Take Breaks:** Step away from your project when you need to recharge. Go for a walk, stretch, or binge-watch your favourite show guilt-free.
- **Be Kind to Yourself:** Writing is hard work, and progress isn't always linear. Celebrate small victories, and don't beat yourself up over bad days.
- **Pace Yourself:** Set realistic goals and remember that slow and steady wins the race.

**Pro Tip:** Think of writing like running a marathon. Sprinting to the finish line might sound appealing, but pacing yourself ensures you make it without collapsing halfway through.

## Keep It Fun

Writing should feel rewarding, not like a chore. If your current project starts to feel heavy, shake things up to keep the creative juices flowing.

- **Try Writing Prompts:** Pick a random prompt and write a quick scene—it doesn't even have to relate to your book.
- **Join a Fun Challenge:** Participating in a challenge like NaNoWriMo can inject some excitement and give you a supportive community to cheer you on.
- **Work on a Side Project:** If your main book feels like a grind, take a mini-break to work on something else —a short story, a poem, or even a blog post.

**Pro Tip:** Keep a folder of "fun writing" for the days when your main project feels like pulling teeth. A little creative play can remind you why you started writing in the first place.

### A Little Inspiration

Sometimes, a good quote or story can be the boost you need. Here's one to keep in your back pocket:

"Write a little every day, without hope, without despair." – Isak Dinesen (*Out of Africa*)

Even the pros know that steady, consistent effort is the key to success. It's not about being perfect—it's about showing up.

### Wrapping It Up

Staying motivated for the long haul is all about balance. Revisit your reasons for writing, give yourself permission to rest, and find ways to inject fun into the process. Remember, writing a book is a journey, not a sprint—and every word you write brings you one step closer to your goal.

Keep going. You've got this!

## Exercise: Design Your Ideal Writing Routine

Creating a writing routine isn't about following a one-size-fits-all plan—it's about finding what works best for *you*. This exercise will help you craft a routine that suits your goals, schedule, and personality. Think of it as building the perfect recipe for productive writing. Let's get started!

## What to Include in Your Writing Routine

1. **Define Your Writing Goals:**
   - What do you want to achieve this week or month? Maybe it's finishing a chapter, writing 5,000 words, or editing your outline. Whatever it is, make it specific and realistic.

**Pro Tip:** Write down your goals and keep them visible—sticky notes on your desk work wonders.

2. **Identify Your Most Productive Times of Day:**
   - Are you a morning person who thrives on coffee-fuelled creativity? Or do your best ideas come after dark? Find your "golden hours" and plan to write during those times.

3. **Plan for a Distraction-Free Environment:**
   - Choose a spot where you can focus without interruptions. Turn off notifications, tidy your space, and let others know when you're in "do not disturb" mode.

**Pro Tip:** If you can't escape the noise, noise-cancelling headphones and a good playlist can do wonders.**Implementation: Make It Happen**

4. **Commit to Your Schedule:**
   o Decide on a daily or weekly writing schedule that feels achievable. Whether it's 30 minutes every morning or two-hour sessions on weekends, consistency is key.
5. **Test and Tweak:**
   o Stick to your plan for a month and see how it works. Pay attention to what feels good and what doesn't. Adjust your schedule as needed to make it more effective.
6. **Track Your Progress:**
   o Use a planner, app, or simple calendar to mark your writing days and celebrate your streaks.

**Optional Idea: Use a Writing Routine Planner**

To make this process easier, grab a printable or downloadable writing routine planner. It should include sections for:

- **Weekly or Monthly Goals:** What you want to achieve and by when.
- **Daily Writing Times:** Your planned writing slots.
- **Progress Tracking:** Space to log what you accomplished each day.

**Pro Tip:** If you miss a day, don't stress—just pick it up again tomorrow. Progress, not perfection, is the goal.

**Wrapping It Up**

Douglas Owen

Designing your ideal writing routine is all about creating a schedule that works for your life and keeps you moving toward your goals. Once you've got a plan in place, stick with it, adjust as needed, and celebrate your wins along the way. Remember, the best routine is the one that helps you keep writing!

# Chapter 5
# **Developing Characters**

## *Creating a Protagonist*

Your protagonist is the beating heart of your story. They're the one readers will cheer for, cry with, and occasionally shout at when they make questionable choices (because, let's face it, they will). A well-crafted protagonist isn't just the centre of the action—they're the reason readers stick around to see how it all unfolds. Let's dive into what makes a compelling main character.

### Define Their Goals

Every protagonist needs a goal. It's the driving force behind their actions and the thing that keeps the story moving forward. Ask yourself:

- What does your protagonist want?
- Why is it important to them?

This goal could be anything from saving the world (*very ambitious*) to finding their missing cat (*just as noble, really*). Whatever it is, it should feel urgent and meaningful to the character, raising the stakes if they fail.

**Pro Tip:** The goal doesn't have to stay the same throughout the story. Characters often start with one goal, only to discover what they truly need as the plot develops.

### Explore Their Flaws

Perfect protagonists are boring. Nobody wants to read about someone who always makes the right decisions, wins every fight, and never spills coffee on their shirt. Real people are flawed, and your protagonist should be too.

Maybe they're impulsive, or afraid of commitment, or bad at asking for help. Whatever their flaws, these traits should create challenges that make their journey harder—and their eventual growth more satisfying.

**Pro Tip:** A protagonist's flaws don't always need to be negative. A strength, like being overly loyal or ambitious, can become a flaw when it's taken to an extreme.

### Develop Their Backstory

Your protagonist didn't just appear out of thin air (unless they did, in which case, wow, what a story idea!). Who they are today is shaped by their past experiences.

- What's their childhood like?
- What relationships, events, or traumas have defined them?

- How do these things influence their decisions in the story?

You don't need to write a 20-page life history, but knowing their backstory will help you understand their motivations and make their actions feel believable.

**Pro Tip:** Sprinkle backstory into your story naturally—don't dump it all in one go. Readers want hints and breadcrumbs, not a Wikipedia article.

## Focus on Internal and External Conflict

Conflict is the engine of any good story, and your protagonist should have plenty of it.

- **External Conflict:** These are the big challenges happening around them. Think evil villains, natural disasters, or that annoying coworker who keeps stealing their lunch.
- **Internal Conflict:** This is the emotional struggle within your protagonist. Maybe they're fighting self-doubt, guilt, or a fear of failure.

The best stories balance both types of conflict, showing how external problems affect your protagonist internally—and how their internal struggles influence how they handle the outside world.

**Pro Tip:** The resolution of your protagonist's internal conflict often mirrors the resolution of the external one. It's a satisfying way to tie everything together.

**Example Exercise: Build Your Protagonist**

Take a few minutes to write a brief character bio for your protagonist. Include:

- **Their Goal:** What do they want, and why?
- **Their Biggest Fear:** What are they afraid of losing or facing?
- **What's at Stake:** What will happen if they fail?

Here's an example:

- **Name:** Riley Grant
- **Goal:** To win a national baking competition and save their struggling bakery.
- **Biggest Fear:** Failing in front of an audience (and their super-critical mother).
- **What's at Stake:** If Riley doesn't win, they'll lose their bakery and their sense of purpose.

**Wrapping It Up**

A strong protagonist is the key to a memorable story. Give them clear goals, relatable flaws, a meaningful backstory, and plenty of juicy conflicts. They don't have to be perfect—they just have to be human (or at least relatable, if they're an alien, wizard, or sentient cupcake). Now, go create someone your readers will root for!

**Creating an Antagonist**

Your antagonist isn't just a cardboard cut-out villain with a dastardly laugh and a penchant for twirling their moustache. They're a vital piece of your story's puzzle, the force that keeps the protagonist on their toes and raises the stakes to nerve-shredding levels. A well-crafted antagonist doesn't just create conflict—they make your story unforgettable.

## Define Their Motivation

Every antagonist needs a reason for their actions. Nobody wakes up and decides to wreak havoc "just because." In fact, the best antagonists believe they're doing the right thing, even if their methods are questionable (or downright terrible).

- Why are they doing what they're doing?
- What drives them? Is it revenge, love, greed, or a deep-seated belief in their cause?

A believable antagonist with clear motivations can create a more layered and compelling conflict. Bonus points if their goal conflicts directly with the protagonist's, forcing both characters into a tense game of tug-of-war.

**Pro Tip:** Ask yourself how your antagonist justifies their actions. If you can imagine a version of the story where they're the protagonist, you're on the right track.

## Make Them a True Challenge

Your antagonist shouldn't just annoy the protagonist—they should push them to their absolute limits.

- What makes your antagonist a real threat? Is it their strength, intellect, cunning, or sheer determination?
- How do they force your protagonist to grow or change to overcome them?

A strong antagonist raises the stakes and makes victory feel earned. After all, a story where the hero breezes past the villain without breaking a sweat isn't much of a story.

**Pro Tip:** Make sure your antagonist's strengths directly challenge the protagonist's weaknesses. It creates tension and keeps readers hooked.

### Avoid Clichés

We've all seen the overly dramatic "evil for evil's sake" villain. While they might work in certain stories, most antagonists are more interesting when they're complex. Instead of going full "mwahaha," try adding depth:

- Give them a sympathetic trait or backstory that makes readers hesitate to fully hate them.
- Let them have moments of doubt or vulnerability—this can make them feel more human (even if they're not human).

**Example:** In *Black Panther*, Killmonger is ruthless, but his motivations stem from a deeply personal and understandable place. His goals resonate, even if his methods are extreme.

### Create Parallels or Contrasts

One of the most effective ways to design a memorable antagonist is by comparing them to the protagonist. How are they similar, and how are they different?

- **Parallels:** Maybe they share a similar goal but have drastically different methods of achieving it.

- **Contrasts:** Perhaps one values order while the other thrives in chaos (*hello, Batman and the Joker!*).

These connections make the conflict richer and can highlight your story's themes in a deeper way.

### Example: The Joker in *The Dark Knight*

The Joker is a perfect example of a dynamic antagonist. He's the polar opposite of Batman, embodying chaos while Batman represents order and control. The Joker's actions force Batman to confront his own moral boundaries, creating a conflict that's not just physical but deeply philosophical.

### Wrapping It Up

A strong antagonist is just as important as your protagonist. By giving them clear motivations, making them a true challenge, avoiding clichés, and exploring their relationship to the protagonist, you'll craft a character that leaves a lasting impression.

**Pro Tip:** A great antagonist isn't just an obstacle—they're the catalyst that drives your story forward. Now, go create someone readers will *love* to hate!

### Creating Supporting Characters

Supporting characters are like the backup singers in your story. They may not take centre stage, but their presence adds depth, context, and emotional resonance to the protagonist's journey. Done right, they become more than just props— they're memorable, meaningful, and vital to the plot.

Let's explore how to create supporting characters that shine without stealing the spotlight.

**Give Them Purpose**

Every supporting character should serve a purpose in the story. They're not just there to fill space—they need a reason to exist. Ask yourself:

- How do they contribute to the protagonist's journey?
- Do they offer guidance, present obstacles, or provide emotional support?

A well-purposed supporting character keeps the story moving forward, whether they're a mentor, rival, or comedic sidekick.

**Pro Tip:** If a supporting character isn't adding anything significant to the plot, consider combining them with another character to streamline your cast.

**Develop Their Personality**

Avoid the trap of one-dimensional sidekicks. Even supporting characters deserve some love when it comes to their development. Give them:

- **Unique Traits:** Maybe they're the only one in the group who always finds the silver lining—or the one who carries snacks everywhere.
- **Personal Goals:** What do they want, and how does it intersect with the protagonist's goals?
- **Quirks:** A small, memorable detail—like a love for obscure trivia or an aversion to cats—can make them stand out.

**Pro Tip:** Think about how their personality complements (or clashes with) the protagonist. Contrast creates dynamic and interesting interactions.

## Explore Their Relationships

One of the best ways to bring supporting characters to life is through their relationships.

- **With the Protagonist:** Are they a mentor, best friend, rival, or reluctant ally? Strong relationships create emotional stakes, making readers care about what happens to them.
- **With Other Characters:** Do they get along with everyone, or are they the group's wildcard? Secondary relationships can add depth and complexity to your cast.

**Example:** In *The Lord of the Rings*, Samwise Gamgee's loyalty to Frodo isn't just touching—it's crucial to the story. Their friendship carries the emotional weight of the journey, making Sam a standout supporting character.

## Balance the Spotlight

As much as you might love your supporting characters, remember that they're there to enhance the protagonist's story, not overshadow it.

- Keep their subplots relevant to the main narrative.
- Make sure their screen time doesn't distract from the protagonist's journey.

**Pro Tip:** If a supporting character starts stealing the show, it might be a sign they deserve their own story—or that they need to step back a little.

## Wrapping It Up

Supporting characters are the unsung heroes of your story. By giving them purpose, developing their personalities, and exploring their relationships, you can create a cast that enriches your narrative without stealing the spotlight.

Remember, your protagonist might be the star, but it's the supporting characters who often leave readers saying, "I loved that guy!" Now go build a crew of sidekicks, mentors, and frenemies that your readers won't forget!

## Creating Minor Characters

Minor characters might not get much time in the spotlight, but their presence can make a world of difference in your story. They're the little sprinkles of detail that flesh out the world and support the plot without taking over. When done well, these characters leave just enough of an impression to enhance your story's flavour without overwhelming it.

## Focus on Function

Every minor character should have a purpose. Whether they're delivering a crucial piece of information, creating an obstacle, or simply adding colour to the setting, they need to earn their place in the story.

Ask yourself:

- What role does this character play?
- Do they move the plot forward, help develop the main cast, or build the world?

**Example:** The grumpy neighbour who shouts about parking rules might not be crucial to the story, but they could help set the tone of your protagonist's suburban prison—or even deliver an offhand comment that plants a key plot clue.

**Pro Tip:** When in doubt, think of minor characters as tools. They exist to serve the story, not the other way around.

### Avoid Overloading Them with Detail

Minor characters don't need backstories that rival your protagonist's. A few vivid traits are enough to make them memorable without stealing the spotlight.

For example:

- The librarian who always wears mismatched socks and whispers *way* too loudly.
- The barista who calls everyone "champ" but has a terrible memory for names.

These little quirks help minor characters pop without dragging the reader away from the main action.

**Pro Tip:** If you find yourself writing three pages about the bartender's tragic backstory when they only appear in one scene, it might be time to rein it in.

### Keep Them Consistent

Even if a character only shows up a couple of times, they need to feel believable. If the local baker is kind and chatty in one scene but suddenly gruff and reclusive in another, readers will notice.

- Maintain consistent traits, dialogue, and behaviour.
- If their personality changes, make sure it's intentional and justified by the story.

**Example:** If the baker down the street is always humming show tunes, don't forget to slip that in again when they reappear. It's those little details that make minor characters feel real.

### Use Them Sparingly

It's easy to go overboard with minor characters, especially when you're building a rich, detailed world. But too many minor players can clutter the story and confuse readers.

- Only include minor characters when they add value.
- Combine roles where possible to keep things streamlined.

**Example:** Instead of three separate delivery people showing up to interact with your protagonist, merge them into one memorable, chatty courier who becomes a recurring face.

**Pro Tip:** Think of your story like a party—too many guests, and it's hard to remember who's who. Keep the guest list manageable.

### Wrapping It Up

Minor characters are like the seasoning in your story. A dash here and there can add richness and flavour, but too much can overwhelm the dish. Focus on their function, keep them consistent, and give them just enough detail to stand out without stealing the show.

Now go forth and create those quirky librarians, grumpy neighbours, and show-tune-humming bakers—your story (and readers) will thank you!

# Chapter 6
# **Building a World**

## *Establishing the Setting*

The setting is more than just a backdrop—it's the stage where your story unfolds. Whether it's a bustling city, a quiet countryside, or a spaceship zipping through a distant galaxy, your setting shapes the tone, mood, and challenges your characters face. Let's explore how to build a setting that feels vivid and alive.

### The Basics

Start with the location. Where is your story happening, and what's it like? A setting isn't just a place—it's an experience.

### Think About:

- What do the characters see? Skyscrapers glowing in the night? Towering trees in an ancient forest?

- What do they hear? The hum of traffic, the chirp of crickets, or the eerie silence of deep space?
- What do they smell? Freshly baked bread from a corner bakery or the metallic tang of a spaceship's air filters?

Sensory details bring your setting to life, grounding readers in the world you're building.

**Time and Era**

When is your story set? The time period can influence everything from your characters' clothing and speech to the technology and societal norms they encounter.

**Think About:**

- Is your story unfolding in the past, present, or future?
- How does the era shape the challenges your characters face? For example:
- In a medieval fantasy, travel is slow, and news is delivered by messengers.
- In a futuristic sci-fi world, your protagonist might zip across galaxies in seconds but wrestle with interplanetary politics.

**Example:** In *The Hunger Games*, the futuristic dystopian setting of Panem—with its sharp divide between the affluent Capitol and the impoverished districts—not only builds tension but highlights the story's central themes of inequality and rebellion.

**Rules of the World**

For fiction writers, this is where you set the "rules" of your world. Is it bound by the laws of physics as we know them, or does magic come into play? Even nonfiction settings have cultural or social rules that shape the environment.

**Think About:**

- Are there unique features in this world? Maybe gravity is lighter, or time flows differently.
- What customs or traditions define this world? In nonfiction, these might be societal norms like how people greet each other or what they eat.
- What limitations exist? Are there areas characters can't enter or laws that restrict certain behaviours?

The rules of your world add depth and ensure consistency. Once you set them, stick to them!

**Pro Tip: Use Contrast**

The setting isn't static—it can shift and evolve to amplify the story. Contrast is a powerful tool:

- A serene meadow can make an oncoming battle feel more jarring and intense.
- A rainy, chaotic city street mirrors a character's internal turmoil and raises tension.

**Example:** In a horror story, a once-cozy family home becomes chilling when the lights flicker and a shadow moves in the hallway. The change in setting mirrors the shift in tone.

**Wrapping It Up**

Establishing your setting is all about grounding your readers in the "where," "when," and "how" of your story. By layering sensory details, clarifying time and era, and setting consistent rules, you'll create a vivid world that feels as real as your characters.

Now, whether your story takes place in a sleepy village, a bustling metropolis, or a dimension where cats rule the universe, make it a place your readers never want to leave—or can't wait to escape from!

## Creating Mood

Mood is the emotional soundtrack of your story. It's what your readers *feel* as they immerse themselves in your world—whether it's the light-hearted thrill of a sunny summer day or the creeping dread of a foggy graveyard at midnight. A well-crafted mood pulls readers into the scene, amplifying the emotional beats and setting the tone for what's to come.

## Tone and Emotion

Start by deciding how you want your readers to feel in a given scene. The mood should match the tone of your story or moment:

- Is it eerie and foreboding? Then shadows stretch too far, whispers echo, and the air grows cold.
- Is it bright and hopeful? Then the sky is clear, laughter rings out, and the breeze carries the scent of blooming flowers.

The key is consistency. If your overall tone is grim and serious, a sudden shift to slapstick comedy might feel out of place (unless you're writing a dark comedy—then, by all means, go wild!).

**Pro Tip:** Think of mood as a dial. You can subtly adjust it up or down to match the intensity of the scene. A mildly tense dinner party can evolve into a full-blown argument as the mood escalates.

## Setting Cues

Your setting is your best tool for creating mood. Small details can evoke big emotions.

- **Descriptive Details:** Stormy weather, flickering lights, or long shadows can set the stage for tension. On the flip side, golden sunlight, chirping birds, and warm breezes can bring comfort and joy.
- **Lighting:** Bright, natural light feels safe and welcoming, while dim or uneven lighting creates unease.
- **Sounds and Smells:** Think beyond visuals. The creak of a floorboard, the rustle of leaves, or the smell of woodsmoke can make a setting come alive.

**Example:** In a mystery novel, a cobblestone street slick with rain, the distant sound of footsteps, and a single flickering lamppost instantly establish an ominous mood.

## Character Perception

How your characters interact with their environment can shape the mood.

- A bustling market might feel exciting to a wide-eyed adventurer but overwhelming to someone plagued by social anxiety.
- A quiet forest might be serene to one character and suffocatingly lonely to another.

By showing how your characters perceive their surroundings, you can add layers of depth to both the mood and their personalities.

**Pro Tip:** Think about your character's emotional state. If they're nervous, they'll notice details that amplify their unease —a ticking clock, a closed door, or the distant hum of machinery.

### Example: Hogwarts in *Harry Potter*

J.K. Rowling masterfully shifts the mood of Hogwarts to suit the story. During festive moments, the castle feels warm and magical, with roaring fires and glittering decorations. During darker times, like battles or betrayals, the same castle feels cold, oppressive, and filled with shadows. These shifts show how mood can evolve within the same setting to support the story's tone.

### Pro Tip: Mood Can Change Scene by Scene

Mood isn't a one-size-fits-all deal—it can and should evolve throughout your story. A romantic moment can turn tense with the sound of shattering glass. A cheerful family dinner can take a sombre turn when an unexpected guest arrives.

### Wrapping It Up

Mood is the emotional heartbeat of your story. By carefully crafting tone, using setting cues, and reflecting your characters' perceptions, you can create a world that resonates with readers. Don't be afraid to let the mood shift as your story unfolds—it's one of the most powerful tools for drawing readers in and keeping them hooked.

Now go ahead and turn that sunny meadow into a creepy crime scene—or vice versa!

## Adding Background Details

The devil (and the magic) is in the details. Background details are the small but powerful elements that breathe life into your world, making it feel like a place readers can step into, whether it's a bustling fantasy kingdom, a quiet prairie town, or a real-life historical setting. Let's explore how to use details to create a world that feels authentic, immersive, and memorable.

## Culture and History

Every world, whether fictional or nonfictional, is shaped by its past and its people.

- **For Fiction:** Create traditions, myths, or historical events that define your world. Does your society celebrate a yearly festival? What stories are whispered around campfires? These elements provide depth and a sense of authenticity.
- **For Nonfiction:** Research the cultural or historical context of your setting. What was happening politically or socially during this time? What customs, landmarks, or events would have influenced daily life?

**Example:** In a fantasy world, a crumbling statue might commemorate a long-forgotten hero, hinting at past wars and values. In a memoir, mentioning the music popular at the time adds historical flavour and nostalgia.

**Pro Tip:** Think of culture and history as the roots of your story. They don't need to be visible at all times, but they should inform how your world and characters grow.

### Daily Life

It's the little things—what people eat, wear, and do in their downtime—that make a world feel lived-in.

- What's on the dinner table? Is it roasted boar with wild herbs or takeout pizza eaten on the couch?
- What do people wear? Are they dressed for survival, fashion, or comfort?
- How do they entertain themselves? Card games, magical duels, Netflix binges?

Adding these details doesn't just ground your story—it also gives readers clues about the culture and values of your world.

**Pro Tip:** A quick, vivid snapshot of daily life can speak volumes. A street vendor selling spicy skewers or a child chasing a tin can down a cobbled alley instantly paints a picture without needing pages of explanation.

### Use All the Senses

Readers want to experience your world, not just see it. Engage all the senses:

- **Sight:** The crimson banners flapping in the wind or the glint of a sword under moonlight.
- **Sound:** The distant rumble of thunder, the chatter of a market, or the eerie creak of a floorboard.
- **Smell:** Freshly baked bread, acrid smoke, or the earthy scent of rain.
- **Touch:** The scratch of coarse fabric, the coolness of marble underfoot, or the sticky warmth of summer air.

**Example:** In *The Night Circus* by Erin Morgenstern, readers can almost taste the caramel popcorn, feel the chill of the night air, and hear the soft hum of carnival music. The sensory details make the circus a vivid and unforgettable setting.

### Show, Don't Tell

Avoid the temptation to unload all your world-building in one go. Instead, sprinkle details naturally into the story. Let the world reveal itself through the characters' actions, dialogue, and observations.

### Examples of "Showing" Details:

- A character brushes dust from a centuries-old tapestry, hinting at the room's age and history.
- A snippet of a folk song hummed by a villager reveals cultural traditions.
- A passing mention of a crumbling monument hints at forgotten wars or past glory.

**Pro Tip:** Trust your readers to pick up on the clues. They don't need every detail spelled out—leave space for their imagination to fill in the gaps.

**Wrapping It Up**

Background details are the secret sauce that makes a story's world feel alive. By weaving in culture, history, daily life, and sensory elements, you create an immersive environment that keeps readers hooked. Just remember to balance detail with story—enough to enrich, but not so much it overwhelms.

Now, go sprinkle some caramel popcorn into your world—or whatever else makes it pop!

**Things to Remember**

World-building isn't about dumping all your ideas onto the page at once—it's about layering setting, mood, and details to create an immersive experience. Whether you're building a fantastical land of wizards or painting a picture of life in a small prairie town, focus on what makes your world unique and how it enhances your story.

Now, grab your notebook (or crystal ball) and start building a world your readers will never want to leave!

# Chapter 7
# Structuring Your Story or Argument

## *Understand the Importance of Structure*

Structure is the unsung hero of writing. It's not flashy or glamorous, but without it, your story or argument could end up as a tangled mess that leaves readers scratching their heads. Think of structure as the backbone—it holds everything in place, keeping your writing upright and purposeful. Without it? Well, you've got a soggy sandwich, and no one wants that.

### Why Structure Matters

- **Clarity for Readers:** A well-structured piece ensures your readers can follow along without having to double back and reread every other sentence. It's like providing a clear map for your journey, so no one gets lost on the way to your brilliant conclusion.
- **Keeps Things Engaging:** Structure helps pace your writing, doling out just enough information to keep

readers hooked without overwhelming them. Think of it as layering a story or argument—one juicy detail at a time.

- **Shows You Know Your Stuff:** A strong structure gives readers confidence that you're in control of your material. Even if your ideas are complex, good structure makes them digestible.

## What Happens Without Structure?

Ever tried reading something that jumps from one idea to the next without warning? It's like watching a squirrel hop from branch to branch—confusing and a bit exhausting. A lack of structure leaves readers frustrated and more likely to abandon your work.

## Pro Tip: Start with an Outline

Before you dive into writing, sketch out the basic structure. For stories, this could mean noting key plot points. For arguments, list the main ideas and the evidence you'll use to support them. It doesn't have to be perfect—just enough to give you direction.

## Wrapping It Up

Structure may not be the star of the show, but it's the stage that lets your ideas shine. A strong backbone for your writing ensures readers stay engaged, understand your points, and make it to the end feeling satisfied—not lost in a sea of confusion. So, build that structure and let your story or argument stand tall!

## Learn the Basics of Story Arcs

A story arc is the backbone of a great narrative, giving it shape, flow, and a satisfying sense of progression. Think of it like the recipe for a perfect cake—you need the right ingredients (characters, conflict, resolution) in the right order for everything to come out just right. One of the most reliable recipes for storytelling is the classic three-act structure, but if you're feeling bold, there are other story arcs to explore too!

**The Three-Act Structure**

The three-act structure is a tried-and-true storytelling method that breaks your story into three main parts:

- **Act 1: The Setup**
  - This is where you introduce your characters, establish the setting, and plant the seeds of conflict.
  - Think of it as the opening act of a play—you're setting the stage and giving readers a reason to care.
  - By the end of this act, there's usually an "inciting incident" that kicks off the story and makes readers eager to know what happens next.

**Example:** In *The Lion King*, Act 1 is when we meet Simba, learn about his royal future, and witness the inciting incident—Mufasa's tragic death.

- **Act 2: The Confrontation**
  - This is the meat of your story. Your protagonist faces obstacles, confronts challenges, and learns valuable lessons along the way.

- The stakes should escalate, keeping readers on the edge of their seats.

**Example:** Act 2 in *The Lion King* includes Simba's exile, his carefree life with Timon and Pumbaa, and his eventual realisation that he must return to save the Pride Lands.

- **Act 3: The Resolution**
  - Everything comes to a head. The protagonist confronts the final challenge, the loose ends are tied up, and readers get the satisfaction of seeing how it all turns out.

**Example:** Act 3 of *The Lion King* is the climactic showdown with Scar, Simba reclaiming his place as king, and the Pride Lands returning to balance.

**Why the Three-Act Structure Works**

It's simple, effective, and provides a clear roadmap for almost any story. Whether you're writing a novel, a screenplay, or a short story, this structure ensures your plot has a logical flow and a satisfying payoff.

**Other Story Arcs**

Feeling adventurous? There are plenty of other story arcs to explore:

- **The Hero's Journey:** Popularized by Joseph Campbell, this arc is perfect for tales of transformation and adventure. It takes your protagonist on a cyclical journey of departure, trials, and return. Think *Star Wars* or *The Lord of the Rings*.

- **Freytag's Pyramid:** A five-part structure that includes exposition, rising action, climax, falling action, and denouement. Great for more intricate, literary works.
- **Non-Linear Arcs:** If you're feeling bold, play with time! Jump between past and present, or start with the climax and work backwards. It's a challenge, but when done well, it can be incredibly rewarding.

### Pro Tip: Choose What Works for Your Story

There's no one-size-fits-all approach to story arcs. The three-act structure is a fantastic starting point, but don't be afraid to mix things up or try a different framework if it suits your narrative better. Just make sure your story still has a clear flow that keeps readers engaged.

### Wrapping It Up

Story arcs are the blueprint for a satisfying narrative. The three-act structure is a classic for good reason, but exploring other arcs can add depth and uniqueness to your storytelling. Whether you're crafting an epic adventure or a heartfelt drama, a strong arc will guide your characters—and your readers—through an unforgettable journey.

### Master Persuasive Flow for Nonfiction

Nonfiction may not feature sword fights or fiery dragons, but it still needs a structure that keeps readers hooked. Whether you're writing a self-help guide, an essay, or a memoir, a strong persuasive flow ensures your argument lands with impact. Without it, you risk losing readers faster than a poorly timed Wi-Fi outage.

Let's break down how to structure your nonfiction piece so it's logical, engaging, and, most importantly, convincing.

**The Persuasive Flow**

Think of this as your nonfiction roadmap. Follow these steps to guide your readers smoothly from your opening hook to a satisfying conclusion:

1. **Start with a Hook:**
   - Grab attention right away with something interesting, surprising, or relatable.
   - Use an anecdote, a compelling statistic, or a provocative question to make readers lean in and want to know more.

**Example:** Opening with "Did you know that 80% of people abandon their New Year's resolutions by February?" immediately sets the stage for an article on sticking to goals.

2. **Present Your Main Point (or Thesis):**
   - Lay out your central argument or purpose clearly and concisely. This is the backbone of your piece—the idea you want your readers to walk away with.
   - Keep it sharp and direct, like the opening line of a TED Talk.

**Example:** "This guide will show you how to turn short-lived resolutions into lifelong habits."

3. **Build Your Case:**
   - Support your main point with clear, logical arguments. Use examples, research, and evidence to back up your claims.
   - Organize your points in a way that builds momentum, leading your readers step by step to your conclusion.

**Pro Tip:** Stick to a logical order. If your arguments feel scattered, readers will lose focus faster than you can say "where was I going with this?"

4. **End with a Powerful Conclusion or Call to Action:**
   - Wrap things up by summarizing your key points and driving home your thesis.
   - Leave readers with a strong final impression—a call to action, a thought-provoking question, or a memorable takeaway.

**Example:** "By following these three simple steps, you'll create habits that stick—no more abandoned goals!"

### Keep It Flowing Smoothly

Transitions are the glue that holds your arguments together. Without them, your piece risks feeling disjointed, like a clunky shopping cart with a wobbly wheel.

- **Use Transition Words:** Words like "next," "however," and "therefore" can help bridge your ideas and guide readers through your argument.
- **Signal Shifts in Focus:** Introduce new sections with a sentence that hints at what's coming. For example,

"Now that we've explored why resolutions fail, let's look at how to make them stick."

- **Check for Flow:** Read your work out loud to catch any awkward jumps or gaps in logic. If it doesn't sound smooth, it probably isn't.

## Wrapping It Up

Nonfiction may not have dragons, but it still needs a strong, persuasive flow to keep readers engaged and convinced. Start with a hook, build a clear argument with solid evidence, and end with a powerful conclusion. Smooth transitions will keep your ideas connected and ensure your piece reads like a well-oiled machine—not that wobbly cart everyone avoids at the grocery store.

Now go out there and craft an argument so strong even a dragon would nod along!

## Use Structure to Build Tension or Momentum

Good writing is like a roller coaster—it pulls readers in, keeps them gripping the edges of their seats, and delivers a thrilling ride all the way to the end. Whether you're writing fiction or nonfiction, structure plays a vital role in building tension or momentum, keeping readers eager for what comes next. Let's look at how to use structure to ramp up excitement and deliver those satisfying payoffs.

## In Fiction: Building Tension

Fiction thrives on rising stakes and mounting tension. Your structure should gradually increase the pressure on your protagonist, making obstacles tougher and consequences greater with each step.

## How to Build Tension with Structure:

- **Raise the Stakes:** Start with smaller conflicts and gradually escalate them. Each challenge should push the protagonist closer to their breaking point.
- **Introduce Uncertainty:** Keep readers guessing—will the protagonist succeed, or will things go horribly wrong? A surprising twist or a cliffhanger can keep them flipping pages.
- **Layer Conflicts:** Don't rely on a single problem. Combine external challenges (like a villain or natural disaster) with internal struggles (like self-doubt or guilt) for a richer story.

**Example:** In *The Hunger Games*, the structure ramps up tension by moving from Katniss's quiet life in District 12, to the terrifying spectacle of the Capitol, to the life-or-death stakes of the arena. Each stage introduces higher stakes, building to a nail-biting climax.

**Pro Tip:** Think of tension like a rubber band. Stretch it slowly over the course of your story, letting it snap only at the climax for maximum impact.

## In Nonfiction: Building Momentum

In nonfiction, your goal is to guide readers step by step to a satisfying conclusion or breakthrough. Each point should logically build on the last, creating a sense of progress and leading to that all-important "aha!" moment.

## How to Build Momentum with Structure:

- **Start with the Basics:** Lay the groundwork with foundational ideas or context. Readers should feel confident they understand the basics before moving on.
- **Stack Your Points:** Each argument or piece of evidence should flow naturally from the previous one, deepening the reader's understanding.
- **Save the Best for Last:** Place your most compelling points or solutions toward the end, so readers finish on a high note.

**Example:** In a self-help book about productivity, the structure might start by addressing common pitfalls, move to simple strategies for improvement, and end with a powerful framework for transforming your daily habits. Each section builds logically on the last, creating a sense of momentum.

**Pro Tip:** Think of nonfiction momentum like assembling a puzzle. Each piece adds clarity, and by the final chapter, the full picture comes into view.

### Wrapping It Up

Whether you're writing fiction or nonfiction, structure is your secret weapon for keeping readers engaged. In fiction, use structure to crank up the tension, pulling readers deeper into the story with every turn of the page. In nonfiction, let your structure create a natural flow that builds understanding and excitement, culminating in a big "aha!" moment.

Now go ahead and give your writing that roller-coaster edge—just make sure your readers are buckled in for the ride!

### Stay Flexible

Structure is important—it keeps your story or argument on track and ensures readers don't wander off confused. But here's the thing: writing isn't paint-by-numbers. Sometimes, you need to bend the rules, shuffle things around, or even toss your plan out the window when inspiration strikes. Think of structure like a recipe—it gives you the framework, but you're allowed to add extra spice or adjust the ingredients to suit your taste.

**Why Flexibility Matters**

- **Writing Evolves:** No matter how perfect your outline seems at first, your story or argument might take unexpected turns as you write. Maybe a character develops a mind of their own, or new research points you in a different direction. Being flexible lets you follow those surprises.
- **Creativity Needs Space:** Sticking too rigidly to a plan can stifle creativity. Give yourself permission to experiment, take detours, or rework sections if they feel off.
- **Every Story Is Unique:** Not every story or argument fits neatly into a cookie-cutter structure. What works for one piece might not work for another, so don't be afraid to tweak the formula to suit your needs.

**How to Stay Flexible**

1. **Treat Your Outline as a Guide, Not a Rulebook:**
   - Your outline is there to help, but it's not set in stone. If a new idea pops up that makes your story or argument stronger, go for it!

**Pro Tip:** Think of your outline as a travel itinerary. It's great to know your destination, but sometimes, an unexpected side trip can make the journey even better.

2. **Listen to Your Gut:**
   - If a scene or argument isn't working, don't force it. Take a step back, reassess, and try a different approach. Your instincts are often right.
3. **Embrace Rewrites:**
   - Adjusting your structure during revisions is normal —and often necessary. The first draft is for figuring things out; the second (or third) is for making it shine.
4. **Keep the End in Mind:**
   - Flexibility doesn't mean aimlessness. While you can adjust the journey, always keep your final goal or message in focus.

### Think of It Like Cooking

You wouldn't skip the eggs in a cake recipe, but you might decide to add a splash of vanilla or swap chocolate chips for nuts. Structure works the same way. Stick to the essentials (beginning, middle, and end), but feel free to adjust the details to fit your taste.

**Pro Tip:** If your adjustments aren't working, don't panic. You can always return to the original recipe and try again. That's what drafts are for!

### Wrapping It Up

Structure is there to support your writing, not hold it hostage. Stay flexible, trust your instincts, and let your story or argument evolve naturally. Sometimes the best ideas come when you veer off the planned path—so don't be afraid to explore. After all, the most delicious dishes are the ones made with a little experimentation!

## Know When to Break the Rules

Rules are great—until they aren't. Once you've got the basics of structure down, it's time to embrace your inner rebel and get creative. Non-linear timelines, surprise endings, or quirky approaches to an argument can take your writing from predictable to unforgettable. The trick is knowing how to bend the rules without breaking your readers' brains.

## Why Break the Rules?

- **To Surprise Your Readers:** Doing something unexpected keeps your audience engaged and excited. A well-timed twist or unconventional format can make your story or argument truly memorable.
- **To Fit Your Unique Vision:** Some stories or topics call for an approach that doesn't follow traditional structures. Breaking the rules lets you tell your story the way it's meant to be told.
- **To Stand Out:** In a sea of cookie-cutter narratives and essays, a bold choice can set your work apart.

**Example:** *Pulp Fiction* breaks the rules with its non-linear timeline, but viewers still piece the story together—and that's part of its charm.

## How to Break the Rules (Without Losing Your Readers)

1. **Master the Basics First:**

- You can't break the rules effectively if you don't understand them. Learn the traditional structures before experimenting—think of it as knowing how to play the melody before improvising the solo.

**Pro Tip:** A strong foundation gives you the confidence to take creative risks without losing control of your story or argument.

2. **Keep It Clear:**
   - Creativity is great, but not at the expense of clarity. If readers are confused about what's happening or can't follow your argument, they'll lose interest fast.
   - Use markers like chapter headings, time stamps, or clear transitions to help guide readers through unconventional structures.

**Example:** A memoir might jump between childhood and present day, but clear headings like "1979" or "Today" help readers keep track.

3. **Choose Your Moments Wisely:**
   - You don't have to throw out the rulebook entirely. Breaking one or two rules can be enough to make your writing stand out while keeping the rest of the structure intact.

**Pro Tip:** If you're going for a twist ending or a big structural shake-up, make sure it's worth it. A twist that doesn't feel earned can leave readers frustrated.

4. **Test It on Others:**

- Share your work with beta readers or a trusted friend. If they're confused, your creativity might need a little tweaking to ensure your audience can follow along.

## What Does Breaking the Rules Look Like?

- **Non-Linear Timelines:** Jumping back and forth in time, like in *The Time Traveler's Wife*.
- **Unconventional Arguments:** Using a playful or conversational tone to present a serious topic (hello, Bill Bryson!).
- **Surprise Endings:** Dropping a twist that reframes everything, as in *The Sixth Sense*.
- **Experimental Formats:** Structuring your story as diary entries, text messages, or even a series of interviews.

## Wrapping It Up

Breaking the rules can elevate your writing from good to extraordinary, but it's a balancing act. Learn the basics, keep clarity front and centre, and experiment in ways that serve your story or argument—not just for the sake of being different.

So go ahead, colour outside the lines—just don't lose the plot (literally). Your readers will thank you for the ride!

# Chapter 8
# Writing Engaging Scenes or Chapters

## Writing Action

Action scenes are the adrenaline rush of your story—the moments where the stakes rise, the pace quickens, and readers are flipping pages as fast as their eyes can scan. But writing action isn't just about explosions or sword fights—it's about immersing readers in the heart-pounding, edge-of-your-seat intensity of the moment. Let's break it down.

## Clarity Is Key

Nothing pulls readers out of an action scene faster than confusion. If they're scratching their heads trying to figure out who's doing what, they won't be feeling the tension.

- **Use Short, Sharp Sentences:** Short sentences mimic the quick, frantic energy of action. "He ran. She followed. The door slammed shut." See how punchy that feels?

- **Avoid Overloading with Detail:** While it's tempting to describe every punch, kick, or crash, too much detail slows the pacing. Focus on the key movements that drive the action forward.

**Pro Tip:** After writing an action scene, reread it and ask yourself: Can I picture this clearly? If not, simplify!

### Build Tension

Great action doesn't just drop out of the sky—it builds. The moments before the action explodes are just as important as the chaos itself.

- **Raise the Stakes Gradually:** Start with subtle hints of danger or conflict—a loaded glance, a creaking door, a character's rising heartbeat—and then let things escalate.
- **Make Readers Anticipate:** Draw things out a little. A character reaching for a hidden weapon or the slow, deliberate sound of footsteps can ratchet up the tension before the action erupts.

**Pro Tip:** Think of tension like a rubber band—stretch it until it's about to snap, then unleash the action.

### Show, Don't Tell

Action is best experienced, not narrated. Let readers *feel* the chaos by putting them in the thick of it.

- **Describe Sensory Details:** What does the character see, hear, smell, or feel? Is the room filled with smoke? Can they hear the dull roar of blood in their ears?

- **Focus on Reactions:** Show how characters respond to the action. Are they gasping for breath, bracing for impact, or wincing in pain?

**Example:** Instead of saying, "The explosion was loud," try, "The blast shattered the air, ringing in his ears as the heat singed his skin."

## Use Strong Verbs

Passive descriptions drain energy from action scenes. Strong verbs pack a punch.

- Swap "he was hit by the ball" for "the ball slammed into his chest."
- Avoid weak fillers like "started to" or "began to." Instead of "She started to run," go with "She sprinted."

**Pro Tip:** Verbs are your best friend in action scenes. Use them wisely, and your writing will leap off the page.

### Ideas for Action Scenes

- **Use Breaks and White Space:** Short paragraphs or single-sentence lines can mimic the rhythm of fast-paced action, visually speeding up the scene for readers.
- Example:

The door crashed open.

He turned—too slow.

The fist connected.

- **Introduce Reflection or Hesitation:** Slowing down the pace for a brief moment of internal thought can make the next burst of action feel even more intense.
- Example: A character pauses to catch their breath, thinking, *I can't keep this up much longer,* just before the enemy charges again.
- **Balance Internal and External Elements:** Action isn't just physical—it's emotional too. Combine the external movements (dodging punches, leaping fences) with the internal experience (fear, determination, panic).

**Example:** "Her legs burned as she sprinted through the alley, heart pounding in her chest. *Don't stop. Don't look back.* Behind her, the echo of boots on cobblestones grew louder."

### Action That Packs a Punch

When done right, action scenes aren't just exciting—they're unforgettable. Focus on clarity, tension, sensory immersion, and strong verbs, and your readers will feel every punch, every leap, and every heartbeat. Now, get writing—because that chase scene isn't going to write itself!

### Writing Dialogue

Dialogue is the secret sauce of storytelling. It's where characters come to life, relationships take shape, and the plot moves forward in a way that feels natural and engaging. But writing great dialogue isn't as easy as letting your characters chatter away—it's all about crafting purposeful, believable conversations that hook your readers.

## Make It Purposeful

Every line of dialogue should earn its place on the page. If it's not advancing the plot, revealing a character's personality, or building tension, it might be worth cutting.

### Examples of Purposeful Dialogue:

- Advancing the plot: "If we don't find that key by midnight, the entire plan is ruined."
- Revealing character: "I don't care about the money—I just want to make my dad proud."
- Creating tension: "Why didn't you tell me the truth before?"

**Pro Tip:** Use dialogue to show what's happening rather than explaining it outright. Instead of, "She was angry at him," try, "I can't believe you did this. Again."

## Keep It Natural

Great dialogue sounds like real speech—just better. It's polished enough to avoid the "ums" and "likes" of everyday conversation, but not so formal it feels stiff.

### Tips for Natural Dialogue:

- Keep sentences short and conversational. Real people don't speak in long, complicated monologues (unless they're giving a speech).
- Avoid info-dumping. Instead of "As you know, our grandmother passed away last year and left us the

house," try, "You've been avoiding Grandma's house ever since we inherited it."

- Add quirks or habits unique to each character's voice —like a tendency to use slang or avoid contractions.

**Pro Tip:** Read your dialogue out loud. If it sounds awkward coming out of your mouth, it'll feel just as awkward on the page.

### Show Subtext

What characters say is important, but what they *don't* say can be even more revealing. Subtext adds depth to your dialogue by hinting at hidden emotions, thoughts, or conflicts.

### How to Show Subtext:

- Use hesitation or pauses: "I... I didn't think you'd notice."
- Include body language: "Sure, I'm fine," she said, gripping her coffee cup until her knuckles turned white.
- Play with tone or sarcasm: "Oh, great idea. Because your plans always work out so well."

**Pro Tip:** Think about what your characters want versus what they're willing to admit. Subtext happens when their words don't quite align with their true intentions.

### Vary the Flow

Good dialogue has rhythm. Too many short exchanges can feel choppy, while too many long speeches can drag. Mixing things up keeps readers engaged.

**Example of Varied Flow:**

- Quick back-and-forth:
- "Did you hear that?"
- "Hear what?"
- "Shh. Listen."
- Longer monologue:
- "When I was a kid, I used to come here with my dad. We'd spend hours fishing by the lake. I haven't been back since he passed, and... it's harder than I thought it would be."

**Pro Tip:** Use pacing to match the scene's tone. Snappy dialogue works well in action scenes, while slower, reflective dialogue suits emotional moments.

**Ideas for Better Dialogue**

1. **Use Dialogue Tags Sparingly:**
   - Stick to simple tags like "said" or "asked." Readers tend to skim over them, which keeps the focus on the conversation. Overly descriptive tags like "exclaimed" or "whispered dramatically" can feel distracting.
2. **Break It Up with Action or Description:**
   - Ground conversations in the scene by showing what characters are doing while they talk. For example:
   - "I'll call him tomorrow," she said, fiddling with the strap of her purse. "Or maybe the day after. I don't know."
3. **Read It Aloud:**

○ Test your dialogue for authenticity by reading it out loud. Does it sound like something a real person would say? If not, tweak it until it flows naturally.

**Pro Tip:** When dialogue is in quotes, that means the person is speaking. If the text is in italic, then they are thinking. Avoid the Thought Out Loud syndrome that many first time authors are using. Let your punctuation say it for you.

Dialogue is your chance to make your characters' voices sing —literally, if you're writing a musical. Keep it purposeful, natural, and layered with subtext, and your readers will hang on every word. Now go give your characters something to talk about!

### Writing Transitions

Transitions are the bridges that connect your scenes and chapters, keeping the narrative smooth and your readers engaged. Done well, they make your story feel like a seamless journey rather than a bumpy bus ride where the driver keeps slamming the brakes. Let's dive into how to write transitions that keep readers turning the pages.

### Create a Hook

The best transitions start with a strong ending. Whether it's a shocking cliffhanger, an emotional gut punch, or an intriguing question, give readers a reason to keep going.

### Examples of Compelling Hooks:

- A question: "But what was waiting for her on the other side of the door?"

- A revelation: "That's when he realised the map was upside down."
- A cliffhanger: "She turned the corner—and froze."

**Pro Tip:** End a scene or chapter with a hint of what's to come. Think of it as dangling a carrot just out of reach. But don't do it all the time, for it becomes exhausting for the reader.

### Connect Ideas

Transitions aren't just about moving from one place or time to another—they're about showing the relationship between scenes. Help readers understand how one moment leads to the next.

### Ways to Connect Ideas:

- **Shared Themes:** Tie scenes together with a recurring idea, like hope or loss.
- **Character's Thoughts:** Use internal monologue to reflect on the previous scene and set up the next one.
- **Visual Details:** A storm ending one scene might carry into the next with a character wiping rain off their coat.

**Example:** If a character ends a scene by staring at an empty photo frame, the next scene might begin with a flashback to the last time the frame held a picture.

### Avoid Over-Explaining

Readers don't need every detail spelled out—leave room for them to connect the dots. A good transition skips the boring parts (we don't need to see your character walk down every hallway) while still making the narrative easy to follow.

**Pro Tip:** Trust your audience. If you leap forward in time or change location, a quick sentence like, "Two days later, in Paris," is all they need.

### Play with Time and Space

Transitions often signal shifts in time, location, or perspective. Make these shifts clear, but don't let them feel clunky.

### Tips for Smooth Shifts:

- **Time:** Use phrases like "Later that evening" or "The next morning" to orient readers.
- **Location:** A quick mention of setting ("In the bustling café...") helps ground the reader.
- **Perspective:** If you're switching points of view, start with a distinctive detail that signals the new character's voice or experience.

**Pro Tip:** Experiment with starting new chapters in the middle of action to immediately grab attention. For example: "The knife was already at her throat when she opened her eyes."

### Ideas for Effective Transitions

1. **Internal Monologue or Reflection:**
   - Let a character's thoughts bridge the gap between scenes. Example: "The smell of the coffee reminded him of home, but that was a memory he didn't have time to dwell on now."
2. **Jump Into Action:**

- Begin a new chapter or scene mid-action to hook the reader right away. Example: "He hit the ground running, the stolen briefcase clutched to his chest."

3. **Parallel Imagery or Repeated Phrases:**
   - Use a recurring image or phrase to tie scenes together. Example: A story that ends one scene with a flickering candle could start the next with the glow of a sunrise.

## Keep It Moving

Great transitions don't just connect—they enhance. By creating hooks, connecting ideas, trusting your readers, and playing with time and space, you'll keep your narrative flowing effortlessly. Now, go build some literary bridges that are so smooth, readers won't even notice they've crossed them!

# Chapter 9
# **Staying Motivated**

## Overcoming Writer's Block

Writer's block—it's like staring at a blank page that stares back at you with smug indifference. But here's the thing: writer's block isn't the end of your creativity. It's just your brain's way of telling you something needs a tweak. The trick is not to panic, but to tackle it head-on with a few simple strategies.

### Identify the Cause

Before you can fix writer's block, it helps to figure out what's causing it. Are you stuck because:

- **The Plot Feels Wobbly?** Maybe you're unsure what happens next, or the direction feels wrong.
- **Burnout Has Caught Up?** If you've been writing non-stop, your creative well might need a refill.

- **Fear of Imperfection?** That inner critic telling you it's not good enough can freeze you in your tracks.

**Pro Tip:** Once you've identified the cause, you can take targeted action. If the plot's unclear, brainstorm possibilities. If it's burnout, rest. If it's fear, remind yourself that first drafts don't have to be perfect.

## Change Your Perspective

Sometimes a scene just needs a fresh angle. Shake things up by:

- Writing from a different character's point of view. What would this moment look like through their eyes?
- Changing the setting. Could this confrontation happen in a crowded café instead of a living room?
- Switching the tone. If it feels too heavy, try writing it as light-hearted banter—or vice versa.

**Pro Tip:** Experimentation is low stakes. If the new angle doesn't work, no harm done. But it might surprise you and unlock a creative door.

## Set Small Goals

Don't try to write the perfect chapter all at once—it's too overwhelming. Instead, break it into bite-sized pieces:

- Start with a single sentence. Just one.
- Expand that into a paragraph.
- If full-on writing feels too daunting, brainstorm a list of ideas or jot down a rough outline.

Small wins build momentum, and before you know it, you're back in the flow.

**Take a Break**

Sometimes the best way to move forward is to step away for a while. A change of scenery can work wonders for a stuck mind.

- Go for a walk and let nature jog your creativity.
- Take a shower—some of the best ideas show up when you least expect them.
- Try a completely different activity, like baking or doodling, to let your subconscious work its magic.

**Pro Tip:** Breaks are productive when they're intentional. Avoid spiralling into endless "breaks" that are really procrastination in disguise.

**Ideas to Jumpstart Creativity**

- **Use Writing Prompts:** A good prompt can nudge your imagination in an unexpected direction. For example, "Write about a character who finds an old, mysterious key."
- **Skip the Stuck Part:** If one scene feels impossible, write a different one you're excited about. You can always return later.
- **Try Timed Writing Sprints:** Set a timer for 10 minutes and write as fast as you can without stopping to edit. It's amazing what a little pressure can do to shut up your inner critic.

**Wrapping It Up**

Writer's block isn't a creative death sentence—it's a speed bump. With a mix of reflection, experimentation, and small, intentional steps, you'll get past it. So go ahead, try a fresh perspective, take a purposeful break, or just write that one sentence. The rest will follow!

## Dealing with Self-Doubt

Ah, self-doubt. That pesky little voice whispering, *"Is this even good?"* or, worse, *"Should you even bother?"* It's the uninvited guest at every writer's table. But here's the thing: self-doubt is a part of the process, not a sign you're failing. The trick is learning to quiet that voice—or at least turn it into a constructive critic instead of a heckler.

### Acknowledge It's Normal

Every writer, from newbies to seasoned pros, wrestles with self-doubt. Yes, even your favourite authors have stared at their drafts thinking, *This is absolute garbage.*

**Why It Matters:** Recognising that doubt is part of the creative journey takes the sting out of it. You're not alone, and you're not failing—self-doubt just means you care about what you're writing.

**Pro Tip:** When self-doubt creeps in, remind yourself, *"If Stephen King can have bad days, so can I."*

### Separate Creation from Criticism

Writing and editing use different parts of your brain. Trying to do both at the same time is like pressing the gas and the brakes simultaneously—it just stalls you out.

**How to Do It:**

- Write freely without worrying if it's perfect. First drafts are *supposed* to be messy.
- Save the nitpicking and revisions for later drafts when you can look at your work with fresh eyes.

**Pro Tip:** Post a sticky note near your workspace that says, *"Write first, edit later."* It's a simple mantra that can keep you moving forward.

### Focus on Progress, Not Perfection

Perfection is overrated. What matters is moving forward, even if it's just a small step.

### Celebrate Small Wins:

- Finished a chapter? That's worth a victory dance.
- Wrote three days in a row? Treat yourself to a fancy coffee.

Progress builds momentum, and momentum quiets self-doubt.

**Pro Tip:** Keep a progress tracker—a calendar, a notebook, or an app. Seeing your streaks of effort, even on tough days, can be incredibly motivating.

### Remind Yourself of Your Why

When doubt hits hardest, take a moment to reflect on why you started writing in the first place. Was it to tell a story that's been burning in your mind? To inspire others? To prove to yourself that you can?

**Why It Works:** Reconnecting with your passion can reignite your motivation and drown out negative self-talk.

**Pro Tip:** Write down your reasons for writing and keep them somewhere visible. On the tough days, they'll remind you why you're doing this in the first place.

**Ideas for Managing Self-Doubt**

1. **Keep a Journal of Positivity:**
   - Write down positive feedback from beta readers, kind comments from friends, or moments when writing felt joyful.
   - On tough days, flip through these pages for a boost of encouragement.
2. **Use Affirmations:**
   - Simple phrases like, *"It's okay to write a bad first draft,"* or *"Done is better than perfect,"* can help quiet negative thoughts.
   - Repeat them to yourself when doubt rears its head.
3. **Join a Writing Group:**
   - Connect with fellow writers who can offer encouragement, feedback, and a reminder that you're not alone in this journey.
   - Plus, it's nice to have someone else say, *"No, this doesn't suck,"* when you're second-guessing everything.

Self-doubt is persistent, but it doesn't have to call the shots. With the right mindset and strategies, you can keep writing even when that little voice in your head tries to tell you otherwise. Now, go remind self-doubt who's boss—you've got a story to tell!

## Practical Tools for Staying Motivated

Writing can feel like running a marathon—long, exhausting, and occasionally tempting you to lie down and quit. The good news? With the right tools and habits, you can keep your motivation strong and your progress steady. Let's dive into some practical strategies to help you stay on track, one word at a time.

## Create a Routine

Consistency is the secret weapon of every productive writer. By setting a regular schedule, you train your brain to expect writing time, making it easier to get started each day.

- **Why It Works:** A routine reduces procrastination because writing becomes a habit, not a choice you have to make every day.
- **How to Do It:** Choose a time of day when you're most focused (morning, lunchtime, evening—whatever works for you) and block it off as dedicated writing time.

**Pro Tip:** Pair your writing session with a ritual to get into the zone—brew a cup of tea, play a specific playlist, or light a candle. It's like telling your brain, *"Hey, it's writing time!"*

## Track Your Progress

Nothing fuels motivation like seeing how far you've come. Progress tracking gives you a visual reminder that all those little writing sessions add up to something big.

- **Tools to Try:**
- A simple notebook to jot down daily word counts.

- Apps like Scrivener or Wordly for tracking progress.
- A calendar where you mark writing days with a big, satisfying X.

**Pro Tip:** Set small, achievable goals—like "500 words a day" or "3 writing sessions a week." Every time you hit a goal, it's another reason to celebrate.

### Reward Yourself

Who doesn't love a good reward? Celebrating your writing milestones keeps the process fun and gives you something to look forward to.

- **Ideas for Rewards:**
  - Your favourite snack after finishing a chapter.
  - A relaxing break to binge your favourite show.
  - A new book, fancy notebook, or shiny pen to fuel your creativity.

**Pro Tip:** Tie rewards to specific goals. For example, treat yourself to a dinner out when you finish your first draft—it'll give you extra motivation to get there!

### Ideas for Staying Motivated

1. **Set Up a "Streak Tracker":**
   - Keep a visual record of how many days in a row you've written. Apps like Streaks or a simple wall calendar work wonders.
   - Seeing those streaks grow is surprisingly motivating—you won't want to break the chain!
2. **Find a Writing Buddy:**

- Partner up with a fellow writer for accountability. Check in regularly, swap encouragement, and celebrate each other's wins.
- Even virtual writing sprints together can make a big difference.

3. **Switch Up Your Environment:**
   - Writing in the same spot every day can feel stale. A change of scenery can re-energize your creativity.
   - Try a café, park, library, or even just a different room in your house.

**Pro Tip:** If you're feeling stuck, try moving your writing session outdoors—fresh air works wonders for a tired brain.

Staying motivated doesn't have to be a struggle. With a routine, progress tracking, and a few well-earned rewards, you'll keep moving forward—even on the tough days. Now, set up that streak tracker and get ready to crush your next goal!

Part 3
# Editing and Revising

# Chapter 10
# Self-Editing Basics

**Cutting Fluff**

Fluff is like the packing peanuts of your manuscript—it takes up space but doesn't add much value. Removing fluff makes your writing leaner, sharper, and more engaging for readers. It's all about saying more with less, and trust me, your readers (and your editor) will thank you for it.

**Spot Unnecessary Words**

Filler words like "really," "very," "just," or "in order to" sneak into sentences and bloat them without adding meaning. Most of the time, you can cut them, and the sentence will still make perfect sense—if not better sense.

**Examples:**

- "She was very tired" becomes "She was tired."
- "He just wanted to help" becomes "He wanted to help."

**Pro Tip:** Do a "fluff sweep" by searching your document for filler words like "just," "very," or "actually." You'll be amazed at how often they pop up!

## Avoid Redundancies

Redundancies are the pesky habit of saying the same thing twice. Phrases like "unexpected surprise" or "end result" are repetitive and can easily be trimmed to one strong word.

### Examples:

- "The final outcome was clear" becomes "The outcome was clear."
- "She nodded her head" becomes "She nodded."

**Pro Tip:** When in doubt, ask yourself: *Am I saying the same thing twice?* If yes, simplify!

## Trim Repetition

You don't need to hammer the same idea home repeatedly—your readers are smarter than you think. Say it once, say it well, and move on.

### Example:

- Instead of: "The room was dark. It was so dark that she couldn't see anything. Darkness filled every corner."
- Try: "The room was pitch black."

**Pro Tip:** Repetition can work for emphasis in dialogue or dramatic moments, but use it sparingly—it's like hot sauce, not ketchup.

## Ideas to Cut Fluff

1. **Highlight and Delete Filler Words:**
   - Search your manuscript for "just," "really," "very," and similar culprits. Try deleting them and see how much crisper your sentences feel.
2. **Simplify Overwritten Descriptions:**
   - Example: "She was completely and utterly exhausted" can become "She was exhausted."
3. **Use Editing Tools:**
   - Tools like ProWritingAid or Hemingway Editor can highlight unnecessary words and overcomplicated sentences, helping you spot fluff you might miss (but they are not perfect - exercise caution when using them).

Cutting fluff isn't about stripping your writing bare—it's about letting your best ideas shine without the clutter. When every word serves a purpose, your readers stay engaged, and your prose becomes irresistible. Now grab those scissors (metaphorically speaking) and start trimming!

## Tightening Prose

Tight prose is like a strong cup of coffee—it delivers a punch without any fluff. It's clean, powerful, and gets straight to the point, ensuring every word on the page pulls its weight. By tightening your prose, you'll create writing that's sharp, impactful, and a pleasure to read.

## Use Strong Verbs

Verbs are the engine of your sentences, so don't settle for

weak ones. Strong, action-packed verbs add energy and clarity to your writing.

**Examples:**

- Replace "She walked slowly" with "She crept."
- Change "He said loudly" to "He yelled."

**Why It Matters:** Weak verbs rely on extra words to convey meaning, while strong verbs get the job done in one punchy word.

**Pro Tip:** If you find yourself leaning on adverbs (words ending in "-ly"), it's often a sign you need a stronger verb. Also be careful about tag words, for some have different meanings and can confuse the reader.

### Simplify Sentences

Long, winding sentences can confuse readers and dilute your point. Breaking them into shorter, punchier sentences makes your writing clearer and easier to follow.

**Examples:**

- Overcomplicated: "In the dimly lit room that smelled faintly of lavender, she slowly lowered herself into the creaky chair, which groaned under her weight."
- Tightened: "The dim room smelled of lavender. She eased into the creaky chair, which groaned."

**Why It Matters:** Shorter sentences make your writing more digestible and allow key details to stand out.

**Pro Tip:** Read your sentences aloud. If you run out of breath or lose track of what you're saying, it's time to simplify.

## Avoid Overwriting

Less is often more. Overwriting happens when you describe too much, bogging down the story and leaving nothing for the reader's imagination. Trust your audience to fill in the gaps.

**Examples:**

- Overwritten: "The sky, which was a brilliant shade of sapphire with streaks of fluffy, cloud-like white, stretched endlessly above them."
- Tightened: "The sapphire sky stretched above them."

**Why It Matters:** Overwriting slows pacing and risks losing readers in a tangle of unnecessary words.

**Pro Tip:** Focus on the most vivid or essential details, and let readers connect the dots.

## Ideas to Tighten Your Prose

1. **Swap Passive Voice for Active Voice:**
   - Passive: "The cake was eaten by her."
   - Active: "She ate the cake."
   - Active voice is clearer and puts the subject in charge, making sentences more direct.
2. **Cut Overused Adjectives and Adverbs:**
   - Example: Instead of "He walked quickly to the door," write "He hurried to the door."
3. **Use Editing Tools or Tricks:**

- Apps like Hemingway Editor can highlight overly complex sentences and passive voice.
- Print your manuscript and highlight long sentences or weak verbs for a closer look.

Tightening prose doesn't mean stripping away your style—it's about cutting the excess and making your words pack a punch. With strong verbs, clean sentences, and just the right amount of detail, your writing will shine. Now, go trim the fat and let your story leap off the page!

**Checking Consistency**

Consistency is the unsung hero of great writing. Readers may not consciously notice when everything aligns, but they'll definitely spot when it doesn't. Whether it's a character's mysteriously changing eye colour or a timeline that doesn't quite add up, inconsistencies can yank readers out of your story faster than a misplaced comma. Here's how to keep your writing polished and immersive.

**Character Details**

Characters are the heart of your story, so their traits and behaviours need to remain steady. A character who starts with blue eyes shouldn't magically end up with brown ones unless it's a plot point (in which case, tell us!).

**Tips for Consistency:**

- Keep track of physical traits like hair colour, height, and scars.
- Monitor speech patterns and quirks—if a character is

sarcastic in one scene, they shouldn't suddenly sound like a Shakespearean poet in another.

- Remember relationships. A cousin in Chapter 1 shouldn't inexplicably become a best friend by Chapter 5.

**Pro Tip:** Create a "character cheat sheet" with all key details and keep it handy while editing - Excel is good for this, and Scrivener has a (basic) character sheet available as well.

## Plot Logic

Your story's events should flow in a way that makes sense. If readers spot a contradiction—like someone holding a coffee mug in one hand and a sword in the other during a duel—they'll stop to question the logic, breaking their immersion.

## Tips for Plot Consistency:

- Check your timeline. Make sure events happen in an order that's logical and possible within your world.
- Ensure cause and effect align. If a character escapes through a locked door, explain how they got it open.
- Watch for unresolved plot threads. If you set up a mystery in Chapter 3, make sure it's addressed by the end.

**Pro Tip:** Print a chapter-by-chapter summary and review it for plot holes or contradictions.

## Formatting and Style

Consistency isn't just about what you're saying—it's also about how you're saying it. Fluctuations in formatting or style can distract readers and make your manuscript look unpolished.

**Tips for Formatting and Style Consistency:**

- Stick to one tense (past or present) throughout your story unless there's a clear reason for a shift.
- Keep point of view steady within a scene. Head-hopping between characters without warning can confuse readers.
- Check formatting for uniformity. Are chapter headings styled the same way? Are dialogue tags formatted consistently?

**Pro Tip:** If your story involves flashbacks or journal entries, use formatting (like italics or indents) to distinguish them—but make sure you use the same style every time.

**Ideas to Stay Consistent**

1. **Create a Style Sheet:**
   - Track character traits, timelines, locations, and any world-building details. A simple table or spreadsheet can save you hours of hunting through your manuscript.
2. **Use the "Find" Function:**
   - Search for recurring terms or phrases to ensure they're used consistently. For example, if you call a character's home "the estate" in one chapter and "the manor" in another, choose one term and stick to it.
3. **Double-Check the Basics:**

- Review chapter headings, scene breaks, and dialogue formatting. Uniformity here makes your manuscript look professional and easier to read.

Consistency might not be the most glamorous part of editing, but it's one of the most important. A well-aligned story keeps readers immersed and shows you've done your homework. So, grab your checklist, channel your inner detective, and make sure every detail lines up perfectly!

# Chapter 11

# **Restructuring**

Sometimes, your manuscript's "bones" need a little rearranging to make the whole thing stronger. Restructuring isn't about tweaking a sentence here or there—it's about stepping back and asking if your story or argument flows logically, keeps readers engaged, and delivers its message effectively. Think of it as a house renovation: sometimes you just need new paint, but other times, you have to knock down a wall to make the space work.

**Reevaluate the Order**

The way you've arranged your scenes, chapters, or arguments might feel natural to you, but does it make sense for the reader?

- **Ask Yourself:** Are the events unfolding logically? Would the story be more exciting or the argument clearer if things happened in a different order?

- **Test Different Arrangements:** Try moving a climactic scene earlier to grab attention or repositioning a quieter moment to give readers breathing space after intense action.

**Pro Tip:** Pretend you're a reader encountering the story for the first time. What questions might they have at each stage, and does your structure answer them in the right order?

### Tighten the Timeline

If parts of your manuscript drag, it's time to streamline.

- **Spot Unnecessary Delays:** Are there scenes or sections that stall progress without adding much value? For example, do you really need a full chapter about a character walking to the grocery store unless something crucial happens along the way?
- **Speed Things Up:** Combine minor events or condense long explanations into a single, snappy paragraph.

**Pro Tip:** Pacing is key. Action-packed scenes need a brisk pace, while emotional moments can linger—but not too long!

### Cut or Combine Scenes

Sometimes, less is more. Repetition or weak scenes can dilute your message or story.

- **Eliminate What's Not Working:** If a scene doesn't move the plot forward, reveal character, or support your argument, it's a candidate for the chopping block.

- **Merge Weak Sections:** If two scenes feel too similar or lack energy on their own, consider combining them into one stronger, more dynamic moment.

**Pro Tip:** Don't throw deleted scenes away! Save them in a separate file—you might find a use for them later.

### Strengthen Transitions

A great manuscript flows seamlessly from one section to the next. If your transitions are clunky, readers might feel jolted out of the story.

- **Make Connections Clear:** Tie scenes or arguments together with thematic links, character motivations, or shared imagery.
- **Avoid Over-Explaining:** A simple sentence or visual cue can bridge sections without slowing the pace.

**Pro Tip:** Read the last paragraph of one scene and the first of the next to ensure they flow naturally. If they feel disconnected, smooth the gap.

### Ideas to Restructure Your Manuscript

1. **Print a Chapter or Scene Summary:**
   - Write a one-sentence summary for each chapter or scene, then shuffle them around to see if a different order improves the story.
2. **Identify Slow or Unnecessary Sections:**
   - Ask: Does this scene advance the plot or argument? If not, it's time to cut or rethink it.
3. **Use Colour-Coded Sticky Notes:**

○ Assign colours to key plot points, arguments, or themes and map them out visually. This helps you spot imbalances or gaps in your structure.

Restructuring might feel daunting, but it's the foundation of a polished manuscript. With a little effort and creativity, you'll find the flow that makes your work truly shine. So grab those sticky notes and start rearranging—it's like puzzle-solving for writers!

## Enhancing Themes

Themes are the heartbeat of your work, providing emotional and intellectual depth. Whether your theme is love conquers all, the perils of power, or the joy of finding a decent cup of coffee, it's what gives your story or argument its purpose. Deep revision is the perfect time to refine and amplify your themes, making sure they resonate with readers in subtle but powerful ways.

## Clarify the Central Theme

Before you can enhance your theme, you need to know what it is. Ask yourself: *What is this story or argument really about?*

- **Focus on Consistency:** Every part of your manuscript should contribute to or reflect the central theme. If your story is about redemption, does every major plot point and character choice support that?
- **Avoid Overcrowding:** Too many competing themes can muddy your message. Stick to one or two core ideas and let them shine.

**Pro Tip:** Write your central theme in one sentence (e.g., *"The courage to face your past leads to freedom"*). Keep it visible while revising to stay on track.

### Reinforce Through Subtext

Themes don't have to hit readers over the head. Subtlety is your friend—let your theme emerge through recurring details, imagery, and actions.

- **Recurring Imagery:** Repeating symbols like a bird in flight, the colour red, or a broken clock can hint at your theme without spelling it out.
- **Dialogue and Actions:** What characters say and do should align with the theme. For example, a theme of resilience might be reflected in characters who keep trying despite setbacks.
- **Setting as a Metaphor:** The world around your characters can echo the theme. A crumbling house might symbolise a deteriorating relationship or hidden secrets.

**Pro Tip:** Readers love discovering hidden layers. Subtle thematic hints invite them to dig deeper, which keeps your work lingering in their minds long after they've finished.

### Remove Conflicting Messages

Secondary elements—subplots, character choices, or settings—should support your main theme. If they clash, it creates confusion and dilutes your message.

- **Examine Subplots:** Does a side story fit your central

theme, or does it distract from it? If it doesn't contribute, it might need tweaking or cutting.

- **Align Character Arcs:** Each character's journey should reinforce the main idea, even if it's from a contrasting angle (e.g., a redemption theme might include a character who fails to achieve redemption, highlighting its importance).

**Pro Tip:** Conflicting messages aren't always bad if done intentionally. For example, a story about moral ambiguity might thrive on clashing perspectives—but make sure it's clear that's the goal.

**Ideas to Enhance Themes**

1. **Review Each Scene or Section:**
   - Ask yourself: *Does this contribute to my theme?* If not, consider adjusting the scene or cutting it entirely.
2. **Add Symbolic Details or Motifs:**
   - Incorporate recurring objects, colours, or phrases that subtly reinforce your theme. For example, in a story about freedom, recurring imagery of open doors or wide landscapes might emphasise the message.
3. **Highlight Character Decisions or Outcomes:**
   - Show how pivotal moments in the story reflect your theme. A protagonist choosing forgiveness over revenge, for instance, drives home a theme of healing.

Enhancing your themes is like tuning a musical instrument—it ensures everything in your story or argument plays in harmony. By clarifying your central message, weaving it subtly through your work, and cutting distractions, you'll create a piece that resonates deeply with readers. Now, go ahead and fine-tune your masterpiece—because themes are where the magic happens!

## Refining Style

Your writing style is the personality of your manuscript—it's what makes it unique and keeps readers coming back for more. Whether your tone is snarky, heartfelt, or somewhere in between, refining your style during revisions ensures that your voice is authentic, engaging, and polished. Let's dig into how to make your style shine.

## Tone Consistency

Tone sets the mood and atmosphere of your writing, so keeping it consistent is crucial. A light-hearted piece shouldn't suddenly veer into heavy, sombre territory (unless it's intentional and carefully executed).

### How to Check for Tone Consistency:

- **Match the Mood:** Does the tone fit the scene or section? For example, a suspenseful moment calls for tension, not casual banter.
- **Watch for Jarring Shifts:** Sudden changes in tone can confuse readers. If your manuscript flips between humour and seriousness without a clear purpose, it might need smoothing out.

**Pro Tip:** Highlight tone-shift areas as you read. If something feels out of place, tweak the language to bring it in line with the rest of the piece.

## Vary Sentence Structure

Monotonous sentence structures can make even the most exciting scenes feel flat. Mixing short and long sentences adds rhythm and energy to your writing.

### How to Vary Structure:

- Use short sentences to create tension or urgency. Example: "She ran. Fast. Too fast."
- Use longer sentences to slow things down or add depth to a moment. Example: "She sank into the chair, her breath catching as the weight of the day finally settled over her shoulders like a heavy blanket."
- Alternate between the two for dynamic pacing, especially in action scenes or emotional moments.

**Pro Tip:** Read your writing out loud to catch repetitive rhythms. If every sentence has the same cadence, rework a few to add variety.

## Eliminate Clunky Phrasing

Awkward or overly complex sentences can trip up readers and pull them out of the story. Smooth, natural phrasing keeps them immersed.

### How to Spot and Fix Clunky Sentences:

- Look for sentences that are overly wordy or hard to follow. Example: "The sight that presented itself before her was one that she found utterly bewildering." Tighten it to: "The sight bewildered her."

- Simplify complex ideas where possible.
- Avoid phrases that sound forced or unnatural—rewrite them in a conversational style if appropriate.

**Pro Tip:** If a sentence feels "off," try rewriting it three different ways. One of them will almost always hit the mark.

### Check for Repetition

Repetitive words or ideas can dull your writing, even if the rest of your style is strong. Variety keeps things fresh and engaging.

### How to Avoid Repetition:

- Highlight frequently used words and phrases in your manuscript. If you've said "glanced" or "dark" five times in a single chapter, it's time to get creative with synonyms or rephrase.
- Watch for repeated ideas. If you've already described a character's loneliness, you don't need to hammer it home in every scene.

**Pro Tip:** Tools like "Find and Replace" in your word processor can help you locate repeated words quickly.

### Ideas for Refining Style

1. **Read Sections Aloud:**
   - Awkward phrasing or unnatural tone shifts often stand out when you hear the words instead of reading them silently.

2. **Highlight Repeated Words:**
   ○ Use a highlighter or editing tool to track overused phrases and replace them with fresh alternatives.
3. **Rewrite Formal or Stiff Sentences:**
   ○ If a sentence feels too academic or robotic, rewrite it in a natural, conversational tone (if it fits the context).

Refining your style is about more than just fixing awkward sentences—it's about ensuring your unique voice shines through while keeping readers engaged. By maintaining tone consistency, varying sentence structure, and polishing your prose, you'll leave readers wanting more. Now grab your metaphorical paintbrush and get ready to refine your masterpiece!

# Chapter 12

# **Feedback and Critiques**

## Working with Beta Readers

Beta readers are your story's first audience, your test readers, and your canaries in the literary coal mine. They're not editors or professional critics—they're everyday readers who help you see your book from a fresh perspective. Their feedback can highlight big-picture issues like plot holes, pacing problems, and character inconsistencies. Here's how to make the most of their insights.

## What Beta Readers Do

Beta readers aren't there to nitpick grammar or comma placement (though they might notice the odd typo). Their focus is on the *experience* of reading your book:

- **Overall Story:** Does the plot hold together? Are there any glaring holes or confusing moments?

- **Characters:** Do the characters feel like real, relatable people? Are their actions believable?
- **Pacing:** Does the story move too slowly, or are there moments where it feels rushed?
- **Engagement:** Did they want to keep reading, or did their attention start to wander?

**Pro Tip:** Encourage beta readers to approach your manuscript as they would a published book—reading naturally and sharing honest reactions.

### Choosing the Right Beta Readers

Not all beta readers are created equal. To get the best feedback, choose people who:

- **Enjoy Your Genre:** A romance fan might not appreciate your sci-fi epic, and vice versa. Find readers who are familiar with the type of story you're telling.
- **Will Be Honest:** You want constructive criticism, not endless praise or overly harsh feedback. Look for readers who will point out what works and what doesn't in a thoughtful way.
- **Aren't Too Close to You:** Your best friend or grandma might struggle to give unbiased feedback. Aim for people who can offer objective insights.

**Pro Tip:** Online writing communities or social media groups can be great places to find beta readers if you're struggling to recruit locally. One such online community, Scriptophobia.com, is starting up in Beta early 2025. A good reason to join is during Beta, they are free!

## Asking the Right Questions

Beta readers need guidance to provide useful feedback. A list of specific questions can help focus their responses. Here are some examples to get started:

- Were you hooked from the beginning? If not, where did you lose interest?
- Did the characters feel real and relatable? Were there any characters you didn't connect with?
- Were there parts of the story that felt slow, confusing, or unnecessary?
- Were there any moments that surprised or delighted you?

**Pro Tip:** Avoid overwhelming beta readers with too many questions. Prioritise 5-10 key areas where you're seeking input.

## Ideas for Working with Beta Readers

1. **Start Small:**
   - Begin with a group of 2-5 beta readers. Too many opinions at once can get overwhelming, and smaller groups are easier to manage.
2. **Ask for Specific Feedback:**
   - If you're unsure about a particular element—like whether your ending is satisfying or if a subplot works—let your beta readers know upfront.
3. **Look for Trends:**
   - One person might dislike a character, but if several beta readers point out the same issue, it's worth

paying attention. Trends in feedback often indicate areas that need improvement.

Working with beta readers is a collaborative step that can transform your manuscript. They'll point out the things you're too close to see, helping you shape a stronger, more engaging story. So send out your draft, arm them with questions, and get ready to learn from their fresh eyes!

## Finding Critique Partners

Critique partners are like your creative workout buddy—they know the struggles of writing, share your passion for stories, and are there to spot your blind spots. Unlike beta readers, who approach your work as readers, critique partners are fellow writers who can dive into the nuts and bolts of your manuscript. They'll help you refine your work, and in return, you'll do the same for them.

## Benefits of Critique Partners

Critique partners bring a writer's eye to your work, which means they:

- **Spot Technical Issues:** Plot holes, weak dialogue, or inconsistent character arcs—things that can slip by unnoticed when you're too close to your own story.
- **Offer Creative Insights:** They might suggest plot twists, deeper character motivations, or ways to amp up tension that you hadn't thought of.
- **Keep You Accountable:** Knowing someone's waiting for your next chapter can be just the push you need to keep writing.

**Pro Tip:** A good critique partner doesn't just point out problems—they help you brainstorm solutions and cheer you on when you nail it.

## Where to Find Them

Finding the right critique partner can feel like dating—you need someone who clicks with your style and goals. Here are some great places to connect:

- **Writing Groups:** Local or online writing groups often include critique exchanges. Check with your library, community centres, or sites like Meetup.
- **Online Communities:** Platforms like Scribophile, Absolute Write, and Reddit's writing forums are excellent for finding like-minded writers.
- **Social Media:** Twitter, Facebook writing groups, and even Instagram can connect you with potential partners. Look for hashtags like #WritingCommunity.

**Pro Tip:** When reaching out, introduce yourself, share your genre, and describe the kind of critique you're looking for. Being clear upfront helps avoid mismatched expectations. There is also a new platform that opens up for Beta testing early 2025 called Scriptophobia.

## Setting Expectations

Clear communication is the foundation of a great critique partnership. Before diving in, set guidelines for:

- **Focus Areas:** Let them know what you need most. For example:

- "I'm struggling with pacing—let me know if any scenes drag."
- "Do my characters' motivations feel believable?"
- **Timeline:** Decide how quickly you'll exchange work and provide feedback. Life gets busy, but setting realistic deadlines helps keep things on track.
- **Tone of Feedback:** Some writers prefer blunt honesty; others need a gentler approach. Share your preferences to avoid misunderstandings.

**Pro Tip:** Be specific about what you need. A vague request like "Tell me what you think" might result in unfocused feedback.

### The Give-and-Take Dynamic

Critique partnerships work best when the exchange is balanced. Be as thoughtful with your feedback as you hope they'll be with yours.

- **What to Look For:** Plot holes, character development, clunky dialogue, or inconsistencies.
- **How to Deliver Feedback:** Start with what's working, then dive into areas for improvement, and finish on a positive note. It's not just good manners—it's good motivation.

**Pro Tip:** Use the "sandwich method": Start with a positive, discuss improvements in the middle, and end with another positive. Example: "I loved the tension in Chapter 3, but the pacing felt a little slow in the middle. Your dialogue at the end was spot-on, though!"

## Ideas for Using Critique Partners Effectively

1. **Refine Specific Sections:**
   - Share tricky scenes or chapters you're unsure about to get targeted advice before sending your full manuscript to beta readers.
2. **Schedule Regular Swaps:**
   - Commit to monthly or bi-weekly exchanges to keep momentum and accountability. Consistent feedback keeps your story moving forward—and theirs too!

A critique partner isn't just someone who reads your work—they're a collaborator who helps you grow as a writer. With clear communication, a give-and-take approach, and mutual respect, critique partnerships can become one of your most valuable tools. Now go find your literary gym buddy and start swapping those chapters!

### Working with Editors

When it's time to take your manuscript to the next level, professional editors are your secret weapon. With their expertise, they can refine your work, catch errors you've overlooked, and help your story shine. But working with an editor is more than just handing over your manuscript—it's a collaborative process that requires preparation and a willingness to embrace honest critique.

### Types of Editing

There are different types of editing, and knowing which one you need will save you time and money. Each focuses on a specific stage of your manuscript's journey:

1. **Developmental Editing:**
   - This is the big-picture edit, where your editor looks at structure, pacing, character arcs, and themes.
   - They might suggest cutting or rearranging scenes, deepening character motivations, or enhancing your central themes.
   - Ideal for early drafts that need a solid overhaul.
2. **Line Editing:**
   - This edit focuses on the language itself—how your sentences flow, the tone, and the overall clarity of your writing.
   - Expect suggestions to refine your phrasing, tighten wordy sentences, and enhance your voice.
   - Great for polishing a manuscript that's structurally sound but needs a little finesse.
3. **Copy Editing:**
   - This is the nitty-gritty stage: grammar, punctuation, spelling, and consistency in style (like how you capitalize terms or format dialogue).
   - Perfect for a nearly finished manuscript to ensure it's error-free and polished.

**Pro Tip:** If you're unsure which type of editing you need, ask an editor to review a sample of your manuscript and recommend the best path forward.

**Finding the Right Editor**

Not all editors are created equal, so it's important to find one who's a good fit for your project.

- **Specialize in Your Genre:** A thriller editor might not be the best fit for your steamy romance novel.

Look for someone with experience in your specific genre.

- **Check Client Reviews:** Read testimonials or reach out to past clients to gauge the editor's style and reliability.
- **Request a Sample Edit:** Many editors offer a short sample edit to show you how they work. This is a great way to see if their approach aligns with your vision.
- **Test Multiple Editors:** Get five editors to perform a sample edit on the same three pages. Compare them. Take the one who shows the most. Don't fall for the one who strokes your ego.

**Pro Tip:** Trust your instincts. If an editor's feedback feels more discouraging than constructive, they might not be the right fit for you.

### What to Expect

Editors are there to improve your manuscript, not sugar-coat it. Be prepared for feedback that's honest, thorough, and sometimes a little hard to hear.

- **Editorial Letters:** Developmental editors often provide a detailed summary of their suggestions, outlining what's working and what isn't.
- **Inline Comments:** Line and copy editors will usually add comments directly to your manuscript, highlighting specific issues and offering fixes.
- **Collaborative Process:** Editing isn't about "fixing" your work—it's about enhancing it. You can discuss suggestions and push back if something doesn't feel right.

**Pro Tip:** Take a breath before diving into your editor's notes. It's normal to feel defensive at first, but remember—they're on your team, and their goal is to make your book the best it can be.

**Ideas for Working with Editors**

1. **Start with Developmental Editing:**
   - Focus on big-picture issues first. There's no point polishing sentences if entire scenes might get cut or restructured later.
2. **Budget and Plan:**
   - Editing can be pricey, so research rates and plan your budget accordingly. Know your timeline too—editors often book months in advance.

**Pro Tip:** Don't rush the process. Each stage of editing takes time, and skipping steps can lead to missed opportunities for improvement.

Working with an editor is like having a trusted guide for your manuscript's final stretch. They'll challenge you, inspire you, and help your story reach its full potential. With the right editor by your side, your manuscript will be ready to take on the world—or at least that publisher's desk!

**Processing Feedback**

Receiving feedback can feel like walking into a room full of people discussing your outfit—you might hear a mix of helpful suggestions, surprising insights, and the occasional, "What were you *thinking*?" But feedback isn't a critique of you; it's a chance to improve your manuscript. Learning how to handle differing opinions and make smart choices about what to change is a crucial skill for every writer.

## Look for Patterns

One piece of feedback might just be a personal opinion, but when multiple people flag the same issue, it's a sign worth paying attention to.

- **Examples of Patterns:**
- If three beta readers say your opening chapter feels slow, it's time to consider tightening it.
- If several critique partners point out that a character's motivations are unclear, it's worth reworking their arc.
- **Why It Matters:** Patterns help you separate one-off preferences from actual problem areas in your story.

**Pro Tip:** Create a simple chart or list to track repeated feedback. Seeing the overlap makes it easier to prioritize changes.

## Stay Open-Minded

It's tempting to bristle at critique—your manuscript is your baby, after all. But feedback is about making your book better, not tearing you down.

- **How to Stay Open:**
- Read the feedback through once without reacting. Let it sink in before you decide how you feel about it.
- Assume good intentions. Most people giving feedback genuinely want to help, not nitpick for the sake of it.
- **Focus on the Work, Not You:** A comment like "This

scene feels flat" isn't a jab at your talent—it's an invitation to explore how the scene could improve.

**Pro Tip:** If a piece of feedback stings, take a day or two before responding or revising. Distance can make it easier to see the critique objectively.

## Trust Your Vision

Not all feedback will fit your goals for the story—and that's okay. You're the author, and you know what you want your book to say.

- **When to Trust Your Gut:**
    - If a suggestion doesn't align with your theme or intended audience, it's fine to ignore it.
    - If the feedback would drastically change the heart of your story, consider whether it's worth the trade-off.
- **Balancing Vision with Feedback:** Be open to suggestions, but remember that you don't have to take every piece of advice—just the ones that truly strengthen your work.

**Pro Tip:** Ask yourself, "Does this feedback help me achieve what I set out to do?" If the answer is no, move on.

## Ideas for Processing Feedback

1. **Create a Feedback Summary:**
    - Compile all the comments you receive into a single document. Group similar suggestions together to spot patterns.

      ◦ Mark suggestions as "Must Fix," "Consider," or "Pass" based on their relevance and importance.

2. **Take a Break:**
      ◦ After receiving feedback, give yourself a day or two to step away. Processing it objectively is easier when emotions aren't running high.

**Pro Tip:** Keep the feedback summary handy as you revise. It acts as a checklist and helps you stay focused on what matters most.

Processing feedback can be a rollercoaster of emotions, but it's also one of the most rewarding parts of the writing process. By identifying patterns, staying open-minded, and trusting your vision, you'll turn critique into a powerful tool for improvement. So take a deep breath, dive in, and remember—you've got this!

### Giving Feedback

Providing feedback isn't just about helping another writer—it's also a fantastic way to sharpen your own skills. By analysing someone else's work, you'll gain insights into storytelling, pacing, and character development that you can apply to your own writing. Plus, giving thoughtful critiques builds trust and camaraderie in the writing community.

### Be Constructive

Critiques should help the writer improve, not leave them feeling defeated. The goal is to offer helpful suggestions while recognising what's already working.

- **Focus on Both Strengths and Weaknesses:** Highlight areas where the writing shines, and offer solutions for parts that could be stronger.
- **Frame Suggestions Positively:** Instead of, "This is boring," try, "This scene could feel more dynamic with a bit of tension or conflict added."

**Pro Tip:** Always ask yourself, "Would this feedback motivate me to keep writing if I received it?"

### Be Specific

Vague feedback like "This didn't work for me" or "I liked it" isn't all that useful. Specificity is key to providing actionable suggestions.

- **Examples of Specific Feedback:**
  - "The pacing in this chapter felt slow because there was a lot of description without much action."
  - "This dialogue really captures the character's personality—I'd love to see more of that in other scenes."
- **Why It Matters:** Specific comments help the writer know exactly what to adjust or keep.

**Pro Tip:** If you can, point to a specific sentence or paragraph to illustrate your feedback.

### Balance Honesty with Encouragement

Honesty is crucial in a critique, but so is encouragement. Nobody wants to hear only what's wrong with their work—it's just as important to acknowledge what's going well.

- **Start with the Positives:** Begin by pointing out something you enjoyed or thought worked well.
- **Tactfully Address Areas for Improvement:** Phrase critiques as suggestions rather than absolutes. For example, "Consider adding more tension here" instead of "This part doesn't work."

**Pro Tip:** Ending with encouragement helps soften the sting of constructive criticism and leaves the writer feeling motivated to revise.

### Ideas for Giving Feedback

1. **Use the "Sandwich Method":**
   - Start with a positive comment, discuss areas for improvement, and finish with another positive. Example:
   - Positive: "Your opening really hooked me—I love the suspense!"
   - Improvement: "The middle felt a bit slow; maybe tighten up the pacing by cutting some of the internal monologue."
   - Positive: "Your descriptions are vivid and really bring the setting to life."
2. **Reflect on Your Experience as a Writer:**
   - Think about the kind of feedback that's helped you improve in the past. Use that as a guide for how you critique others.

Giving thoughtful feedback takes effort, but it's one of the most valuable skills you can develop as a writer. It strengthens your relationships with fellow authors and helps everyone—

including you—improve. So grab your critique pen, aim for kindness and clarity, and watch your writing community flourish!

I have worked with several editors and will tell you, they are all different.

My first book (may it rest in peace) went through an editor who swore they were good (don't they all). After receiving back edits and incorporating them, the book bombed due to the editing. From that point on, I swore to be more cautious.

It was not until my stint with Duke and St. Joseph University that I felt comfortable enough to do most of the edits on work published through my publishing company. The problem is, I still have to rely on outside editors for my own work.

So, beware the editor who makes it look like your writing is sunshine and roses. Always go with the one who marks the crap out of it.

# Part 4

# The Business Side

# Chapter 13

# **Understanding Publishing Options**

Pros and Cons of Having an Agent

Landing a literary agent can feel like finding the golden ticket in a chocolate bar—it's exciting and full of possibilities. However, while an agent can open doors and provide much-needed expertise, it's not always the best path for every writer. Let's break down the pros and cons so you can decide if having an agent aligns with your publishing goals.

**Pros**

1. **Access to Traditional Publishers**
   - Many traditional publishers won't look at unsolicited manuscripts, meaning your dream of being on a bookstore shelf might hinge on having an agent.
   - Agents come armed with a Rolodex of editor contacts and established relationships, increasing your chances of getting noticed.

**Pro Tip:** If your dream is to see your book in major retail stores or snag a deal with a Big Five publisher, an agent is practically a must.

2. **Contract Negotiation Expertise**
   - Publishing contracts are full of legal jargon and complex terms—an agent knows how to navigate these waters.
   - They'll fight for better royalties, rights, and advances, ensuring you're not shortchanged.

**Pro Tip:** Agents are particularly good at protecting your long-term interests, like retaining rights to future editions or adaptations.

3. **Career Guidance**
   - Agents often act as career coaches, advising on what projects to pursue and how to grow your author platform.
   - They're also great for navigating market trends—suggesting tweaks to make your book more appealing to readers and publishers.

**Pro Tip:** Think of your agent as your partner in building not just a book, but a writing career.

4. **Advocacy and Support**
   - Difficult conversation with a publisher? Tight deadlines? Your agent will handle the messy bits, leaving you free to focus on writing.
   - Agents champion your work, ensuring editors and publishers give it the attention it deserves.

**Pro Tip:** A good agent isn't just a business ally—they're your cheerleader when self-doubt creeps in.

5. **Networking Opportunities**
   - Agents are deeply connected in the industry and can introduce you to editors, publicists, and even other authors.
   - These relationships can lead to more opportunities, like anthologies, collaborations, or speaking gigs.

**Pro Tip:** Your agent's network is an extension of yours—don't underestimate the doors this can open.

**Cons**

1. **Finding an Agent is Difficult**

   - It's a competitive market, and literary agents receive hundreds (if not thousands) of queries every year.
   - You'll need a polished manuscript, a killer query letter, and patience to withstand the rejections that might come your way.

**Pro Tip:** Research agents who represent your genre and personalise your query to increase your chances.

2. **Commission Fees**

   - Agents typically take 15-20% of your earnings, which can add up over time.

- While their expertise is often worth the investment, it's something to factor into your financial expectations.

**Pro Tip:** Remember, agents only make money when you do—they're incentivised to help your book succeed.

### 3. Lack of Creative Control

- An agent might suggest changes to your manuscript to make it more marketable, which can sometimes feel at odds with your artistic vision.
- Publishers might also have their own demands, and your agent may advocate for those over your preferences.

**Pro Tip:** Be clear about your non-negotiables with your agent to ensure your vision remains intact.

### 4. Not Always the Right Fit

- An agent who doesn't understand your genre or career goals can lead to frustration or missed opportunities.
- Like any professional relationship, mismatches happen, and they can be hard to navigate.

**Pro Tip:** Don't rush into signing with the first agent who offers representation. Take the time to find someone who truly gets you and your work.

### 5. Delays in the Process

- Once your manuscript is in an agent's hands, they'll shop it to publishers—a process that can take months, sometimes longer.
- Even after a deal is signed, the traditional publishing timeline can add years to the process.

**Pro Tip:** Use the waiting period to start your next project. Publishing is a marathon, not a sprint.

Agents can be invaluable guides through the often-complicated world of traditional publishing, but they're not the only option. Take the time to weigh these pros and cons against your personal goals and resources to determine if working with an agent is the right path for you.

### Traditional Publishing

Traditional publishing is the path many writers dream of—it's the classic route where a publisher takes your manuscript, polishes it to perfection, and puts it on bookstore shelves. But while the rewards can be enticing, this option comes with its share of challenges. Let's break down the pros, cons, and key things to consider.

### Pros

1. **Professional Team**
   - With a traditional publisher, you gain access to experienced editors, designers, and marketing experts. They'll help refine your manuscript, create a professional cover, and promote your book effectively.
   - You're not going it alone—there's a whole team behind you to ensure your book shines.

**Pro Tip:** Use this opportunity to learn from the pros. Their expertise can elevate not just this book but your overall writing skills.

2. **Wide Distribution**
   - Traditional publishers ensure your book gets prime placement in physical bookstores, libraries, and major online retailers.
   - Their established networks make it easier for your book to reach a large audience.

**Pro Tip:** Getting into brick-and-mortar stores is no small feat, and traditional publishers have the connections to make it happen.

3. **Advance Payment**
   - Many traditional deals come with an advance, which is an upfront payment against future royalties. This can provide financial security while you work on your next project.

**Pro Tip:** Advances vary widely, so temper your expectations. The size of the advance doesn't define your success.

4. **Industry Credibility**
   - A traditional publishing deal adds a layer of professional validation. It shows that industry experts believe in your work.
   - This can boost your profile with readers, reviewers, and future publishers.

**Pro Tip:** Use your traditional publishing experience as a credential when pitching future projects or building your platform.

### 5. Marketing Support
- Publishers handle much of the marketing for you, from creating promotional campaigns to organizing book launches and events.
- While you'll still need to promote your book, having a professional team backing you up makes it much easier.

**Pro Tip:** Collaborate with your publisher's marketing team to maximize their efforts. Share ideas and be proactive about engaging with readers.

### Cons

### 1. Difficult to Break Into
- The traditional publishing path is competitive. To even get in the door, you'll likely need a literary agent to champion your manuscript.
- The process of querying agents and publishers can be long and filled with rejections.

**Pro Tip:** Research agents and publishers thoroughly. Tailor your submissions to those who specialize in your genre for a better chance of success.

### 2. Long Timeline
- From signing a contract to seeing your book on shelves, the process can take 1–2 years—or longer.

- Traditional publishing requires patience, as everything from editing to printing follows a carefully planned schedule.

**Pro Tip:** Start working on your next project during the waiting period to make the most of your time.

3. **Limited Creative Control**
   - Publishers often have the final say on key elements like your book's title, cover design, and even some aspects of the content.
   - While their choices are usually market-driven, it can feel frustrating if you're attached to a particular vision.

**Pro Tip:** Be open to feedback, but don't hesitate to advocate for your core ideas. Communication is key.

4. **Lower Royalties**
   - Traditional publishing typically offers lower royalty percentages compared to self-publishing.
   - While the publisher takes on more financial risk, it means you earn less per book sold.

**Pro Tip:** Focus on volume—traditional publishing's wide distribution can lead to more overall sales, even with smaller royalties.

5. **Rights Ownership**
   - Publishers often retain significant rights, including foreign translations, audiobook production, and film adaptations.

○ You might lose some control over how your work is used in the long term.

**Pro Tip:** Carefully review contracts to understand which rights you're giving up and consider negotiating terms where possible.

**Ideas to Consider**

- **Research Agents and Publishers:**
  - ○ Look for agents and publishers who specialize in your genre. Study submission guidelines carefully to make the best impression.
- **Prepare a Strong Query Package:**
  - ○ A compelling query letter and a concise, engaging synopsis are essential to stand out in a crowded market.
- **Evaluate Contracts Thoroughly:**
  - ○ Understand the fine print, especially when it comes to royalty percentages, rights, and expectations for marketing efforts. If needed, consult a publishing lawyer for advice.

Traditional publishing offers a wealth of resources and expertise, but it also comes with its share of trade-offs. Understanding the process and weighing the pros and cons will help you decide if this path aligns with your goals.

**Small Press Publishing: Pros and Cons**

If traditional publishing feels like trying to win the lottery and self-publishing seems a bit too DIY, small press publishing could be your Goldilocks option—not too big, not too small, but just right. Small presses combine professional support with a more personal touch, but they're not without their quirks. Let's dig into the pros and cons so you know what you're signing up for.

## 1. Pros of Small Press Publishing

- **Personalized Attention:**
  - Small presses often feel like boutique operations, where you're more than just another name on a spreadsheet. Expect hands-on collaboration and real conversations about your manuscript.
  - You'll likely have more say in decisions like cover design, title choices, and even marketing approaches—no faceless committees here.

**Pro Tip:** If you're someone who likes being involved in the process but doesn't want to handle everything yourself, a small press can be the perfect fit.

- **Niche Market Expertise:**
  - Many small presses carve out a niche—whether it's LGBTQ+ romance, hard sci-fi, or Canadian regional history. They know their audience and how to reach them.
  - This can be especially helpful if your book targets a specific or underserved market.

**Pro Tip:** Find a small press that already publishes books like yours. Their experience in your genre is a huge asset.

- **Faster Timelines:**

- Unlike traditional publishing, which can take years, small presses often move faster, meaning your book could hit shelves in months rather than millennia.

**Pro Tip:** Use this time advantage to build momentum, like planning your launch strategy early or engaging with potential readers on social media.

- **Flexibility:**
  - Small presses often embrace innovation. Whether it's experimenting with formats (like audiobooks) or targeting unconventional audiences, their agility can work in your favour.

**Pro Tip:** If you have a bold idea for how your book could be marketed or sold, small presses are more likely to entertain it than big publishers.

- **Community Building:**
  - Small presses pride themselves on building a sense of family among their authors. Networking opportunities with other writers can lead to collaborations, inspiration, or simply someone to vent to about comma splices.

**Pro Tip:** Connect with other authors at the press. They can offer tips, share experiences, or help amplify your book's reach.

- **Less Gatekeeping:**

- Small presses are often open to debut authors, unconventional ideas, or projects that might not fit into a big publisher's "profit margin spreadsheet."

**Pro Tip:** Don't be afraid to pitch a project that's a little outside the box—it might be just what a small press is looking for.

### 2. Cons of Small Press Publishing

- **Limited Distribution:**
  - Small presses may lack the resources to secure placement in big bookstore chains or libraries, which could mean more reliance on digital sales or local outreach.
  - You might not see your book on the shelves at Indigo or Barnes & Noble without some hustle.

**Pro Tip:** Partner with independent bookstores or attend local author events to get your book into physical spaces.

- **Smaller Marketing Budgets:**
  - Don't expect a massive marketing campaign. You'll likely need to take on a lot of promotional work yourself, from managing social media to organizing book signings.

**Pro Tip:** Be proactive. Collaborate with the small press's marketing team and supplement their efforts with your own initiatives.

- **No Advances:**

- o Small presses can't afford advances. You'll be banking on royalties instead.

**Pro Tip:** Focus on long-term earnings rather than upfront cash. A steady trickle of royalties can add up over time if your book finds its audience.

- **Varied Reputation and Quality:**
  - o Not all small presses are equal. Some are stellar; others might lack the professionalism or experience to support your book properly.

**Pro Tip:** Check reviews, author testimonials, and previously published books to ensure the press has a track record of quality work and good author relationships.

- **Limited Resources:**
  - o With smaller teams and budgets, editing, design, and distribution might not have the same polish as a large publisher's output.

**Pro Tip:** Don't hesitate to ask questions about what resources and support you can expect before signing a contract.

### 3. Ideas to Consider When Working with Small Presses

1. **Research Thoroughly:**
   - o Treat choosing a small press like hiring a contractor—you want proof of their professionalism and results. Look at books they've published and how they've marketed them.
2. **Understand Your Contract:**

- Read every line of the contract carefully, especially regarding royalties, rights, and marketing expectations. Don't hesitate to consult a publishing lawyer if needed.

3. **Assess Fit for Your Genre:**
   - Does the press specialize in your type of book? If they know your genre inside and out, they're more likely to understand how to market it successfully.

4. **Be Prepared to Promote:**
   - Small presses can't do it all, so plan to be your book's loudest cheerleader. Develop your platform, connect with readers, and promote creatively.

5. **Build Relationships:**
   - Make the most of the small press's tight-knit environment. Collaborating with their team and other authors can boost your career and give you a support network.

Small press publishing offers a unique middle ground between traditional and self-publishing. With the right partnership, you can enjoy the personal attention of a small team while still reaping the rewards of professional publishing. Just make sure you're ready to roll up your sleeves and contribute to the effort!

**Pay for Publication (Hybrid Publishers)**

If traditional publishing feels like climbing Everest and self-publishing feels like setting up camp solo, hybrid publishing might be the cosy lodge in between. Hybrid publishers offer the professional support of traditional publishing while giving you more control over your book—at a price. Here's what you need to know about this unique option.

## 1. What is Hybrid Publishing?

- **Definition:** Hybrid publishing is a blend of traditional and self-publishing. Authors pay for services such as editing, design, and marketing, but retain more creative control over their book.
- **No Shared Responsibilities:** It's not a team effort—authors fund all the production and marketing costs, while the publisher handles the technical and distribution-heavy aspects.

**Pro Tip:** Think of hybrid publishing as co-producing a movie—you're investing in your project, but you have a staff of (hopefully) professionals doing all the heavy lifting.

## 2. Pros of Hybrid Publishing

- **Professional Services:**
  - With hybrid publishing, you get access to high-quality editing, cover design, formatting, and marketing—services that rival traditional publishers.
  - This professional polish can make a huge difference in how your book is received.
- **Creative Control:**
  - Want to veto a cover design? Adjust pricing? Hybrid publishing allows more say in decisions compared to traditional publishers, but it will cost you.

**Pro Tip:** This is your chance to blend professional expertise with your unique vision. Use it wisely.

- **Faster Timeline:**
  - Tired of waiting years to see your book in print? Hybrid publishers often move faster, meaning your work could be published within months.

**Pro Tip:** Use the faster timeline to plan your promotional efforts, like pre-launch campaigns or social media teases.

- **Wider Distribution:**
  - Many hybrid publishers have established connections with distributors and online retailers, making it easier for your book to reach readers.

**Pro Tip:** Ask about specific distribution plans when signing a contract. Visibility is key.

- **Credibility Boost:**
  - Working with a reputable hybrid publisher adds legitimacy to your book compared to going completely solo.

## Cons of Hybrid Publishing

- **Cost:**
  - Hybrid publishing isn't cheap. Services can range from a few thousand dollars to significantly more, and the upfront investment can be daunting.

**Pro Tip:** Treat it like a business decision—consider your budget and potential return on investment carefully.

- **Varied Quality:**

- Not all hybrid publishers are created equal. Some provide excellent services, while others cut corners or make big promises they can't deliver.

**Pro Tip:** Research, research, research. Look for testimonials and examples of books they've published before signing anything.

- **Profit Sharing:**
  - Despite footing the bill, you'll often split royalties with the publisher, which can eat into your earnings.

**Pro Tip:** Negotiate terms wherever possible and make sure the royalty split feels fair given your level of investment.

- **Perception Issues:**
  - Hybrid publishing sometimes carries the stigma of being a "vanity press" (a model where authors pay to be published with little added value).

**Pro Tip:** Work with a well-regarded hybrid publisher to avoid this perception. Their reputation becomes your reputation.

### How to Evaluate a Hybrid Publisher

- **Reputation:**
  - Look up reviews, ask for author testimonials, and assess the quality of books they've published. Red flags include vague contracts and poor communication.
- **Transparency:**

- A trustworthy hybrid publisher will clearly explain their fees, services, and what you can expect in return. Avoid anyone who dodges questions or overhypes results.

**Pro Tip:** If it sounds too good to be true ("We guarantee bestseller status!"), it probably is.

- **Distribution and Marketing:**
  - Check their marketing and distribution strategies. Do they have access to bookstores? How much of the promotional effort will fall on you?
- **Contracts:**
  - Review the contract carefully. Look for clarity on costs, royalties, and rights. Seek legal advice if necessary.

**Pro Tip:** Ensure you retain key rights, such as the ability to publish sequels or sell film and foreign language adaptations.

### Ideas for Authors Considering Hybrid Publishing

- **Budget Wisely:**
  - Know your financial limits and account for all potential costs, including marketing, printing, and promotional activities.
- **Retain Control:**
  - Don't hand over more creative or legal control than necessary. Your book should remain *yours*.
- **Do Your Homework:**
  - Contact authors who've worked with the hybrid

publisher to get honest feedback about their experience.

- **Prepare to Promote:**
  - Hybrid publishers may offer marketing help, but much of the legwork will fall on you. Build your platform and plan your promotional strategy early.

**Pro Tip:** Think of your marketing as part of your investment—success depends on your effort as much as theirs.

Hybrid publishing can be a powerful option for authors who want professional support without sacrificing creative control, but it requires careful research and a willingness to invest time, effort, and money. With the right partner, you can produce a polished, successful book while staying true to your vision.

### Self-Publishing

Self-publishing has become a game-changer for authors who want to take matters into their own hands. If you like the idea of being the CEO of your own book, this path gives you full creative freedom and control. But with great power comes great responsibility—and, well, a lot of work. Let's look at the pros, cons, and a few tips to help you decide if this route is right for you.

### Pros

1. **Creative Control**
   - You're the boss. From cover design to pricing to formatting, every decision is yours to make.
   - Want a bright pink dragon on your cover or

chapters named after snack foods? Go for it! There's no committee telling you no.

**Pro Tip:** While creative freedom is great, don't skip professional input on things like editing or design. Your creative vision still needs polish to shine.

2. **Faster Timeline**
   - Unlike traditional publishing, where you could be waiting years, self-publishing lets you hit "publish" as soon as your book is ready.
   - Got a story burning a hole in your brain? Self-publishing means readers can get their hands on it much sooner.

**Pro Tip:** Faster doesn't mean skipping steps. Professional editing and design take time, so plan your timeline wisely.

3. **Higher Royalties**
   - Platforms like Amazon KDP, IngramSpark, and Draft2Digital allow you to keep a larger chunk of the profits compared to traditional publishers.
   - If you sell directly to readers, you can earn even more without middlemen taking a cut.

**Pro Tip:** Balance your pricing—competitive prices attract readers, but you still want a solid return on your effort.

4. **Niche Audience Targeting**
   - Self-publishing is perfect for books with highly specific or smaller audiences. Think local history,

niche non-fiction, or quirky genres traditional publishers might overlook.

- ○ If you know your audience and where they hang out, you can reach them directly.

**Pro Tip:** Use targeted ads, social media groups, or mailing lists to connect with your specific readers.

5. **Ownership of Rights**
   - ○ You retain full control of your intellectual property, meaning you can sell film rights, audiobooks, or foreign translations without asking anyone's permission.
   - ○ You own it all—your ideas, your words, and your future opportunities.

**Pro Tip:** If your book takes off, you'll be in a stronger position to negotiate with publishers or media producers down the road.

**Cons**

1. **Upfront Costs**
   - ○ Self-publishing isn't free if you want a professional result. Editing, cover design, and marketing all cost money, and you're footing the bill.
   - ○ Cutting corners here could result in a book that doesn't sell well—or worse, damages your reputation.

**Pro Tip:** Budget smartly. Prioritize professional editing and cover design—they're the two most important elements for a polished, marketable book.

2. **Time-Intensive**
   - You'll need to wear multiple hats: writer, project manager, marketer, and accountant. If you're not organized, it can quickly become overwhelming.
   - Learning to navigate publishing platforms, marketing tools, and design software is a job in itself.

**Pro Tip:** Outsource where you can. Hiring freelancers for editing or design can save you time and stress.

3. **Limited Distribution**
   - Getting your book into physical bookstores or libraries can be a challenge without the distribution power of a traditional publisher.
   - Many brick-and-mortar retailers prioritize traditionally published books.

**Pro Tip:** Approach indie bookstores directly or work with print-on-demand services like IngramSpark to improve your chances of getting shelf space.

4. **Marketing Challenges**
   - Self-publishing means you're in charge of getting the word out about your book. If you're not promoting, your book won't sell.
   - Building an author platform and figuring out marketing strategies takes time and effort.

**Pro Tip:** Start building your platform before you publish. Grow an audience through social media, newsletters, and reader communities so you have readers ready to buy when your book launches.

5. **Perception Hurdles**
   - Despite the growth of self-publishing, some readers and reviewers still see it as "less credible" compared to traditional publishing.
   - A poorly produced self-published book can reinforce these biases, so quality is key.

**Pro Tip:** Treat your book like a professional product. High-quality editing, a great cover, and proper formatting will ensure it stands alongside traditionally published works.

**Ideas to Consider**

1. **Use Trusted Platforms:**
   - Platforms like Amazon KDP and IngramSparkare reliable options for distributing your book worldwide.
2. **Budget for Success:**
   - Allocate funds for professional services like editing, cover design, and marketing. Think of it as an investment in your book's success.
3. **Build Your Platform:**
   - Start marketing before you publish. Use social media, newsletters, or even create a website to connect with readers and build buzz around your book.

**Pro Tip:** Don't try to do it all at once. Focus on the platforms where your readers spend the most time.

Self-publishing gives you the freedom to create, publish, and market your book exactly the way you want. It's an empowering choice for authors who are willing to invest time, effort, and a little bit of cash to bring their work to life. With the right approach, self-publishing can be both rewarding and profitable—and you'll own every step of the journey.

When I finished my first novel, I explored several publishing options. Hybrid publishers were one of them, but honestly, most of them seem more interested in separating authors from their money than anything else—even if a few honest ones might exist.

I'll never forget an experience I had about ten years ago at a library event for authors. One of the speakers was beaming with pride over his book, but after his talk, he approached me for advice. At the time, I'd just launched my publishing company, and he wanted my opinion on hybrid publishers.

He handed me a copy of his book, explaining that he'd paid over $8,000 for the work they'd done. Curious (and maybe a little horrified), I took a closer look. The cover was a mess—just a mishmash of royalty-free images: a plane, a woman with long hair, and a palm tree. Even the text looked off. Out of habit, I measured the layout, and sure enough, the text alignment was uneven and tilted.

When I opened the book, the printing inside was even worse. The text on the pages was tilted by seven degrees—not exactly a professional look. I pointed this out to him, and he was shocked. He hadn't even noticed before.

Trying to help, I suggested using a local printer for future runs. That's when he dropped another bomb: his contract with the hybrid publisher forced him to buy all copies directly from them. Their printing costs were 25% higher than a local printer I'd found, locking him into an overpriced arrangement.

To this day, I still wonder if he ever managed to get out of that contract. It was a hard lesson in why it pays to be cautious when choosing a publisher.

# Chapter 14
# **Building Your Platform**

### **Understanding What an Author Platform Is**

An author platform isn't just a fancy buzzword—it's your bridge to readers, publishers, and the wider world. Think of it as your visibility, reputation, and ability to connect with people who want to read *your* work. Whether you're an aspiring author or already have a few books under your belt, building a platform helps you share your stories and make sure readers know where to find them.

**Talking Points:**

- **Definition:**
  - Your author platform is the sum of all the ways you connect with your audience. It's how visible you are, how you engage with readers, and how you spread the word about your work.
  - A strong platform boosts your reach and makes it easier to market and sell your books.

**Pro Tip:** Imagine your platform as a stage—when you step onto it, you're showing readers who you are, why they should care about your books, and where to get them.

- **Purpose:**
  - Your platform builds trust and credibility. Readers buy books from authors they feel connected to or intrigued by.
  - Publishers also care about your platform. Even if you're traditionally published, having an established audience makes you more appealing.

**Pro Tip:** Whether your audience is ten people or ten thousand, engagement matters. Readers who love your work are more likely to spread the word for you.

- **Not Just Social Media:**
  - An author platform is more than just your Facebook posts or Instagram Reels. It's a collection of tools and activities that make you accessible and visible to readers.

**Elements of a Strong Platform can include:**

- **Author Website:** Your home base with information about you and your books.
- **Newsletters:** A direct line to readers' inboxes to share updates, sneak peeks, and special content.
- **Social Media:** Platforms like Instagram, TikTok, Facebook, or Twitter where you can connect in real time.

- **Speaking Engagements:** Events, panels, or workshops where you share your expertise or stories.
- **Media Coverage:** Interviews, articles, or guest blog posts that help spread the word about your work.

**Pro Tip:** Treat your platform like a buffet. You don't need to be *everywhere*. Pick the tools that fit your strengths and audience.

**Ideas to Get Started:**

1. **Reflect on Your Audience:**
   - Who are your readers? Are they fans of fantasy, non-fiction, romance, or memoirs? Where do they hang out—Facebook groups, Instagram, YouTube?
   - Once you understand who your audience is, you'll know where to focus your efforts.

**Example:** If you write YA fiction, TikTok's BookTok community might be your goldmine. If you're a non-fiction author, LinkedIn or newsletters might make more sense.

2. **Assess Where You Are Now:**
   - Take stock of what tools you already have in place. Do you have a website? Are you active on social media? Do you send out newsletters?
   - Write down what's working well and what areas you want to improve or build on.

**Pro Tip:** Start small. If you're missing a website or newsletter, don't panic. Focus on one platform at a time and grow from there.

A strong author platform doesn't appear overnight, but with a little planning and consistency, it becomes a powerful tool to connect with readers and build your writing career. Remember, you're not shouting into the void—you're creating a space where your readers can find *you*.

## Social Media for Authors

Social media can feel like juggling flaming swords while riding a unicycle, but when done right, it's a fantastic way to connect with readers, build your audience, and promote your work. The trick is finding the platforms that work best for you and creating content that feels authentic, engaging, and (most importantly) not like a constant sales pitch.

## Choosing the Right Platforms

Not all social media platforms are created equal, and thankfully, you don't need to be on all of them. Focus on 1–2 platforms that align with your strengths and where your readers are most active.

- **Instagram:** Perfect for visual content. Share book covers, writing updates, aesthetic images, and behind-the-scenes shots. Think of it as your book's highlight reel.
- **Twitter (X):** Great for quick updates, writing tips, and connecting with other writers using hashtags like #amwriting or #WritersCommunity. Bonus: It's also perfect for sharing snarky one-liners.
- **Facebook:** Useful for building a loyal reader community with author pages, groups, and event promotion. Perfect if you want to run giveaways, host live readings, or share regular updates.

- **TikTok:** The home of BookTok, where short, creative videos about books and writing have gone viral. If you enjoy quick, fun content (like book reveals or "day in the life of an author" clips), this platform is gold.
- **LinkedIn:** A solid choice for non-fiction authors, business professionals, or anyone wanting to connect with thought leaders and expand their professional network.

**Pro Tip:** Pick the platform you're most comfortable with and where your audience hangs out. It's better to excel at one than spread yourself thin across five.

### Creating Engaging Content

Let's face it: nobody wants to follow someone who *only* talks about their book. The key to social media success is balance —mix promotional content with updates, personality, and value for your audience.

- **Mix It Up:** Combine posts about your books with personal stories, writing tips, or interactive questions. For example:
  - A snippet from your current work-in-progress.
  - "What's your favourite book to re-read?" (Everyone loves a good book debate.)
  - A quick writing tip or your go-to productivity hack.
- **Tell a Story:** Share your writing journey. Readers love to see what goes on behind the scenes—your successes, struggles, and even funny mishaps.
- **Avoid Over-Promoting:** Social media is about building relationships, not shouting *"BUY MY BOOK!"*

every five seconds. Focus on engaging with your audience, not just selling to them.

**Pro Tip:** Think about what you enjoy seeing from other authors—chances are your readers want the same kind of content from you.

### Staying Consistent

Posting regularly doesn't mean posting *constantly*. Quality always beats quantity, so aim to show up consistently with meaningful content.

- **Create a Schedule:** Use tools like Buffer, Hootsuite, or Later to plan posts in advance so you're not scrambling every day.
- **Set Realistic Goals:** If three posts a week feels doable, start there. Don't burn yourself out trying to post every day.
- **Repurpose Content:** A great blog post can become a series of tweets. A fun Instagram Reel can also work on TikTok. Work smarter, not harder.

**Pro Tip:** Consistency builds trust. Even a steady trickle of posts will help keep you on your audience's radar.

### Ideas for Engaging Content

- **Share Behind-the-Scenes Moments:**
  - Post photos of your writing space, progress updates, or snippets of your current draft.
- **Engage Your Readers:**

- Ask questions, run polls, or hold live Q&A sessions. Readers love being part of your process.
- **Use Hashtags Strategically:**
  - Hashtags increase visibility. Use relevant ones like #WritingCommunity, #Bookstagram, #BookTok, or genre-specific tags like #FantasyAuthor or #RomanceReaders.

**Pro Tip:** Not sure what to post? Start with these quick ideas:

- "What I'm working on this week…"
- "Here's a snippet from my upcoming book—let me know what you think!"
- "Five books I'm loving right now."

Social media doesn't have to feel overwhelming. Start small, focus on building real connections, and remember to be yourself. Readers don't just want to know about your books—they want to know *you*.

### Creating an Author Website

Your author website is your digital "home base"—it's where readers, media, and publishers come to learn about you and your work. Think of it as your online calling card. Whether you're a tech whiz or someone who gets nervous just opening a new tab, building a professional and functional website is easier than you might think.

### Why You Need a Website

- **Your Personal Headquarters:**

- Your website is where everything about you and your writing comes together in one place. Readers can find your books, learn about your journey, and (hopefully) fall in love with your work.
- **Credibility and Control:**
  - A professional website gives you credibility. It tells readers, reviewers, and publishers that you're serious about your career.
  - Unlike social media platforms, which you don't own, your website gives you full control of your content and image.

**Pro Tip:** If someone Googles your name, make sure they find *you* first, not an outdated social media account or a random photo from high school.

### Essential Elements of an Author Website

- **Homepage:**
  - This is your first impression, so keep it clean, welcoming, and to the point. Include quick links to your books, a short bio, or any big news like a book launch or upcoming event.
- **About Page:**
  - Share your bio, but don't make it read like a resumé. Readers want to connect with *you*, so sprinkle in some fun details—like your love of coffee, cats, or that time you got lost on a research trip.
  - Highlight your writing journey: How did you get started, and what drives you to write?
- **Books Page:**

- Showcase your books with their covers, brief descriptions, and links to purchase. Make it easy for readers to click and buy.
- If you have multiple books, organize them by series, genre, or release date.

- **Blog/News Page (Optional):**
  - A blog can be a great way to share updates, writing tips, or thoughts on your genre. If blogging feels like too much work, a "News" page for occasional announcements works just fine.

- **Contact Page:**
  - Include an email address, contact form, or links to your social media. Make it easy for readers, event organizers, or media outlets to reach you.

**Pro Tip:** Your website doesn't have to be complicated—focus on clarity, user-friendliness, and making sure the important info is easy to find.

### Design and Functionality

- **Keep It Clean and Simple:**
- Avoid cluttered layouts, distracting colours, or flashy animations. Readers are here for *you* and your books —don't let a messy design get in the way.
- **Mobile-Friendly:**
- A lot of readers will visit your website on their phones, so make sure it looks just as good on a small screen as it does on a computer. Most website platforms offer mobile-friendly templates to make this easy.

**Pro Tip:** Pretend you're a reader seeing your site for the first time. Can you find your books and contact info in a few clicks? If not, simplify.

**Ideas to Get Started**

- **Choose a Platform:**
  - Use user-friendly tools like Squarespace, WordPress, or Wix. They offer templates that look professional without requiring any coding skills.
- **Build Your Mailing List:**
  - Add a newsletter sign-up form on your homepage or in a pop-up. Offer a free short story, bonus chapter, or behind-the-scenes content as an incentive.
- **Create a Media Kit:**
  - Include a downloadable media kit with your bio, professional author photo, book descriptions, and any relevant links. This makes it easy for event organizers or reviewers to feature you.

**Pro Tip:** If you're intimidated by the tech side, start simple. Launch with the basics (a homepage, an about page, and a books page), and build out the extras later.

A good author website doesn't need to be flashy or expensive —it just needs to work. Keep it simple, keep it professional, and most importantly, keep it *you*. Readers are looking for an author to follow, and this is your chance to give them a place to land.

**Developing Your Personal Brand**

Your personal brand is how readers see you, remember you, and connect with you. It's more than just your books—it's *you*. Your voice, your personality, and what makes you stand out as an author all come together to create your brand. Think of it like your signature style, but instead of just clothes, it's everything from your social media presence to the way you write your author bio.

**What is a Personal Brand?**

- **How You're Perceived:** Your personal brand is the "you" readers experience—whether they see your posts on social media, browse your website, or read an interview.
- **Reflecting Your Identity:** It should match your voice, genre, and personality. A romance author might lean into warmth and charm, while a thriller writer might go for something sharp and intense.

**Pro Tip:** Your brand isn't just for readers—it helps you, too. It's a guide for how you present yourself and ensures consistency wherever your name pops up.

**Finding Your Author Voice**

Your voice is the tone and personality you project, and it should be consistent across everything you share—whether that's a tweet, a blog, or an author event.

- **Decide on Your Tone:**
    - Are you approachable and funny? Thoughtful and professional? Witty and sarcastic? Pick a tone that

reflects who you are and what your audience expects.

- **Match Your Genre:**
  - Your tone should align with your work. A horror author probably wouldn't crack jokes all the time, while a children's author would keep things fun and light-hearted.

**Example:** A historical fiction author might present themselves as knowledgeable and detail-oriented, while a fantasy writer might embrace a whimsical, imaginative tone.

**Pro Tip:** Don't overthink it—your voice is *you*. Write and share as you naturally would, and the right readers will connect with it.

### Visual Branding

Visual consistency helps readers instantly recognize you, your work, and your content. It's like giving your brand a "look" that readers come to expect.

- **Choose Consistent Colours and Fonts:**
  - Use the same colours, fonts, and design styles across your website, social media banners, book covers, and promotional materials. It makes you look professional and cohesive.
- **Imagery Matters:**
  - Whether you're posting on Instagram or designing a website header, choose visuals that fit your tone and style. For example:
  - A dark, moody palette for a thriller author.
  - Bright, playful images for a children's author.

**Pro Tip:** Free tools like Canva can help you create branded graphics, ads, and headers without needing a design degree.

**What Makes You Unique?**

Readers connect with *people*, not polished sales pitches. Your quirks, passions, and values are what set you apart, so don't hide them.

- **Share Your Interests and Personality:**
  - Do you love coffee? Cats? Hiking? Share it! Small personal details make you relatable.
  - Highlight what you care about—whether it's a passion for storytelling, strong female leads, or a love for 80s sci-fi movies.
- **Stand Out:**
  - What makes your work or process different? Maybe you write fantasy with a comedic twist, or you're a retired chef writing foodie mysteries. Lean into what makes you unique.

**Example:** "Fantasy author crafting magical worlds with a touch of humour and heart."

**Pro Tip:** Share stories from your writing journey. Readers love hearing about your challenges, victories, and "aha!" moments —it makes you human.

**Ideas to Get Started**

1. **Write a Personal Branding Statement:**
   - Summarize your voice and style in one or two sentences. For example:

- *"I write contemporary romance novels with strong female leads and lots of laughs."*
- *"Thriller author turning everyday moments into nightmares you can't put down."*

2. **Design Branded Content:**
   - Use tools like Canva to create consistent social media graphics, website headers, and ads.
3. **Share Your Writing Journey:**
   - Post updates about your process, behind-the-scenes glimpses of your writing life, or fun facts about your books.

**Pro Tip:** Be yourself. Readers can spot a fake from a mile away. Authenticity builds trust, and trust keeps readers coming back for more.

Developing your personal brand is about showcasing *you—*your voice, your style, and the things that make you unique. It's not about being perfect; it's about being memorable. Your audience isn't looking for a marketing machine—they're looking for *you*.

**Building an Email Newsletter**

An email newsletter might sound old-fashioned compared to shiny social media platforms, but trust me—it's one of the most reliable tools an author can have. Why? Because unlike social media algorithms that hide your posts, an email lands directly in your readers' inboxes. No distractions. No guesswork. Just you and your audience, building a connection one email at a time.

**Why Newsletters Matter**

- **Direct Access to Readers:**
  - Social media is great, but let's be honest—it's unpredictable. With a newsletter, you control when and how you connect with your readers. No algorithms to fight. No scrolling to get lost in.
- **Build Long-Term Relationships:**
  - A newsletter allows you to stay in touch with your audience, share your progress, and keep them engaged between book releases.
  - Think of it like writing to a group of friends who are *really* excited about your stories.

**Pro Tip:** Your email list belongs to *you*, unlike followers on social media. If a platform shuts down tomorrow, your subscribers are still there. And if you host the email list on your website, you don't have to worry about spam or emails leaking to bad characters on the internet.

**What to Include**

The beauty of a newsletter is that it's yours to shape. But if you're stuck, here are a few ideas to keep it fresh and engaging:

- **Writing Updates:**
  - Let readers know how your latest book is coming along—word count milestones, challenges you've overcome, or a sneak peek at the next big twist.
- **Exclusive Content:**
  - Reward your subscribers with something special:
  - Free short stories, bonus chapters, or deleted scenes.

- Early cover reveals or excerpts before anyone else sees them.
- **Personal Touches:**
  - Share a bit about your life, your writing process, or funny anecdotes. Readers love connecting with the *person* behind the book.

**Example:** "I hit 40,000 words this week and celebrated with a giant slice of cake. In case you're wondering—yes, the cake was chocolate."

**Pro Tip:** Keep your emails conversational and upbeat, like you're chatting with an old friend.

**How to Grow Your List**

Building a newsletter list takes time, but these tips will help you get started:

- **Offer Incentives:**
  - Give readers a reason to sign up by offering something valuable, like:
    - A free first chapter of your book.
    - An exclusive short story or resource they can't get anywhere else.
- **Promote Everywhere:**
  - Spread the word about your newsletter:
  - Add a sign-up form to your website's homepage.
  - Mention it in your social media posts, author bio, or book acknowledgements.
  - Include a link in the back of your books. Readers who finish your work are already hooked!
- **Make It Easy:**

- Don't make readers hunt for the sign-up button. Use tools like pop-ups (non-annoying ones, please) or clear calls to action:
- "Want a free short story? Join my newsletter here!"

**Pro Tip:** Focus on quality, not quantity. A smaller list of loyal readers is better than a big list of people who don't open your emails.

### Ideas to Get Started

- **Choose a Platform:**
  - Use email management tools like **Mailchimp**, **MailerLite**, or **ConvertKit** if your CMS does not have one available. They make it easy to set up, design, and send newsletters.
- **Set a Schedule:**
  - Decide how often you'll send newsletters—monthly, bi-weekly, or tied to milestones like a book launch.
  - Consistency matters more than frequency. Readers should know when to expect an email from you.
- **Start Simple:**
  - Your first email doesn't need to be fancy. Introduce yourself, tell readers what they can look forward to, and thank them for joining.

**Pro Tip:** Treat your newsletter subscribers like VIPs. Give them exclusive content, early updates, or sneak peeks to keep them feeling special.

Building an email newsletter might seem like extra work, but it's an investment in your audience and your career. Keep it friendly, offer value, and, most importantly, *have fun with it*. Your readers are signing up because they love your work—now give them a reason to stick around.

## Engaging with Your Audience

Writing a book is one thing—getting readers to connect with you and stick around for the next one is where the magic happens. Engaging with your audience isn't about shouting "Buy my book!" into the void. It's about building real relationships and creating a space where readers feel valued. When done right, your audience becomes your most loyal supporters and biggest cheerleaders.

### Be Responsive

- **Reply and Interact:**
  - Answer questions, reply to comments, and thank readers who reach out. Whether it's on social media, your website, or through email, readers appreciate an author who takes the time to connect.
  - A simple "Thanks for reading!" can go a long way toward building loyalty.
- **Make It Personal:**
  - If someone leaves a glowing comment about your book, don't just hit "like"—give them a thoughtful reply. Readers love knowing you *see* them.

**Pro Tip:** Think of reader engagement as a conversation, not a broadcast. The more you interact, the stronger your connection will be.

## Create Community

- **Start a Reader Group:**
  - Platforms like Facebook are perfect for building a private group where readers can hang out, discuss your books, and share their love for your stories.
- **Host Events:**
  - Live streams, virtual book clubs, or writing challenges bring readers together. They get to know you better and bond with each other, which strengthens their connection to your work.
- **Encourage Interaction:**
  - Ask for reader opinions or feedback:
  - "What should I name my next character?"
  - "Which of my covers do you like better?"
  - Fans love contributing and feeling like part of your journey.

**Pro Tip:** A strong community can feel like a mini fan club—nurture it, and it'll grow.

## Offer Value

Keep your readers invested by sharing content that feels valuable, not just promotional.

- **Share Writing Tips:**
  - Whether it's advice for aspiring writers or a behind-the-scenes look at your process, readers enjoy learning from you.
- **Book Recommendations:**
  - Share the books you're currently reading or loving.

Readers trust your taste, and this keeps your content fresh and engaging.

- **Exclusive Updates:**
  - ○ Offer sneak peeks of upcoming projects, cover reveals, or behind-the-scenes tidbits about your books. Readers love feeling like they're getting something special.

**Pro Tip:** Offer content that answers this question for readers: "Why should I stick around?" If it's interesting, fun, or valuable, they will.

**Ideas to Get Started**

1. **Run Giveaways or Contests:**
   - ○ Give away signed copies of your book, exclusive swag, or early access to a short story. This builds excitement and encourages engagement.
2. **Create a Hashtag:**
   - ○ Encourage readers to share photos of your book using a unique hashtag. For example, #YourBookTitle or #ReadingWith[YourName]. It's free marketing and builds community.
3. **Host Virtual Events:**
   - ○ Hold live Q&A sessions where readers can ask about your books, writing process, or favourite snacks.
   - ○ Collaborate with other authors for interviews or panel discussions—readers love seeing authors interact.

**Pro Tip:** Focus on building relationships, not just selling books. Readers who connect with you as a person are far more likely to become lifelong fans and tell their friends about your work.

Engaging with your audience doesn't have to be complicated or time-consuming. Be present, be real, and show readers that you value them. When you treat readers like part of your journey, they'll be cheering for you every step of the way.

# Chapter 15

# Querying Agents and Publishers

## Understanding the Querying Process

Querying might sound like sending a message in a bottle and hoping someone reads it, but it's much more strategic than that. It's your chance to introduce yourself and your book to agents or publishers who might help bring your story to the world.

### What Querying Is

- **The Process:**
  - Querying involves submitting your manuscript (or a portion of it) to literary agents or publishers for consideration. Think of it as the professional handshake that says, "Hi, I wrote this book, and you're going to love it."
- **The Query Letter:**
  - Your query letter is the key to opening the door. It's a short, polished pitch that introduces your

book, hooks the reader, and explains why they should care. In other words, it's your chance to convince them your manuscript is worth reading.

- Some publishers do not want a full fledged letter, but supply a form for you to put information in. Be prepared for this if it comes up.

**Pro Tip:** A great query letter doesn't ramble. Be clear, be professional, and leave them wanting more.

### Who to Query

Not all submissions are the same, so it's important to target the right people.

- **Literary Agents:**
  - Agents act as the gatekeepers to the world of traditional publishing. They pitch your manuscript to large publishers, negotiate contracts, and advocate for your career.
  - Most major publishers don't accept submissions without an agent, so this route is essential if you're aiming for the big leagues.
- **Traditional Publishers:**
  - These are the major publishing houses you know—Penguin Random House, HarperCollins, and the like. Most require submissions through an agent.
  - Smaller traditional publishers may allow direct submissions without an agent. Check their submission guidelines carefully.
- **Small Press Publishers:**
  - Small presses are often more accessible for debut

authors. They focus on niche markets or specific genres and often accept direct submissions.

o While they may not have the reach of a large publisher, they often provide more personalized attention.

**Pro Tip:** Querying is not a "spray and pray" situation. Research agents and publishers who specialize in your genre and target audience. Sending a thriller to a romance-focused agent is a quick trip to the rejection pile.

### Know Your Goals

Before you hit send on your query, get clear on what you're aiming for:

- **Literary Agent:**
  o If you want access to major traditional publishers, an agent is your best path.
  o Agents also provide valuable career advice, contract negotiation skills, and connections within the industry.
- **Small Press Submission:**
  o If you're focused on smaller, niche publishers, you can submit directly. This option can be a great fit for genres with passionate readers or for authors who want more hands-on support.
- **What Feels Right for You:**
  o Do you want the prestige and distribution power of a large publisher, or the flexibility and accessibility of a small press? There's no wrong answer—only what works for your goals.

**Pro Tip:** Write down your publishing goals before you start querying. Whether it's getting an agent or landing a deal with a small press, knowing your destination will help guide your approach.

Querying doesn't have to feel like shouting into the void. With a polished query letter, clear goals, and some strategic research, you'll increase your chances of getting the right person's attention. It's not about luck—it's about putting yourself and your book in front of the right people.

## Writing Effective Query Letters

A query letter is your ticket to getting an agent or publisher interested in your book. Think of it as your professional elevator pitch—short, snappy, and designed to make them say, *"I need to see more."*

## Purpose of a Query Letter

- A query letter introduces you and your book to an agent or publisher.
- Its sole purpose? To convince them to request your manuscript. It's not the place for rambling life stories or unnecessary fluff—it's a business letter with a splash of personality.

**Pro Tip:** Treat your query letter like a movie trailer—it's all about hooking the reader with the highlights, not spoiling the entire plot.

## Essential Elements of a Query Letter

1. **Greeting:**

- Address the agent or editor by name. A little research goes a long way here—no "Dear Sir/Madam" or "To Whom It May Concern."
- Example: *"Dear Ms. Williams,"*

2. **The Hook:**
   - Start strong. Write one or two sentences that immediately grab their attention and introduce the premise of your story.
   - Example: *"When shy librarian Jane discovers a portal in her basement, she's thrust into a realm of dragons, betrayal, and questionable life choices."*

3. **The Pitch (The Summary):**
   - This is the heart of your letter. Briefly summarize your book's plot, focusing on:
   - **Protagonist:** Who is your main character?
   - **Conflict:** What challenge or problem are they facing?
   - **Goal and Stakes:** What do they want, and what happens if they fail?
   - Example: *"When Jane stumbles into a magical war between rival dragon clans, she must choose sides and embrace her inner courage. If she fails, the portal—and her world—will be destroyed."*

4. **Your Bio:**
   - Include any relevant writing credentials, like previous publications, awards, or experience. If you're a debut author, don't panic—just mention something personal that connects you to the story.
   - Example: *"This is my debut novel, inspired by my lifelong obsession with dragons and my time spent working in libraries."*

5. **The Closing:**

- Thank them for their time and let them know your manuscript is ready. Be polite, professional, and confident.
- Example: *"Thank you for considering my novel. The full manuscript is available upon request, and I look forward to hearing from you."*

## Tone and Style

- Keep it **professional, clear, and concise**—no more than one page. Agents and editors receive hundreds of queries, so get to the point quickly.
- **Tailor your query** to each agent or publisher:
  - Mention why you're submitting to them. Did you see a tweet about their love for dragon stories? Reference it.
  - Show you've done your homework—it proves you're serious.

**Pro Tip:** Avoid overloading your letter with too many characters, subplots, or details. Stick to the main plotline and keep it clean.

## Key Tip:

Keep it short, compelling, and polished. Agents and editors have limited time—make every word count!

## Perfecting Your Pitch

Think of your pitch as the appetizer to your book—it's small, irresistible, and leaves them wanting more. Whether you're submitting a query, attending a writer's conference, or awkwardly cornering someone who *just might* be an agent, a polished pitch is your secret weapon.

## What a Pitch Is

- A pitch is a short, punchy summary of your book that highlights the core premise and hooks the listener or reader's interest.
- It's used in two key places:
  - **Verbal pitches:** At conferences, networking events, or chance meetings.
  - **Query materials:** Often included in query letters or submission packages.

**Pro Tip:** Your pitch isn't the full story. It's the hook that gets someone to ask, *"Tell me more!"*

## Elements of a Strong Pitch

1. **One-Sentence Logline:**
   - Boil your book down to one compelling sentence that captures the essence of your story.
   - Example: *"A retired detective must solve one last case when his best friend's disappearance unravels a dark conspiracy."*
2. **Highlight the Stakes:**
   - What's the protagonist's goal? What's standing in their way? What happens if they fail? Stakes are what keep the listener or reader invested.
   - Example: *"If he doesn't uncover the truth, the conspiracy will destroy not only his friend but the entire city."*
3. **Unique Selling Point:**

- What makes your story stand out? Is it the fresh twist, the unusual setting, or your unique voice? Make it clear why your book isn't "just another story."
- Example: *"A time-travelling librarian fights aliens with enchanted books—because who needs swords when you've got Shakespeare?"*

**Pro Tip:** Avoid trying to cram everything into your pitch. Stick to the protagonist, the conflict, and the stakes. Leave subplots and minor characters for later.

### Practice Makes Perfect

- **Rehearse Aloud:**
  - Say your pitch out loud until it rolls off your tongue naturally. If you stumble, simplify.
- **Test It on Others:**
  - Run your pitch by friends, writing peers, or anyone willing to listen. If they look confused, tweak it. If they say, *"That sounds awesome!"* you're on the right track.
- **Be Confident and Ready:**
  - Whether it's at a conference or a random coffee shop chat, you never know when you'll need to pitch your book. Practise until you can deliver it smoothly and enthusiastically.

**Pro Tip:** Write several versions of your pitch and refine it. Trim it down, tighten the wording, and polish it until it shines. A great pitch is sharp, clear, and impossible to ignore.

A strong pitch isn't just about getting someone interested—it's about making them *need* to know what happens next. Keep it short, sharp, and irresistible, and you'll have them hooked before they know it!

## Preparing Your Work for Submission

Submitting your work is like preparing for a big interview: you want to look sharp, follow the rules, and leave the best impression possible. Agents and publishers are busy people, so your submission needs to be professional, polished, and exactly what they've asked for.

## Polish Your Manuscript

- **Complete and Polished:**
  - Don't even think about submitting until your manuscript is finished and thoroughly edited. This isn't the time for "good enough"—it needs to shine.
- **Get Feedback:**
  - Beta readers can catch plot holes and clunky dialogue, while a professional editor can polish your prose. Fresh eyes are your best friend.

**Pro Tip:** Run your manuscript through one last proofread before submission. Typos are like spinach in your teeth—no one wants to see them.

## Follow Submission Guidelines

Agents and publishers love rules, and ignoring them is the fastest way to land in the rejection pile.

- **What to Check:**
  - **Word Count Limits:** Make sure your manuscript fits within the expected length for your genre.
  - **Formatting:** Stick to industry standards unless told otherwise:
    - Double-spaced.
    - 12pt font (usually Times New Roman).
    - Standard 1-inch margins.
  - **Requested Materials:** Check exactly what they want:
    - Query letter.
    - Short synopsis.
    - Sample chapters (e.g., first three chapters or first 50 pages).
    - Full manuscript.
  - **Follow Instructions to the Letter:**
    - If they say "send the first 10 pages pasted into the email," don't send 11 pages in an attachment. Details matter.

**Pro Tip:** Submission guidelines vary widely. Read them twice —*then* hit send.

### Write a Synopsis

The synopsis is your book in miniature form—a clean, concise summary that covers all the major beats.

- **What It Includes:**
  - Major plot points, big twists, and the resolution (yes, you need to give away the ending).
  - A clear overview of the story arc, including the protagonist's journey and stakes.

- **Length:**
    - Typically less than one page, single-spaced. Keep it clear, simple, and to the point. If you cannot do this, did you really write the manuscript?

**Pro Tip:** Avoid being vague. Agents don't want teasers like, *"Will they survive? Read to find out!"* Give them the full story, spoilers and all.

### Prepare a Submission Package

Your submission package is like your toolkit—everything an agent or publisher needs to see you and your book in the best light.

- **What to Include:**
    - **Query Letter:** Your polished, one-page pitch.
    - **Synopsis:** The brief, no-nonsense summary of your book.
    - **Sample Chapters:** Only send the chapters or word count they request. If they want the first three chapters, don't send chapters four and five "just in case."
    - **Author Bio (if required):** A short paragraph about you, focusing on relevant writing experience, publications, or what inspired the book.

**Pro Tip:** Save each part of your package as a separate file, clearly labelled. Example: *"YourName_BookTitle_Synopsis.pdf"*

### Key Tip:

Submission guidelines can feel like a test, and in some ways, they are! Follow them to the letter, show your professionalism, and you'll set yourself apart in the slush pile.

## Researching Agents and Small Press Publishers

Querying without research is like playing darts blindfolded. Sure, you might hit the target, but chances are you'll end up far from where you want to be. Researching agents and small press publishers helps you find the best fit for your work, save time, and increase your chances of success.

## Finding the Right Fit

Not all agents and publishers are created equal, and submitting your YA romance to someone who only works with crime thrillers is a guaranteed "No, thanks." Here's how to narrow your search:

1. **Look for Representation in Your Genre:**
   - Agents and publishers typically specialize in specific genres.
   - Research their preferences to ensure your book aligns with what they're seeking.
   - Example: If your manuscript is a fantasy epic, look for agents who've successfully sold similar works.
2. **Track Records Matter:**
   - Seek agents or publishers with a history of working with authors like you, whether you're a debut novelist or a seasoned pro.
   - Look for evidence of deals or successes within your genre or niche.
3. **Use Research Tools and Resources:**
   - **QueryTracker:**

- A user-friendly database to find and track literary agents and publishers.
- Includes submission data from other writers, so you know what to expect.
- **Manuscript Wish List (MSWL):**
  - A website and hashtag (#MSWL) where agents and publishers specify what they're currently looking for.
  - Example: An agent might tweet, "Looking for fresh takes on dystopian fiction with a romantic twist." That's your cue if it matches your book!
- **Publisher's Marketplace:**
  - Offers detailed information about agents, publishers, and deals.
  - A subscription-based resource, but invaluable if you want to dig deep into publishing trends.
- **Agency Websites:**
  - The goldmine of information. Check client lists, submission guidelines, and recent news about the agency.
  - Bonus: Some agencies share success stories or insights into their approach.

**Pro Tip:** A little detective work goes a long way. Researching agents and publishers not only helps you target the right ones but also demonstrates professionalism and genuine interest in your submission.

**Red Flags to Avoid**

The publishing world has its fair share of bad apples. Stay alert for these common red flags:

1. **Agents or Publishers Asking for Money Upfront:**
   - Legitimate agents are paid through commission (typically 15–20% of your earnings), not upfront fees.
   - Similarly, publishers shouldn't charge for reading your manuscript or basic publishing services.
2. **Poorly Reviewed or "Vanity" Presses:**
   - Vanity presses charge authors for publication and often provide little value in return.
   - Look up reviews or reach out to authors who've worked with the press to ensure it's reputable.
3. **Too Good to Be True Promises:**
   - Beware of agents or publishers guaranteeing success or best-seller status. Publishing is unpredictable, and no one can make those claims honestly.
4. **Lack of Transparency:**
   - If an agent or publisher is vague about their submission guidelines, track record, or fees, consider it a red flag.

**Pro Tip:** Check forums like Writer Beware or Absolute Write Water Cooler to verify the legitimacy of agents and publishers. Other writers' experiences are a great resource for identifying potential scams.

**Organizing Your Research**

Once you've found promising agents and publishers, it's time to get organized. Submitting willy-nilly isn't just ineffective—it's chaotic.

1. **Create a Spreadsheet:**
   - Track key details about each agent or publisher, such as:
     - Name and contact info.
     - Genre preferences.
     - Submission guidelines.
     - Date of submission and response times.
     - Notes on interactions (e.g., feedback, requests for more materials).
     - This helps you stay on top of your querying efforts and prevents double submissions.
2. **Categorize by Priority:**
   - Divide your list into tiers:
     - **Tier 1:** Dream agents or publishers.
     - **Tier 2:** Great fits, but not your top choices.
     - **Tier 3:** Good options for later rounds if Tier 1 and Tier 2 don't pan out.
   - Start with Tier 1 and work your way down.

**Pro Tip:** Colour-code your spreadsheet to easily track where each submission stands. Green for "Sent," yellow for "Requested Material," red for "Rejection." It turns a tough process into something visually satisfying.

### Building Relationships Before Querying

Networking isn't just for corporate events—it can make a big difference in the querying process.

1. **Follow Agents and Publishers on Social Media:**
   - Many agents share insights, tips, and even submission preferences on platforms like Twitter.
   - Engaging with their content (respectfully!) can

make you a familiar name when your query hits their inbox.

2. **Attend Conferences or Workshops:**
   - Writing conferences often include pitch sessions with agents and publishers.
   - Even if you don't pitch, attending panels and workshops can provide valuable insights into the industry.

**Pro Tip:** Networking doesn't mean spamming agents' DMs. Engage meaningfully, not aggressively.

### Why Research Matters

Research is about more than finding a match—it's about setting yourself up for success:

- **Professionalism:** Tailored submissions show agents and publishers you've done your homework.
- **Confidence:** Knowing your submission is going to the right person builds your confidence as a writer.
- **Efficiency:** Targeting the best fits saves you time and energy in the long run.

**Pro Tip:** Think of querying as dating—you wouldn't propose on the first date, so don't send a query without knowing if you're a match.

Researching agents and small press publishers might take time, but it's an investment in your writing career. With a little effort and a lot of organization, you can increase your chances of finding the perfect home for your book.

### Handling Rejections and Next Steps

Rejections are like taxes and mosquito bites—unavoidable and not particularly fun. But in the world of querying, they're part of the process. Learning to handle rejections with grace and determination is a key skill for any writer aiming to get published.

**Expect Rejections**

Let's get this out of the way: rejections happen to everyone. Yes, *everyone*.

- **It's Not Personal:**
    - Agents and publishers aren't rejecting *you* as a person. They're making business decisions based on their preferences, market trends, and client rosters. Sometimes, your book just isn't the right fit for them, and that's okay.
    - Even the most successful authors have drawers (or inboxes) full of rejection letters. Stephen King? Rejected dozens of times. J.K. Rowling? Turned down by 12 publishers. You're in good company.
- **Subjectivity Rules:**
    - Querying is a subjective process. One agent's "not for me" could be another agent's dream manuscript.

**Pro Tip:** A rejection isn't a failure—it's a step closer to finding the person who will champion your work. Stephen R. Donaldson's first book was turned down by 57 publishers, but when it hit the stores, became a world wide success. Don't get deflated by a rejection, just say, "They are not for me, anyway."

**Learn and Adjust**

Rejections are part of the learning curve. Instead of letting them knock you down, use them as a chance to reassess and improve.

- **Re-evaluate Your Query Letter or Pitch:**
  - If you're only getting form rejections (the generic "this isn't a good fit for us" response), it might be time to revisit your query.
  - Ask yourself:
    - Is my hook strong enough to grab attention?
    - Does my pitch clearly convey the stakes and unique elements of my story?
    - Have I targeted the right agents or publishers?
- **Value Constructive Feedback:**
  - Occasionally, an agent will include a personalized note with their rejection. This is gold—treasure it!
  - Sometimes you can ask for a reason why your work was rejected. Be nice about the ask, for they are under no obligation to supply such.
  - Example: *"The pacing felt a bit slow in the opening chapters."* That's a cue to revisit your manuscript and see if there's room for improvement.
- **Don't Overreact:**
  - One rejection (or ten) doesn't mean your book isn't good. It might just mean you haven't found the right match yet.

**Pro Tip:** Consider joining a critique group or asking trusted beta readers to review your query and sample pages. Fresh eyes can help pinpoint areas to tweak.

**Personal Story:** I can't tell you how many manuscripts have been turned down by my publishing company. At first, SC Graham, my submissions coordinator, used to supply reasons for the rejection. After receiving multiple "negative responses" (I read some of them, and found there are a lot of writers out there who are extremely aggressive and mean) the following was put in place:

1. No more personal messages for rejections.
2. All rejections are sent from a no-reply email address that we do not monitor.
3. If an author asks why, they must submit the question through our Q&A form.
4. All responses to the question of why, should start with a "What you did right" section (harder than you think).
5. Give a detailed report on why the work was rejected (an example of one is supplied at the end of the book).

**Keep Querying**

Rejections aren't the end of the road—they're a sign to keep going.

- **Submit in Batches:**
- Most agents recommend querying in small batches of 10–20 agents at a time.
- If you receive no requests for more materials, take a break, rework your query, and try again.
- **Tweak as You Go:**
- Use responses (or lack thereof) to guide your revisions. If you're getting requests for partials but no

further interest, it might be your manuscript that needs fine-tuning.

- **Stay Persistent:**
- Many successful authors queried for months—or even years—before landing representation or a book deal. Patience is key.

**Pro Tip:** Set realistic goals, like sending out three queries per week, to keep momentum without feeling overwhelmed.

### Celebrate Small Victories

Not all rejections are created equal. Sometimes, even a "no" can be a sign you're on the right track.

- **Personalized Rejections:**
- If an agent takes the time to mention what they liked about your submission or why it wasn't a fit, that's a win. It means they saw potential in your work.
- **Requests for Pages:**
- A request for partial or full manuscript means your query letter and pitch are doing their job. Even if the agent ultimately passes, you've cleared a major hurdle.
- **Positive Feedback:**
- Comments like "I loved the voice, but the market is saturated with similar stories" show that your writing is connecting—it's just about timing or finding the right niche.

**Pro Tip:** Celebrate progress, no matter how small. Share your milestones with your writing community—they'll understand and cheer you on!

## Why Rejections Are a Good Thing

Believe it or not, rejections can actually help you grow as a writer.

- **Thickens Your Skin:**
- Writing is a career full of ups and downs. Rejections teach resilience, which is essential for navigating the publishing world.
- **Improves Your Craft:**
- Feedback, even indirect, pushes you to sharpen your skills and refine your work.
- **Clarifies Your Goals:**
- Each rejection brings you closer to finding the right agent, publisher, or path for your book.

**Pro Tip:** Keep a "Rejection Tracker" to log submissions and responses. It turns the process into a manageable game rather than an emotional rollercoaster. Colour-code it if that makes you happy.

Rejections are tough, but they're not the end of the story—they're a part of it. With each query you send and each rejection you receive, you're one step closer to finding the right match for your work. Keep learning, keep growing, and most importantly, keep going. Your success is out there waiting!

## Ideas to Consider

Querying can feel like navigating a maze, but with the right tools and a little creativity, you can make the process smoother—and maybe even a little enjoyable. Here are some practical ideas to help you fine-tune your approach and stay motivated.

## Write Multiple Versions of Your Query Letter

- Think of your query letter as a work in progress. Experiment with different hooks, pitches, or tones to see what resonates best.
- Share these drafts with writing peers, critique partners, or even a friendly beta reader. Honest feedback can uncover what's working—and what isn't.

**Pro Tip:** If multiple people point out the same issue (like an unclear hook), it's worth revising. If they all love it? You're good to go!

## Research Successful Query Letters

- There's no need to reinvent the wheel. Look up query letters that worked for authors in your genre. Websites like **QueryShark** or **AgentQuery** are goldmines of examples and advice.
- Pay attention to structure, tone, and how these letters present the book's stakes. Use them as inspiration, not templates—your voice should still shine through.

**Pro Tip:** Avoid copying a succesful query word for word. Agents have likely seen it, and originality always wins.

## Join Writing Forums and Social Media Groups

- Querying can be lonely, but it doesn't have to be! Connect with other writers who are in the same boat:

- **Writing Forums:** Sites like Absolute Write and Critique Circle are filled with querying writers eager to share advice.
- **Social Media:** Twitter's #WritingCommunity and Facebook writing groups are great places to swap tips and commiserate about rejections.
- **Online Critique Groups:** These can help you refine your query and stay motivated.

**Pro Tip:** Avoid oversharing personal details about agents or publishers online. It's a small industry, and professionalism goes a long way.

### Stay Persistent

- Remember, every "no" brings you closer to that "yes." Rejection is part of the journey, but persistence is what gets you to the finish line.

By mastering your query letters, perfecting your pitches, and preparing stellar submission packages, you'll give your manuscript the best shot at finding a home. Celebrate every small victory, keep learning, and most importantly—don't give up. That "yes" is out there waiting for you!

# Chapter 16

# Self-Publishing and Distribution

### Self-Publishing and Distribution

Self-publishing is like setting out on an epic quest. You're the hero in charge of every decision—choosing your allies (platforms), gathering resources (marketing strategies), and planning the ultimate battle: getting your book into readers' hands. It's exciting, liberating, and occasionally overwhelming, but armed with the right knowledge, you'll be ready to conquer it all.

This chapter breaks down the major self-publishing and distribution platforms, exploring their pros and cons so you can choose the best fit for your goals. Whether you're publishing a fantasy epic, a niche cookbook, or a heartfelt memoir, you'll find strategies and tips to make the most of each option.

I remember my first adventure into self-publishing—it was like stepping into uncharted waters with no map, or attempting to slay a dragon with a filleting knife. Sure, there were some unexpected waves, but every mistake taught me something valuable. Through that time, it became apparent I didn't knew very little about pushing a new book out to the world. I know a lot more now, and continue to learn.

By the end of this chapter, you'll not only know your options but also feel confident about where to start and how to maximize your reach. Ready to dive in? Let's chart your course!

## Amazon KDP (Kindle Direct Publishing)

Amazon KDP is the reigning champion of the self-publishing world. If the self-publishing market were a high school, KDP would be the most popular kid in class. Dominating the scene, it's the go-to platform for authors looking to reach a massive audience without a hefty price tag.

### Overview

- Amazon KDP allows authors to publish **eBooks**, **paperbacks**, and even **hardcovers**.
- It offers exclusive programs like **Kindle Unlimited** and **KDP Select**, which can boost visibility (more on that later with a few tricks).
- Its sheer market dominance makes it almost impossible to ignore if you're serious about self-publishing.

### Pros

- **Massive Reach:**

- Amazon is the world's largest book retailer. Publishing with KDP puts your book in front of millions of potential readers across the globe.
- **Easy-to-Use Interface:**
- Even if tech isn't your strong suit, the KDP platform is intuitive. Uploading and managing your book is relatively pain-free.
- **Generous Royalties:**
- Authors earn either **35% or 70% royalties** on eBooks, depending on factors like pricing and region. That's a sweet deal, especially compared to traditional publishing.
- **No Upfront Costs:**
- Publishing with KDP is free, so you don't have to worry about breaking the bank just to get your book out there.

## Cons

- **Exclusivity with KDP Select:**
- Enrolling in KDP Select means committing to Amazon exclusively for your eBook. While it opens up promotional opportunities, you can't sell your eBook on other platforms during the exclusivity period.
- **Printing Quality for Paperbacks:**
- While acceptable, KDP's print quality might not wow you if you're looking for premium finishes or crisp hardcover aesthetics. For basic novels and non-fiction, it's fine—but for art books or highly visual content, you might need to look elsewhere.

## Marketing Tip

- Enrolling in KDP Select for one three month period is a good idea. This allows you to take advantage of the specials available through that service. But don't keep it going. Once you have reviews, cut off the KDP Select and push your ebook out there to other platforms (more in marketing).
- While KDP Select is great, it is limiting. You cut off a number of other distribution methods and other ways to reach authors. Use it sparingly.

Amazon KDP is a fantastic starting point for self-published authors. Its massive audience and accessible platform make it a no-brainer for many, but as with any tool, its effectiveness depends on your goals. Whether you're testing the waters with your first book or building a long-term publishing empire, KDP is ready to roll.

**Pro Tip:** Do not use expanded distribution for the print version of your book. There are reasons for this, and they will be explained later.

### IngramSpark

If Amazon KDP is the life of the self-publishing party, IngramSpark is the sophisticated guest in the corner sipping artisanal coffee. With a focus on high-quality printing and wide distribution, IngramSpark is the go-to platform for authors looking to get their books into libraries, brick-and-mortar bookstores, and online retailers worldwide.

### Overview

- IngramSpark specialises in **wide distribution,**

making your book accessible to a variety of outlets, including bookstores, libraries, and online platforms.

- It supports both **eBooks** and **print formats** (paperback and hardcover), catering to a range of author needs.

**Pros**

- **Superior Print Quality:**
- If you're dreaming of a book with sharp covers and pages that feel as good as they look, IngramSpark delivers. It's a step above the basics offered by some other platforms (for now).
- **Broad Distribution Network:**
- IngramSpark's global reach includes connections with bookstores, libraries, and retailers that many other platforms can't touch. Want your book on a library shelf or in a local shop? This is the way to do it.
- **Non-Exclusive Agreements:**
- Unlike KDP Select, IngramSpark doesn't tie you down. You're free to distribute your eBook or print book through other platforms simultaneously.

**Cons**

- **Update Fees:**
- While it does not cost anything to add your book to IngramSpark, you only have three months to update the files. After that, making any changes (no matter how small) will cost you $50 USD.
- Example: Fees for making revisions, and adding distribution options, after 90 days.

- **Lower Royalties:**
- IngramSpark operates on a **wholesale pricing model**, which means you earn less per book compared to platforms like Amazon KDP.
- **Steeper Learning Curve:**
- The platform isn't as beginner-friendly as some others. From file formatting to pricing structures, it might take a little extra time (and patience) to figure out.

**Marketing Tip**

- Combine IngramSpark with other platforms for maximum reach. For example:
  - Use **Amazon KDP** for eBooks to dominate the Kindle market.
  - Use **IngramSpark** for print distribution to get into bookstores and libraries.

**Pro Tip:** Before committing, calculate potential earnings using IngramSpark's pricing calculator. Understanding wholesale pricing and discounts can help you make informed decisions about your book's retail price and royalties.

IngramSpark shines for authors who want high-quality print books and wide distribution, especially beyond the Amazon ecosystem. Yes, there are upfront costs and a bit of a learning curve, but the payoff is a polished book with access to markets others might miss. If you're serious about professional-quality publishing and aren't afraid of a little extra work, IngramSpark is a stellar choice.

**History Lesson:** While my company still uses IngramSpark, we use it with specific limitations. No eBook distribution, no returns, lowest royalty for retailers.

This came from a time when one of our authors lined up a signing. The book retailer, seeing returns enabled on Ingram's distribution list, ordered 200 copies of her book. They sold 100, and returned the other 100. We were charged for the returned copies, and due to IngramSpark's terms of service, was charged an extra $20 USD per copy returned. An expensive lesson you do not want to experience. More about this later on.

## Draft2Digital

Think of Draft2Digital (D2D) as the friendly neighbourhood librarian of the self-publishing world. It's approachable, well-organized, and eager to help get your book out there. If managing multiple platforms feels daunting, this eBook aggregator is here to simplify your life and expand your reach —all without charging upfront fees.

### Overview

- Draft2Digital is a **user-friendly aggregator** that distributes your eBooks to multiple retailers, including **Amazon, Apple Books, Kobo, Barnes & Noble**, and more.
- It's designed for authors who want to focus on writing rather than wrangling distribution logistics.

### Pros

- **No Upfront Costs:**

- Draft2Digital only takes a small percentage of royalties from each sale. This means you can publish without breaking the bank.
- **Free Formatting Tools:**
- Not a design whiz? No problem. D2D offers free tools to format your manuscript into professional-looking eBooks. Bonus: You can generate PDF interiors for print editions, but be warry of using it.
- **Wide Reach Across Platforms:**
- With one upload, your book can appear on multiple major retailers, simplifying your distribution process and boosting visibility.

## Cons

- **Percentage of Royalties:**
- While there are no upfront fees, D2D takes a small cut of your earnings. It's fair, but if you're selling in bulk, those pennies can add up.
- **Limited Print Book Options:**
- Draft2Digital partners with Print2Digital for paperbacks, but the service isn't as robust or widely distributed as platforms like IngramSpark.

## Marketing Tip

- I would suggest bypassing Draft2Digital. The options out there have better platforms and easy to use system. For royalties, most are in the same ballpark.
- If you use Draft2Digital, make it one of the last ones you set up for your publication in order to allow for

your work to be put on some other platforms directly by yourself, thus giving you more royalties.

**Pro Tip:** Take advantage of Draft2Digital's **Universal Book Links** to create a single link that directs readers to their preferred retailer. It's a simple way to market your book without spamming multiple URLs.

Draft2Digital is perfect for authors looking for an easy way to distribute eBooks widely without the headaches of managing multiple platforms. It's intuitive, affordable, and loaded with helpful tools. If you're just dipping your toes into the self-publishing waters or looking for a hassle-free aggregator, D2D has you covered.

**History Lesson:** When I tried Draft2Digital years ago, their way to pay Canadian authors and publishers was through a wire payment into your Canadian account. The issue is, your bank will charge you a minimum of $25 to handle such. If your royalty is under that (or less than double) the cost is counter intuitive. They have have moved to cross boarder ACH payments by now, but that also costs them a lot of money, so they may not have. Tread carefully when using them.

### Apple Books

Apple Books is like the upscale boutique of the eBook world—sleek, stylish, and a favourite among loyal Apple users. It might not be as crowded as the Amazon marketplace, but what it lacks in size, it makes up for with a tech-savvy audience that's ready to buy.

### Overview

- Apple Books is Apple's dedicated eBook platform, integrated into its ecosystem and accessible via **iBooks** on iPhones, iPads, and Macs.
- It offers authors an opportunity to reach Apple's loyal customer base without being tied down by exclusivity agreements.

## Pros

- **Loyal Audience with Purchasing Power:**
- Apple users are famously devoted to their devices and are often willing to spend on premium products—including books.
- **No Exclusivity Requirements:**
- Unlike Amazon's KDP Select, Apple Books doesn't demand exclusivity, so you can sell your eBook on other platforms simultaneously.

## Cons

- **Complex Setup for Non-Mac Users:**
- Publishing directly requires **iTunes Producer**, a software that only works on macOS. If you're not a Mac user, you'll need to use an aggregator like **Draft2Digital** to distribute to Apple Books.
- **Smaller Market Share:**
- While Apple Books has a dedicated following, its audience size is smaller compared to Amazon.

## Marketing Tip

- **Exclusive Apple Promotions:** Keep an eye out for promotions or special features on Apple Books that can help boost your visibility.
- **Target Apple Device Users:** Focus your marketing efforts on platforms like Instagram and Facebook, which Apple users frequent, and highlight how your book is optimised for iBooks.

**Pro Tip:** If you're a Mac user, consider uploading directly to Apple Books to retain full royalties. If you're not, don't sweat it —aggregators like **Draft2Digital** make it easy to distribute to this platform.

Apple Books is a sleek and professional platform, ideal for authors targeting an audience with high purchasing power. While it may not boast Amazon's scale, it's a valuable piece of your distribution strategy puzzle, especially if you're looking to diversify your reach.

### Blurb

Blurb is the platform for authors who want their books to double as works of art. If your project is heavy on visuals—like photo books, cookbooks, or art portfolios—Blurb is your new best friend. It's a one-stop shop for creating stunning print books that look like they belong on a coffee table (and maybe in a gallery).

### Overview

- Blurb specializes in **visual-heavy projects**, making it an excellent choice for photographers, artists, and anyone creating books where imagery takes centre stage.

- The platform integrates seamlessly with design tools like **Adobe InDesign** and **Lightroom**, giving you professional-level control over your book's layout.

## Pros

- **Excellent Print Quality:**
- Blurb delivers top-notch print quality, making it ideal for showcasing vivid photography, intricate illustrations, or high-end design work.
- **Design Flexibility:**
- With integration into tools like Adobe InDesign and Lightroom, you can fully customise your book's look, down to the smallest detail.

## Cons

- **High Printing Costs:**
- The superior print quality comes with a price. Blurb's printing costs can make it less practical for traditional novels or books with narrow profit margins.
- **Limited Distribution:**
- Blurb's focus on specialty books means its distribution options are more niche. While they do offer online sales tools, the reach is not as broad as platforms like Amazon KDP or IngramSpark.

## Marketing Tip

- **Leverage Your Niche:** Use Blurb to create standout projects like art portfolios, coffee table books, or collector's editions of your work. These types of books are perfect for direct sales to a specific audience.

- **Direct Sales Strategy:** Pair your Blurb projects with a robust website or online store to sell directly to fans who value quality and uniqueness.

**Pro Tip:** Use Blurb's free book design tools if you're not a pro at Adobe InDesign. They're user-friendly and can still produce stunning results without the steep learning curve.

Blurb is not the platform for every author, but for those creating visually stunning works, it's a dream come true. Its exceptional print quality and design flexibility make it the go-to choice for niche projects that deserve to stand out. If your book is more of a visual masterpiece than a word-driven story, Blurb will help you bring it to life in style.

### BookBaby

BookBaby is like the concierge of self-publishing—a one-stop shop ready to handle everything from formatting to distribution. It's perfect for authors who want professional results without juggling multiple services or learning every detail about publishing on their own. But like any premium service, it comes with a price tag.

### Overview

- BookBaby offers **self-publishing services** for authors who want a polished book with minimal hassle.
- Their services include **editing, formatting, cover design, and distribution**, all wrapped up in convenient packages.

- They handle both **eBooks** and **print formats**, giving authors a variety of options.

**Pros**

- **Broad Distribution Network:**
- BookBaby gets your book into major online retailers like Amazon, Barnes & Noble, and Apple Books, as well as other platforms.
- **Professional Services:**
- Their team can help with editing, custom cover design, and interior formatting, ensuring your book looks its best.
- **No Exclusivity Requirements:**
- Unlike some platforms, BookBaby doesn't lock you into exclusivity agreements. You're free to sell your book elsewhere as well.

**Cons**

- **High Upfront Costs:**
- BookBaby operates on a publishing package model, which means you'll pay for services upfront. These costs can be significant, especially for new authors on a budget.
- **Percentage of Royalties:**
- Even after paying for services, BookBaby takes a percentage of royalties from your sales.

**Marketing Tip**

- **Use the All-in-One Packages Strategically:** If you're not confident in your design or formatting skills, BookBaby's packages can save you time and stress. Just make sure to budget carefully and calculate the potential return on investment.

**Pro Tip:** Review each package carefully to avoid overpaying for services you may not need. For example, if you already have a professional cover, you don't need their design assistance.

BookBaby is a solid option for authors who value convenience and professional results over cost-saving DIY approaches. If you're looking for a seamless process and are willing to invest upfront for high-quality services, BookBaby can help you turn your manuscript into a market-ready book without breaking a sweat. Just be sure to keep an eye on your budget and royalties to ensure it aligns with your publishing goals.

### Lulu

Lulu is like the artisan of self-publishing platforms. While it might not boast the same scale as Amazon KDP or the wide distribution of IngramSpark, it shines in creating **specialty print-on-demand products** like calendars, comics, and unique-format books. If your project veers away from the traditional paperback or eBook, Lulu might be your perfect match.

### Overview

- Lulu focuses on **print-on-demand services**, catering to authors who want creative flexibility with their formats.

- The platform supports a variety of niche formats, making it ideal for projects like photo-heavy coffee table books, calendars, or graphic novels.
- Lulu also offers **distribution options** for print books, though its pricing may be less competitive for mass-market novels.

## Pros

- **Customisable Print Formats:**
- Lulu allows you to design and print books in a wide range of formats and sizes, giving your project a bespoke, professional finish.
- **Good Print Quality:**
- Authors praise Lulu for its sharp printing and sturdy materials, making it a reliable option for high-quality physical products.
- **Wide Print Distribution:**
- Lulu can distribute your print book to major retailers and online stores, ensuring it reaches a broader audience.

## Cons

- **Less Competitive Pricing for Mass-Market Books:**
- While Lulu is fantastic for niche products, its costs may be higher compared to platforms like KDP or IngramSpark for standard novels.
- **Less Intuitive Interface:**
- Some authors find Lulu's interface less user-friendly than competitors, making it trickier to navigate for first-time users.

**Marketing Tip**

- **Pair Lulu with Other Platforms:** Use Lulu for specialty print projects like comics or calendars, while managing your eBook sales through platforms like **Amazon KDP** or **Draft2Digital** for maximum reach.
- **Showcase Unique Offerings:** If you create niche products, highlight them in your marketing efforts to stand out from traditional books.

**Pro Tip:** Test a small print run before committing to large orders. This ensures you're happy with the final product's quality and design.

Lulu excels for authors looking to produce unique, high-quality print-on-demand products that stand out from the crowd. While it may not be the best fit for mass-market paperbacks, its customisation options and solid distribution network make it a valuable tool for specialty projects. Whether you're crafting a stunning photo book or an indie comic series, Lulu's flexibility can help bring your creative vision to life.

**Historical Note:** My first novel when through LuLu because CreateSpace did not print hard cover books. I can attest for their quality, and the price you pay for it. Some time in the future, I'll try KDP's hard cover creation and rate it against Lulu's.

**Google Play Books**

Google Play Books is like the quiet but resourceful sibling in the self-publishing family. It might not dominate the conversation like Amazon or Apple, but with its seamless integration into Android devices and Google accounts, it's a solid platform for reaching tech-savvy readers.

**Overview**

- Google Play Books serves as **Google's platform for eBook sales and distribution**, making your book available to millions of Android users worldwide.
- Unlike some competitors, Google Play Books doesn't require exclusivity, so you can sell your book on multiple platforms simultaneously.

**Pros**

- **Direct Integration with Android and Google Accounts:**
- Your book will be easily accessible to readers on Android devices, which dominate the global smartphone market. Plus, it's linked to users' Google accounts, streamlining the purchasing process.
- **No Exclusivity Requirements:**
- Freedom! You're not tied down to Google Play Books alone and can distribute your eBook wherever you like.

**Cons**

- **Historically Challenging Interface:**
- Google Play Books has a reputation for being a little, shall we say, clunky. Between confusing royalty calculations and the platform's sometimes opaque pricing policies, it can be tricky to navigate for new users, but not impossible.

- **Smaller Audience:**
- While Google is a global giant, its audience for books doesn't quite match up to heavyweights like Amazon or Apple Books.

**Marketing Tip**

- **Optimise Keywords and Metadata:** Since this is Google we're talking about, leverage its search engine roots. Use targeted keywords and well-crafted metadata to increase your book's discoverability on Google Play Books. Think about what your readers are searching for—then make sure your book shows up!

**Pro Tip:** Keep an eye on your pricing. Google Play Books has been known to discount books without warning, which could trigger price-matching on other platforms like Amazon. Be ready to adjust as needed.

Google Play Books may not be the loudest player in the room, but its reach among Android users and lack of exclusivity make it a valuable addition to your publishing toolkit. While the interface may take some getting used to, the potential to tap into Google's vast ecosystem can pay off with a little patience and clever marketing. If you're ready to go global (or at least Android-wide), Google Play Books is worth considering.

**Smashwords**

Smashwords is the indie author's secret weapon, quietly working behind the scenes to distribute eBooks to retailers and libraries that other platforms might overlook. With its straightforward approach and library access, it's an excellent choice for broadening your book's reach—provided you can navigate its formatting rules without pulling your hair out.

## Overview

- Smashwords is an **aggregator** that focuses on distributing eBooks to a variety of platforms, including **Barnes & Noble, Apple Books**, and **library markets** like OverDrive.
- It's designed for authors who want to expand their reach without managing multiple individual accounts on retailer platforms.

## Pros

- **Simple Interface for Distribution:**
- Smashwords streamlines the process of getting your eBook onto multiple platforms, saving you time and effort.
- **Library Market Access:**
- With distribution through **OverDrive**, Smashwords helps you tap into libraries, a valuable but often overlooked market.

## Cons

- **Strict Formatting Guidelines:**
- Smashwords is picky when it comes to formatting. Errors in your manuscript can lead to delays, so double-check before submitting.
- **Takes a Cut of Royalties:**

- Like other aggregators, Smashwords takes a small percentage of your royalties in exchange for its services.

**Marketing Tip**

- **Leverage Library Markets:** Use Smashwords to make your eBook available to libraries, which can bring in new readers who might not otherwise discover your work.
- **Supplement with Other Platforms:** Combine Smashwords with platforms like **Amazon KDP** to cover major retailers while Smashwords handles smaller ones and libraries.

**Pro Tip:** Smashwords offers a free formatting guide— download it and follow it meticulously to avoid delays. If formatting isn't your strong suit, consider hiring a pro.

Smashwords might not have the flash of Amazon or the bespoke polish of IngramSpark, but its library connections and niche reach make it a valuable tool in your self-publishing toolkit. Pair it with smart marketing, and you'll be well on your way to finding your readers wherever they may be hiding.

**Kobo**

Kobo is the indie author's gateway to the world outside the Amazon bubble. With its strong presence in Canada, Europe, and other international markets, Kobo gives authors a chance to shine in regions where Amazon might not dominate. Plus, its intuitive self-publishing platform, **Kobo Writing Life**, makes reaching a global audience easier than navigating IKEA assembly instructions.

## Overview

- Kobo is a leading eBook platform, specialising in both **eBooks and audiobooks**, with a focus on international markets.
- It boasts a robust global distribution network, including partnerships with local retailers in regions where Amazon isn't king.
- **Kobo Writing Life**, Kobo's self-publishing platform, is designed to help authors easily upload, manage, and track their books' performance.

## Unique Features

- **International Focus:** Kobo prioritises markets outside the U.S., providing authors with access to a global audience.
- **Local Partnerships:** It works with local retailers, ensuring a foothold in areas where other platforms may struggle.
- **Kobo Plus:** A subscription service that offers readers unlimited access to eBooks while providing authors with a steady alternative revenue stream.

## Pros of Publishing with Kobo

1. **Global Reach:**
   - Stronghold in **Canada, Europe, and Asia**, making

it ideal for authors targeting international audiences.

- o Partnerships with local retailers expand its reach into non-English-speaking markets.

2. **No Exclusivity:**
   - o Unlike Amazon's KDP Select, Kobo doesn't demand exclusivity. You can sell your eBooks on other platforms simultaneously.

3. **Author-Friendly Interface:**
   - o Kobo Writing Life is straightforward and intuitive, allowing you to manage your books with ease.

4. **Subscription Model Revenue:**
   - o Kobo Plus provides an additional way to earn revenue, tapping into the growing demand for subscription-based content.

5. **Loyal Niche Audience:**
   - o Kobo has a dedicated user base, particularly in regions where it's a market leader.

**Cons of Publishing with Kobo**

1. **Smaller Market Share:**
   - o While Kobo's global reach is impressive, its audience size is still dwarfed by Amazon's behemoth presence.
   - o Its influence is strongest outside the U.S., which may limit its effectiveness for books aimed at American readers.

2. **Limited Marketing Tools:**
   - o Kobo offers fewer promotional tools than platforms like Amazon KDP. There are no countdown deals or advanced ad targeting options.

3. **Subscription Model Pay:**
    - Earnings from **Kobo Plus** are calculated differently, often resulting in lower payments than direct eBook sales.

## Pro Tips for Success on Kobo

- **Localise Your Marketing:**
- Tailor your campaigns to Kobo's core markets, such as Canada, Europe, and Asia. Highlight any regional connections your book might have to resonate with local audiences.
- **Leverage Kobo Promotions:**
- Apply for promotional opportunities directly through Kobo Writing Life. These include genre-based sales and curated promotions that can boost visibility.
- **Consider Translation:**
- Translating your book into other languages could greatly expand your reach in non-English-speaking regions, where Kobo thrives.
- **Experiment with Pricing:**
- Kobo audiences in different regions may have varying expectations for eBook prices. Try different price points to see what works best for your genre and target audience.

## Final Thoughts

Kobo Writing Life is a fantastic option for authors looking to break into international markets without tying themselves down to exclusivity. While it may not rival Amazon's market share, Kobo's dedication to global distribution, flexible terms, and subscription-based earnings offer unique opportunities to indie authors. Whether you're targeting readers in Toronto, Paris, or Tokyo, Kobo has your back—and your book.

# Chapter 17

# **Reviews and Cover Art**

## **Reviews Make or Break Sales**

Let's face it: in the wild, wild world of publishing, reviews are like the cool kids at a party. Everyone gravitates toward the book that's got them, hanging out in clusters on its product page like it's the hottest spot in town. And let's be honest— without reviews, your book is sitting in the metaphorical corner, nursing a punch bowl no one's touched.

Reviews aren't just nice to have—they're essential. For potential readers, they act as the ultimate confidence booster, validating their decision to spend their hard-earned money (and, more importantly, their time) on your masterpiece. A glowing review says, "Hey, this book was worth it," and that reassurance can be the nudge a buyer needs to click that "Buy Now" button.

But it's not only about impressing readers—reviews are the secret sauce that makes the sales machine hum. Platforms like Amazon rely on algorithms, and those algorithms are absolute suckers for engagement. The more reviews your book gets, the more visible it becomes in recommendations and search results. It's the digital equivalent of being bumped to the VIP section of the club.

Even a mix of reviews can work in your favour. A thoughtful three-star review? That can highlight your book's strengths while adding a touch of authenticity. Readers trust books with a variety of opinions more than a suspiciously perfect five-star rating.

In the crowded world of publishing, reviews are your book's ticket to the spotlight. So embrace them, celebrate them, and let them do the heavy lifting of attracting readers while you focus on writing your next bestseller.

## Social Proof Matters

Let's talk about social proof. No, it's not the latest TikTok challenge—it's the idea that people are more likely to try something when they see others raving about it. For books, social proof comes in the form of reviews. Think of them as glowing testimonials from your biggest fans—or, occasionally, brutally honest feedback from your toughest critics. Either way, reviews send a powerful message: this book is worth your time.

Readers are savvy shoppers. Before they hit "Buy Now," they want to know if your book will live up to its snazzy cover and intriguing blurb. Reviews provide that reassurance. A solid batch of endorsements acts like a crowd of enthusiastic cheerleaders, giving hesitant buyers the confidence to give your book a chance. Whether it's a heartfelt five-star review or a cautious three-star critique pointing out the book's charm amidst a few flaws, each review adds weight to your book's credibility.

But here's the catch: numbers matter. A single five-star review from your mum isn't going to cut it. If your book has fewer than ten reviews, it's likely to get overlooked in favour of books that seem more "proven." Readers aren't just checking the star ratings; they're also looking at the quantity. A book with 20+ reviews automatically feels more legitimate. The more reviews you have, the merrier your sales will be.

Now, here's where things get tricky. For most authors, getting reviews feels like trying to solve a Rubik's Cube blindfolded. How do you convince readers to take the time to leave feedback? Even small presses often struggle with this, leaving their authors wondering if they've missed some secret handshake.

The truth is, reviews rarely happen by accident. Sure, a few kind souls will leave spontaneous reviews, but most of the time, you'll need to take proactive steps. This doesn't mean pestering readers like a door-to-door salesperson—it's about making the process easy and appealing.

One strategy is to provide a friendly nudge at the end of your book. A simple line like, "If you enjoyed this story, please consider leaving a review—it helps authors like me connect with readers like you," can work wonders. You can also build relationships with early readers by offering Advance Reader Copies (ARCs) in exchange for honest feedback. Platforms like Goodreads, NetGalley, and Arc Reviewers are great for connecting with these eager readers.

Social media is another invaluable tool. Share your excitement about reviews on your platforms, and encourage readers to tag you when they post theirs. Celebrate every review, even the ones that aren't glowing. Readers love seeing authors engage with their audience—it creates a sense of community and connection.

For those aiming higher, you can approach book bloggers or YouTubers who review in your genre. These influencers have dedicated audiences who trust their recommendations, which can boost your visibility and reviews in one fell swoop.

Let's not forget about the power of persistence. Building a strong review base takes time, effort, and, occasionally, a thick skin. But every review brings you closer to that magic tipping point where potential readers see your book not as a gamble but as a sure thing.

Social proof is the unsung hero of book marketing. It's the force that turns curious browsers into loyal readers and transforms your labour of love into a must-read sensation. Embrace it, nurture it, and watch your sales climb to new heights.

**Boosts Algorithms**

Ah, algorithms—the mysterious, all-powerful forces ruling our digital lives. Whether you're scrolling through a Netflix queue, checking Instagram, or browsing for your next read, algorithms are the wizards behind the curtain, deciding what you see. In the world of bookselling, especially on platforms like Amazon, algorithms are the ultimate matchmakers, introducing readers to books they didn't even know they wanted. And guess what? Reviews are one of the biggest factors in convincing these algorithms that your book deserves a spot in the limelight.

Ever noticed how books with tons of reviews seem to pop up in those "Recommended For You" or "Customers Also Bought" lists? That's no coincidence. Reviews are the breadcrumbs that guide algorithms to your book. Every time a reader leaves feedback, it's like handing the algorithm a glowing neon sign that says, "Hey, people are engaging with this book!" And algorithms? They love engagement. The more reviews your book racks up, the more the platform's recommendation engine takes notice, pushing your title higher in search results and featuring it in curated lists.

It's a virtuous cycle, really. Reviews bring visibility, and visibility brings more reviews. Once your book gets a little traction, the algorithm kicks in to give it a boost, showing it to even more potential readers. Those readers might buy your book, enjoy it, and—fingers crossed—leave their own reviews. And so, the cycle continues, propelling your book further up the ladder of discoverability.

But here's the thing: algorithms aren't sentimental. They don't care how many late nights you spent writing or how much coffee fuelled your creative process. They're purely data-driven. This means even a brilliant book can get buried if it doesn't have the numbers to back it up. That's where reviews come in.

It's not just the quantity of reviews that matters—it's also the consistency. Algorithms love steady streams of activity. If you get a rush of reviews shortly after launching and then nothing for months, the algorithm might assume your book's moment has passed. But if new reviews trickle in regularly, the platform sees your book as active and relevant, keeping it in the spotlight.

So how do you feed the algorithm without sacrificing your sanity? Start by making reviews an integral part of your launch strategy. Encourage early readers to leave honest feedback and remind your audience that reviews are the lifeblood of an indie author's success. Don't be shy about asking; most readers are happy to help if you make it easy for them.

Another tip? Play to the platform's strengths. For example, Amazon's algorithm loves verified purchases. This means reviews from people who bought your book directly through Amazon carry more weight than those from unverified sources. Encourage your network to purchase through the platform and leave a review—it's a win-win for both visibility and credibility.

If your book has a little more mileage on it, keep the momentum going by running occasional promotions, like discounts or free eBook days. These strategies not only attract new readers but also invite fresh reviews, which in turn nudge the algorithm to keep recommending your book.

Let's not forget about diversification. While Amazon is the big player, platforms like Kobo and Apple Books have their own algorithms and unique audiences. Reviews on these platforms can help boost visibility in international markets or niche genres where Amazon might not dominate.

**Pro Tip:** Don't get discouraged if reviews don't pour in overnight. Building that steady stream of engagement takes time, but every review is a step closer to making your book algorithm-approved.

In the end, mastering the algorithm is less about gaming the system and more about showing it that your book has real value. Reviews are the breadcrumbs that lead readers to your door—and with the algorithm's help, that door could open to a whole world of new fans.

## Understanding Amazon Review Rules: What You Need to Know

Amazon reviews are a critical part of selling your book, but the rules governing them can feel like trying to decipher ancient hieroglyphics. Fear not! We're breaking them down so you can navigate the process, collect reviews the *right* way, and avoid landing in Amazon's penalty box.

### 1. No Paid Reviews

**What It Means:**

Amazon strictly prohibits paying for reviews in any form, whether it's cash, gift cards, or that old vase in your attic. This rule is in place to maintain the authenticity and credibility of the review system.

**Example:**

You can't slide someone $50 to write, "This is the best book since sliced bread!" However, giving your book as a free review copy (more on that later) is allowed, provided it's not contingent on a positive review.

**Best Practices:**

- Offer complimentary review copies with no strings attached. Simply ask readers to leave an honest review if they feel inclined.

- Avoid services that promise "guaranteed 5-star reviews." If it sounds too good to be true, it probably violates Amazon's rules.

**Pro Tip:** Build a mailing list or reach out to your reader base to distribute free copies. Be clear that reviews, while appreciated, are voluntary.

## 2. No Reviews from Family or Close Friends

**What It Means:**

Amazon doesn't allow reviews from your mom, cousin, or that friend who's been supporting you since Grade 2. They argue that these relationships could lead to biased reviews.

**Example:**

Your mom writes, "This book is so good, I could cry! The author is my brilliant child!" Amazon's algorithm will sniff out the connection and likely remove the review.

**Best Practices:**

- Politely thank your family and friends for their support but encourage them to share their love for your book offline or on social media instead.
- Focus on gathering reviews from unbiased readers— book bloggers, ARC readers, and your general audience.

**Pro Tip:** Use platforms like NetGalley to reach genuine reviewers outside your immediate circle.

## 3. No Reciprocal Reviews

**What It Means:**

The "I'll scratch your back if you scratch mine" approach doesn't fly on Amazon. Authors cannot exchange reviews with each other, e.g., "I'll give your book 5 stars if you do the same for mine."

**Example:**

You message a fellow author and say, "Loved your book! Want to trade reviews?" While this seems harmless, Amazon's policy sees it as manipulation.

**Best Practices:**

- Instead of trading reviews, trade feedback privately or recommend each other's books in genuine ways (social media shoutouts, newsletters).
- If you want to support another author, purchase their book and leave a thoughtful review, but don't expect one in return.

**Pro Tip:** Join writing communities where honest feedback is encouraged, but be mindful not to cross into quid pro quo territory.

### 4. Disclose Free Review Copies

**What It Means:**

If a reviewer received your book for free, they must disclose this in their review. This ensures transparency and maintains trust among potential readers.

**Example:**

A proper disclosure might look like: "I received a free copy of this book in exchange for an honest review." Anything less transparent could raise Amazon's eyebrows.

**Best Practices:**

- When distributing ARCs (Advanced Reader Copies), kindly remind readers to mention that the book was a free copy in their review.
- Make it easy for reviewers by including a suggested disclosure statement in your correspondence.

**Pro Tip:** Readers are more likely to leave reviews if the process is easy. Include direct links to your book's Amazon page in your email or ARC package.

### 5. No Review Spamming

**What It Means:**

Amazon doesn't allow repeated reviews from the same person or overly promotional reviews stuffed with links and keywords. The goal is to prevent spammy or irrelevant content.

**Example:**

Someone leaves multiple reviews saying, "Great book! Also, check out my blog at www.mypersonalwebsite.com." Amazon will likely remove these reviews for violating the rules.

**Best Practices:**

- Encourage reviewers to leave one honest review per book. No need for them to review it six times just to boost the numbers!

- If you notice suspicious activity (e.g., duplicate reviews), report it to Amazon to protect your book's credibility.

**Pro Tip:** Focus on quality over quantity. A single thoughtful review is worth more than five generic ones.

### 6. No Soliciting Positive Reviews

**What It Means:**

You can ask for reviews, but you can't tell readers to leave a *positive* review. Reviews must be unbiased.

**Example:**

It's fine to say, "I'd appreciate an honest review of my book," but avoid phrasing like, "Please leave a 5-star review!"

**Best Practices:**

- Use neutral language when requesting reviews, like, "If you enjoyed the book, I'd love to hear your thoughts!"
- Avoid pressuring readers—let them share their genuine opinions.

**Pro Tip:** Add a polite review request at the end of your book, such as: "Enjoyed this story? I'd love for you to share your thoughts in a review!"

### 7. Don't Review Your Own Book

**What It Means:**

This one seems obvious, but authors aren't allowed to review their own books. Amazon sees it as a conflict of interest.

**Example:**

You leave a glowing review under a pseudonym like "BookLover1987," praising your literary genius. If Amazon detects this (and they probably will), it'll backfire.

**Best Practices:**

- Focus your energy on encouraging authentic reviews from real readers.
- Resist the temptation to "boost" your rating with a fake account—it's not worth the risk.

**Pro Tip:** Use your author profile to share your excitement about the book instead of attempting to review it. Let your writing speak for itself.

### 8. Reviews Must Be About the Book

**What It Means:**

Reviews need to focus on the content of the book itself—not on shipping issues, Kindle malfunctions, or irrelevant personal opinions.

**Example:**

A review saying, "The book arrived with a bent cover, so 1 star!" isn't helpful to potential readers. While frustrating, these complaints belong in a customer service ticket, not a review.

**Best Practices:**

- Encourage readers to leave thoughtful, content-focused reviews by asking specific questions, like, "What did you think of the characters or plot twists?"
- Gently remind reviewers that logistical complaints should be directed to Amazon's support team.

**Pro Tip:** If you notice unfair reviews unrelated to the book, you can report them to Amazon for removal.

### Final Thoughts

Amazon review rules can feel a bit like navigating a maze, but they're ultimately there to ensure fair play and authenticity. By following these guidelines, you'll build trust with your readers, improve your book's visibility, and avoid the dreaded wrath of Amazon's algorithm.

Remember, reviews are not just stars—they're stories from your readers about how your book made them feel. Encourage them honestly, celebrate each one, and watch your book thrive.

### How to Get Reviews for Your Book

Now it's time to tackle the next big challenge: getting reviews. Reviews are like the word-of-mouth buzz that helps sell your book to readers. But how do you actually get people to take the time to leave them? Let's break down the process, one smart tactic at a time.

### Step 1: Use Advanced Reader Copies (ARCs)

Think of ARCs as your secret weapon. They're early copies of your book that you send to readers in exchange for honest reviews.

**How to Distribute ARCs:**

- **Friends and Fans:** Send ARCs to your mailing list, social media followers, or supportive writer friends.
- **Book Bloggers and Influencers:** Reach out to bloggers and social media influencers who review books in your genre. A simple, polite email works wonders.
- **Services Like Arc Reviewers:** Websites like Arc Reviewers (https://arcreviewers.com) connect authors with readers who are eager to receive and review ARCs. These readers are your target audience, and they're ready to help spread the word.

**What to Include with Your ARC:**

- A clear note explaining the purpose of the ARC and requesting an honest review.
- Links to your book's page on Amazon (or other retailers) to make it easy for reviewers to leave their thoughts.

**Pro Tip:** Give reviewers plenty of time before your launch date to read and post their reviews. A few early reviews can set the tone for your book's debut.

**Step 2: Tap Into the Power of KDP Select**

If you're publishing through Amazon's Kindle Direct Publishing (KDP), enrolling in KDP Select for an initial three months can help you get reviews by giving you promotional tools.

**How KDP Select Works:**

- By enrolling your eBook in KDP Select, you agree to make it exclusive to Amazon for 90 days. In return, you gain access to perks like Free Book Promotion or Kindle Countdown Deals.

**Why It Helps with Reviews:**

- During a Free Book Promotion, readers can download your book for free. While not everyone will leave a review, the influx of downloads increases the odds of receiving feedback.
- Kindle Unlimited readers can also borrow your book, and many of them are frequent reviewers.

**Tips for Maximizing KDP Select Promotions:**

- Announce your free or discounted book on social media and in reader groups.
- Use sites like FreeBooksy or Bargain Booksy to promote your deals and reach more readers.

**Pro Tip:** Be strategic about when you run your promotions—early in your book's launch phase is ideal for building momentum.

**Step 3: Encourage Reviews at the End of Your Book**

The easiest way to get reviews? Just ask! Add a polite request at the end of your book, nudging readers to leave their thoughts.

**What to Include:**

- A heartfelt thank-you for reading your book.
- A short note explaining how reviews help authors like you.
- A direct link to your book's review page on Amazon or other retailers.

**Example Text:**

"Thank you for reading *[Your Book Title]*! If you enjoyed the story, I'd greatly appreciate it if you could leave an honest review. Reviews help other readers discover my work, and I love hearing what you think. Click here to leave your review!"

**Pro Tip:** Keep the tone warm and personal—it feels more genuine and less like a sales pitch.

### Step 4: Engage with Readers on Social Media

Social media isn't just for cat videos and endless scrolling. It's a fantastic way to connect with readers and encourage them to share their thoughts on your book.

**How to Build Relationships:**

- Share behind-the-scenes content, like your writing process or inspiration for the book.
- Host giveaways for signed copies or exclusive content in exchange for reviews.
- Run interactive posts—ask questions about your genre, characters, or themes to spark discussions.

**Pro Tip:** Create a unique hashtag for your book and encourage readers to use it when they share reviews or photos. Something like #YourBookTitleReview can generate buzz and make it easy to track mentions.

## Step 5: Use Book Review Websites

There are plenty of websites dedicated to connecting authors with potential reviewers. While some charge fees, many offer free or affordable options.

### Popular Review Sites to Consider:

- **Goodreads:** A community full of avid readers who love sharing reviews. Create an author profile and engage with your audience.
- **NetGalley:** A platform for distributing ARCs to professional reviewers, librarians, and booksellers.
- **BookSprout:** Offers tools for sending out ARCs and tracking reviews.

**Pro Tip:** Tailor your approach to each platform's unique audience. Goodreads, for example, is more about community engagement, while NetGalley is a professional resource.

## Step 6: Host a Virtual Launch Party

A virtual book launch isn't just a fun way to celebrate—it's also an opportunity to ask readers for reviews.

### What to Include in Your Launch Party:

- Live readings or Q&A sessions to engage your audience.

- Exclusive giveaways where winners agree to leave a review.
- A "thank-you" speech where you explain how reviews help authors and encourage attendees to leave one.

**Pro Tip:** Promote your launch party widely—on social media, in newsletters, and in writing groups—to maximize attendance.

### Step 7: Offer Review Incentives (Within the Rules)

While you can't pay for reviews, you can offer creative incentives that don't break Amazon's guidelines.

**Ideas:**

- Give away free bookmarks or other small swag to readers who post reviews.
- Offer exclusive bonus content, like a short story or deleted scenes, to reviewers.

**Pro Tip:** Always phrase incentives as "thank-yous" for reviews, rather than rewards contingent on posting one.

### Step 8: Leverage Reader Groups and Book Clubs

Reader groups, whether online or local, are full of passionate readers who love sharing their opinions.

**How to Get Involved:**

- Join Facebook groups or forums dedicated to your genre and connect with potential reviewers.
- Reach out to book clubs with an offer of free copies in exchange for group reviews.

**Pro Tip:** Be an active member of these communities—don't just pop in to promote your book. Authenticity goes a long way.

### Final Thoughts

Getting reviews takes time and effort, but the payoff is worth it. From distributing ARCs to running creative promotions, there are countless ways to encourage readers to share their thoughts. By building genuine connections and following best practices, you'll not only gather reviews but also create a loyal audience eager to see what you write next.

So go ahead—start planning your review strategy, and watch your book's reputation grow!

### Covers Speak Words

Let's not sugarcoat it: people *do* judge books by their covers. A captivating cover is often the first impression your book makes, and in the crowded world of publishing, first impressions are everything. If you're a new author trying to stand out, your cover isn't just decoration—it's a billboard screaming, "Pick me!" And remember the old saying, an image is worth a thousand words, make your cover speak about your book, not just a jumble of pictures that mean nothing.

### The Cover is Your Book's First Salesperson

Picture yourself scrolling through an online bookstore or wandering the aisles of a shop. You're bombarded with titles in every genre, each vying for attention. What makes you stop and pick up a book? Nine times out of ten, it's the cover. Good cover art grabs attention and conveys an immediate sense of the book's genre, tone, and professionalism. It tells potential readers, "This is a well-crafted story, and you're in for a treat."

A bad cover, on the other hand, can send the opposite message. Clunky fonts, low-resolution images, or mismatched colours scream amateurism, no matter how brilliant the writing inside might be. Readers might assume the same lack of care in the cover extends to the content. Fair? Maybe not. But perception is reality in the publishing world.

**Setting Expectations with Your Cover**

Your cover is like a promise to the reader. It sets expectations for what's inside and helps them decide if your book is their cup of tea. A dark, moody cover with gothic fonts? Probably a thriller or mystery. A bright, pastel cover with playful lettering? Likely a romance or feel-good fiction.

If your cover doesn't match the content, it creates confusion—and confusion doesn't sell books. Imagine a gritty sci-fi epic with a cartoonish cover that looks better suited for a children's book. Readers expecting light-hearted fun will feel misled, and sci-fi fans might never pick it up in the first place. A well-designed cover ensures your book lands in the right hands.

**The Professional Edge**

For self-published authors especially, professional cover art is a must. Traditional publishers invest in top-notch designers because they know a good cover equals better sales. Indie authors should follow suit. Hiring a professional cover designer might seem expensive, but it's one of the most worthwhile investments you can make in your book.

A professional designer understands the visual language of your genre and knows what works for your target audience. They'll ensure your book stands out on a shelf or thumbnail grid while staying true to genre conventions. Think of it as dressing your book for success.

**Standing Out in a Crowded Market**

The competition in publishing is fierce. Every year, hundreds of thousands of new books hit the market. Your cover art needs to cut through the noise and grab attention in a split second.

This is especially critical online, where your cover will often appear as a thumbnail. Details that look fine on a larger scale might become unreadable or cluttered when shrunk down. A clean, bold design with strong imagery and legible typography is key to making your book eye-catching, even at a smaller size.

**Building Brand Recognition**

If you're planning to write more than one book (and let's hope you are!), your cover art can help build your brand as an author. A cohesive design style across your books can make them instantly recognisable to readers. Think of the matching spines of a book series or an author's signature font and colour palette—it's all about creating a visual identity that sticks.

**Getting the Cover Right**

So, how do you ensure your cover art hits the mark? Start by researching other successful books in your genre. What do their covers have in common? Take note of trends in colour, typography, and imagery. Communicate your ideas to a professional designer, and don't be afraid to ask for revisions if the first draft doesn't quite capture your vision.

### Pro Tip: Test Before You Finalise

Before committing to a cover, consider testing it with your target audience. Post a poll on social media or get feedback from fellow writers. Their input can help you spot issues you might have overlooked and ensure your cover resonates with potential readers.

### The Bottom Line

Good cover art isn't a luxury; it's a necessity. It's the face of your book and the first step in turning browsers into buyers. Whether you're a debut author or a seasoned pro, investing in quality cover design will pay off in sales, visibility, and the professional reputation of your work. So go ahead, judge your book by its cover—and make sure it's one worth showing off.

### Getting Good Cover Art for Your Book: Why It Matters and How to Nail It

Let's face it: your book cover is your handshake with the world. It's what catches a reader's eye as they scroll through an endless list of titles, and it's the first impression that screams, "Pick me!" or, worse, "I was designed in five minutes on a free app." Good cover art can mean the difference between a sale and a shrug, so let's dive into how to get it right.

### Why Cover Art is Non-Negotiable

You wouldn't show up to a job interview in pyjamas, so don't send your book out into the world looking less than its best. A professional, well-designed cover tells readers that you've put time and effort into your book—and that the story inside is worth their investment.

But there's more to it than just aesthetics. A poorly executed cover can:

- Misrepresent your genre (cue the fantasy novel that looks like a romance).
- Signal amateurism to potential readers.
- Land you in hot water legally if you don't understand copyright rules (more on that later).

**Pro Tip:** First impressions matter. Your cover is an investment, not an expense.

### The Pitfalls of DIY Cover Art

We get it—budget constraints are real. But creating your own cover without experience can lead to some, let's say, "interesting" results:

1. **Unintentional Comedy:**
   - Floating heads? Overly stretched text? Mismatched fonts? A bad cover sticks out for all the wrong reasons.
2. **Genre Confusion:**
   - A self-made thriller cover that looks like a children's book? Not a good look. Genre-appropriate imagery and fonts matter!
3. **Legal Nightmares:**
   - Using "free" images without verifying copyright can lead to lawsuits.

- Public domain images can be removed by the creator, leaving you scrambling for replacements—or worse, facing fines.

4. **Technical Problems:**
   - Incorrect dimensions, poor resolution, or colours that print differently can lead to disasters on platforms like Amazon.

**Pro Tip:** Unless you're a professional designer, steer clear of creating your own cover. Your book deserves better!

### Finding the Right Cover Artist

A professional cover artist can make your book shine while ensuring it aligns with your genre, target audience, and personal vision.

### 1. Consider MMT Productions

Looking for a Canadian-based cover art specialist? Check out MMT Productions (https://mmtproductions.ca), an up-and-coming star in the cover art world. Their team works closely with authors to craft custom designs that stand out. Plus, supporting a homegrown talent feels pretty great, eh?

### Why MMT Productions Stands Out:

- Tailored designs that capture the essence of your story.
- Expertise in creating genre-specific covers (no more mistaken genres!).
- Canadian pricing—great quality without breaking the bank in U.S. dollars.

## 2. Vetting Cover Artists

- **Portfolio Review:** Look for artists with a strong portfolio in your genre. A thriller cover artist may not excel at fantasy or romance.
- **Client Testimonials:** Check reviews or ask other authors for recommendations.
- **Clear Communication:** Choose someone who listens to your ideas but isn't afraid to offer professional advice.

**Pro Tip:** Book cover artists early. They're in high demand, especially during pre-holiday and summer publishing seasons.

### The Process: From Idea to Finished Cover

Here's how to work effectively with a cover artist:

1. **Provide a Brief:**
   - Genre, tone, and themes of your book.
   - Specific imagery or symbols you'd like to include (but trust their expertise!).
   - Examples of covers you admire.
2. **Collaborate:**
   - Be open to revisions and feedback. The artist knows how to balance your vision with market trends.
3. **Final Approval:**
   - Ensure the design meets platform specifications (e.g., dimensions for Amazon KDP or IngramSpark).

### Avoiding Legal Trouble: Copyright Matters

Nothing kills your book buzz faster than a copyright claim. Here's what to watch out for:

1. **Royalty-Free Isn't Always Free:**
   - Many "royalty-free" images require a licence, and some prohibit use for commercial products like books.
   - Read the fine print before downloading anything.
2. **Public Domain Pitfalls:**
   - Some authors rely on public domain images, but be warned: creators can sometimes reclaim these works.
   - Imagine having to redo your cover because the "free" art you used is suddenly off-limits.
3. **Stock Image Overuse:**
   - While stock images are legal, they can feel generic or repetitive. Readers may notice if the same image appears on multiple books.

**Pro Tip:** Always ask your cover artist about the source of any images used. Original artwork or properly licensed stock is non-negotiable.

### What Makes a Great Cover?

A great cover does three things:

1. **Attracts Attention:**
   - Bold, clean designs stand out in a sea of thumbnails.
2. **Conveys Genre:**
   - Fonts, imagery, and colour schemes should immediately signal the book's genre.

3. **Tells a Story:**
   - Your cover should intrigue readers enough to want to know more.

**Examples of Cover Art Gone Wrong:**

- The sci-fi novel with a "clipart" rocket and Comic Sans font.
- A horror book featuring a sunny meadow and smiley-faced flowers.
- The fantasy epic with six different fonts crammed onto one cover.

**Pro Tip:** Think you can do a great cover? Don't get caught. Look at Lousy Book Covers (https://lousybookcover.com)

**Making It Work on Your Budget**

You don't need to spend thousands for professional cover art. Here's how to keep costs reasonable:

- **Shop Smart:** Look for freelance artists or smaller studios like MMT Productions that offer competitive rates.
- **Custom vs. Pre-Made Covers:** Pre-made designs can be a budget-friendly option, especially for eBooks.
- **Crowdfunding:** Platforms like Kickstarter or Patreon can help cover design costs while engaging your future readers.

**Pro Tip:** Never skimp on cover art quality. Even on a tight budget, it's better to invest in a professional design than to settle for DIY.

**Final Thoughts**

Your cover art is your book's first ambassador. A polished, professional cover can elevate your book from "meh" to must-read, attracting readers and boosting sales. By working with a skilled cover artist, avoiding copyright pitfalls, and prioritizing genre alignment, you'll set your book up for success—and make your story impossible to ignore.

Now, go forth and design a cover worthy of your incredible book. You've got this!

Part 5

# Beyond the Book

# Chapter 18
# **Building a Writing Career**

## Writing the Next Book

So, you've written your first book—congrats! But don't rest on your laurels for too long. Writing is a skill that thrives on momentum, feedback, and a little creative exploration. Here's how to approach your next masterpiece.

## Momentum Matters

Finishing your first book is an incredible achievement, like crossing the finish line of a marathon. But guess what? The marathon of writing doesn't end there—it's a series of races, and the sooner you lace up for the next one, the better.

Starting your next project while the creative juices are still flowing helps maintain that momentum. Writing consistently hones your skills, keeps your mind sharp, and shows readers (and publishers) that you're serious about your craft. Plus, having more books under your belt increases your chances of building a loyal audience.

Douglas Owen

## Learn from Feedback

Your first book wasn't just a story—it was also a crash course in what works and what doesn't. Pay attention to feedback from beta readers, editors, and even reviews (when they're constructive). Did readers love your witty dialogue? Did they mention that the pacing dragged in Act Two?

Use that information to refine your storytelling approach for book two. Maybe you'll focus on strengthening your plot structure or creating more layered characters. Every piece of feedback is an opportunity to improve, so embrace it as part of the process.

## Experiment with Genre

Feeling bold? Why not shake things up with your next book? Trying out a new genre or blending genres can be a fun way to stretch your creative muscles.

If you've written a mystery, consider adding a romantic subplot or a supernatural twist. If you're a fantasy author, how about a contemporary setting with magical realism? Experimenting can not only broaden your audience but also keep you excited about writing. Just make sure your voice and style remain authentic to you.

## Plan Ahead

If book one taught you anything, it's that writing and publishing take time and organisation. Setting a clear publishing schedule for your next project will keep you on track.

Whether your goal is to release one book a year or every two years, having a timeline helps you manage everything from drafting to marketing. And if you're self-publishing, factor in time for editing, cover design, and formatting. Remember, slow and steady wins the race—and a rushed book rarely makes for a polished read.

**Pro Tip:** Got a burst of inspiration? Capture it! Keep a notebook or digital file handy for jotting down story ideas, snippets of dialogue, or potential titles. It's your personal treasure chest for when you're ready to dive into your next project.

Your next book is an exciting opportunity to grow as a writer and connect with readers on a deeper level. So, take what you've learned, embrace new challenges, and keep that creative momentum going—you've got this!

### Connecting with the Writing Community

Writing may feel like a solo journey, but that doesn't mean you have to go it alone. Building connections with other writers not only boosts your morale but can also open doors you didn't even know existed. From local meetups to online hashtags, the writing community is brimming with opportunities for support, advice, and maybe even collaboration.

### Engage Locally and Online

The writing community is like a treasure chest—you never know what gem of wisdom or encouragement you'll uncover.

### Local Connections:

- Join writing groups in your area to meet authors face-to-face. Public libraries, community centres, and bookstores often host workshops or writing circles.

- Attend in-person events like book launches, author talks, or regional writing conferences. Bonus points if there's free coffee.

## Online Communities:

- **Twitter:** Check out hashtags like #WritingCommunity or #AmWriting to join conversations and connect with writers worldwide.
- **Facebook Groups:** Find genre-specific or general writing groups where you can share tips, ask questions, or celebrate milestones.
- **Discord and Reddit:** Explore writing servers or subreddits like r/writing for niche discussions or virtual writing sprints.

**Pro Tip:** Don't just lurk! Comment, ask questions, or share your journey to become an active part of the community.

### Network Strategically

Think of networking as making new friends, but with a professional twist.

- **Attend Events:** Book fairs, author panels, and virtual writing summits are perfect for meeting editors, agents, and like-minded writers.
- **Follow Up:** Exchanged contact info at an event? Drop a friendly email or social media message to keep the connection going.

- **Be Genuine:** Show interest in others' work and goals —it's not all about you, after all.

**Pro Tip:** Keep business cards handy, even at casual events. You never know when you'll meet someone who can help you— or vice versa.

## Collaborate

Two (or more) heads are often better than one, especially in the creative world.

- **Anthologies:** Contribute a story to a themed collection for exposure and camaraderie.
- **Co-Writing:** Partner on a book or script with another author—it's a fantastic way to share the workload and learn from each other.
- **Guest Posts or Interviews:** Write for fellow authors' blogs or join their podcasts. It's cross-promotion at its finest.

**Pro Tip:** Make sure your goals align before diving into a collaboration. Clear communication is key to keeping the process enjoyable and productive.

## Build Relationships by Giving Back

Networking isn't just about what you can get—it's also about what you can give.

- Share others' books, blog posts, or achievements on social media.
- Offer feedback on drafts or beta-read for someone in your genre.

- Cheer on fellow writers during launches, deadlines, or those "why did I think I could write this?" moments.

**Pro Tip:** Building goodwill with small acts of kindness creates a ripple effect. The more you support others, the more likely they are to support you.

Connecting with the writing community can transform your journey from a lonely trek into an exciting adventure shared with others who understand the ups and downs. Whether you're attending local meetups, diving into online discussions, or collaborating on projects, you'll find that writing becomes even more rewarding when you're part of a supportive network.

### Setting Long-Term Goals

When it comes to writing, long-term goals are your North Star —they guide you, motivate you, and help you steer through the murky waters of publishing. But what does success look like? And how do you stay on track when life, writer's block, and self-doubt inevitably show up? Let's break it down.

### Define Success

What does success mean to *you*? Is it seeing your name on a bestseller list? Earning a steady income from your writing? Maybe it's as simple (and meaningful) as knowing your story has touched someone's heart.

Success in writing isn't one-size-fits-all. Some authors dream of a mansion funded by book royalties; others are happy crafting one perfect novel in their lifetime. Be honest with yourself. Do you crave critical acclaim, reader engagement, financial stability—or all of the above?

**Ask Yourself:**

- Do you want to focus solely on creative freedom, or do you also want a career that pays the bills?
- Are you looking for a global audience or a tight-knit community of devoted fans?
- Do you see yourself juggling writing alongside a day job or going all in?

**Pro Tip:** Write down your definition of success and keep it somewhere visible—a sticky note on your desk, a note on your phone, or a fancy vision board if you're feeling extra creative. Seeing it daily will remind you why you started and where you're headed.

### Create a Roadmap

Dreams are great, but they need structure to become reality. That's where your roadmap comes in.

Take your big goals—like publishing a trilogy or making a full-time income—and break them into smaller, manageable steps. For instance, if you want to write three novels in five years, here's how to make it happen:

1. **Plan Your Timeline:** Map out when you'll draft, edit, and release each book. Be realistic about how much time each step will take (and don't forget to build in breaks).
2. **Set Milestones:** Celebrate each step of the journey— finishing a draft, landing an agent, or hitting "publish" on your first book.

3. **Track Your Progress:** Use tools like spreadsheets, apps, or even a trusty calendar to stay on schedule.

4. **Stay Accountable:** Share your goals with a trusted friend, critique partner, or writing group. They'll help keep you on track when Netflix or procrastination beckons.

**Pro Tip:** Keep your roadmap flexible. Life happens—whether it's an unexpected burst of creativity or a week spent binge-watching your favourite show. Adjust timelines as needed, but don't lose sight of your goals.

### Diversify Your Writing Portfolio

Books are your bread and butter, but diversifying your writing portfolio can open up exciting new opportunities. Think of it as adding sprinkles to an already delicious cake.

Here are some ways to diversify:

- **Freelance Writing:** Offer your skills to magazines, websites, or companies looking for content. This can be a great way to hone your craft and earn some extra cash.
- **Blogging:** Share your insights, journey, or expertise with the world. Blogging builds your platform and connects you with readers.
- **Teaching and Workshops:** If you've got writing tips to share, consider hosting workshops or teaching online classes. Many aspiring writers love learning from published authors.
- **Speaking Engagements:** Writing conferences,

panels, and webinars are fantastic places to share your expertise, network, and grow your audience.

- **Exploring Other Mediums:** Why stop at books? Try your hand at screenwriting, poetry, or even video game narratives. You never know where a new format might take you.

Diversifying isn't just about income—it's also about building a well-rounded writing career. Exploring new avenues keeps your creativity sharp and your skills adaptable.

**Pro Tip:** Start small. Choose one additional project to pursue alongside your book writing and see where it leads. You don't want to overwhelm yourself with too many irons in the fire.

### Revisit and Revise Your Goals

As your writing career evolves, your definition of success might change. Maybe you set out to write literary fiction but discovered a passion for romance. Or perhaps your initial goal of publishing one book a year felt doable, but now you're swamped juggling marketing, freelance work, and that pesky day job.

Revisiting your goals annually ensures they align with where you are now, not where you were five years ago.

### How to Revisit Your Goals:

- Reflect on your achievements—what worked and what didn't?
- Adjust your roadmap to match your current pace and priorities.

- Set new challenges to keep your writing journey exciting and fulfilling.

**Pro Tip:** Use the start of a new year (or your birthday, or your book's publication anniversary) as a natural time to review your goals. It's like hitting the refresh button on your career.

Setting long-term goals doesn't just give your writing career direction—it keeps you motivated through the highs, lows, and inevitable plot twists. Define what success means to you, map out a plan, explore new opportunities, and stay flexible as your career evolves. Writing is a marathon, not a sprint, and every step forward is worth celebrating.

Part 6

# Conclusion

# Chapter 19

# **Your Journey as a Writer**

**Writing, Editing, and Publishing: What You'll Learn**

In the journey of turning your idea into a published book, you'll encounter many challenges and rewarding experiences. This section outlines the comprehensive roadmap provided in this book, offering practical advice and a few laughs to keep the process enjoyable.

**Finding Your Big Idea**

Every great book begins with an idea. The book explores:

- How to brainstorm effectively: Techniques for generating ideas.
- Refining your concept: Identifying themes and ensuring they resonate with readers.
- Testing your idea: How to determine if your story or topic has the potential to captivate an audience.

**Planning and Outlining**

Before diving into writing, planning helps avoid mid-story slumps:

- Types of writers: Are you a "plotter" (detailed planner) or a "pantser" (flying by the seat of your pants)?
- Outlining methods: Traditional outlines, mind maps, or bullet-point lists.
- Structuring your story: Techniques for crafting a beginning, middle, and end that flow seamlessly.

**The Writing Process**

Writing isn't just about putting words on a page; it's about discipline and creativity:

- Overcoming writer's block: Proven strategies to keep the words flowing.
- Finding your voice: Developing a style that feels authentic to you.
- Staying consistent: Creating a writing schedule that works with your lifestyle.

**Editing Like a Pro**

Editing is where the magic happens, transforming a rough draft into a polished manuscript:

- Self-editing basics: Cutting fluff, checking grammar, and ensuring clarity.
- Deep revision techniques: Restructuring chapters, enhancing themes, and refining dialogue.

- Seeking feedback: Working with beta readers, critique partners, or professional editors.

## Publishing Options

Once your manuscript is polished, it's time to consider how to get it into readers' hands:

- Traditional publishing: The process of querying agents and submitting to publishers.
- Self-publishing: Platforms like Amazon KDP, IngramSpark, and Draft2Digital.
- Hybrid publishing: A middle ground that combines aspects of both traditional and self-publishing.

## Marketing and Building Your Audience

Publishing a book is just the beginning. Reaching readers requires strategy:

- Building your author platform: Social media, email newsletters, and personal branding.
- Getting reviews: The importance of early reviews for visibility and credibility.
- Promoting your book: Ideas for virtual and in-person book launches, ads, and partnerships.

## Staying Motivated

Writing is a long game, but persistence pays off:

- Setting realistic goals: Balancing writing with other life commitments.

- Celebrating small wins: Acknowledging progress to stay inspired.
- Learning from setbacks: Using rejection or criticism as fuel for improvement.

## Key Pro Tips Throughout

Sprinkled throughout the chapters are tips like:

- Keep a "treasure chest" of story ideas to draw from when inspiration strikes.
- Use free tools like Canva for cover design mock-ups or Scrivener for drafting and organizing.
- Revisit your goals annually to ensure your writing aligns with your evolving vision.

This book doesn't just teach you how to write—it equips you with the tools, confidence, and motivation to finish your story and share it with the world. Writing is a journey, and you're in the driver's seat. Let's get started!

## Your Journey as a Writer: Learning from the Greats

Writing a book is a bit like wrestling a grizzly bear—terrifying, exhilarating, and often more than a little sweaty. But those who've gone before you prove it's worth the effort. Let's take a page (pun absolutely intended) from the stories of some iconic authors who've turned their scribbled ideas into literary legacies.

## J.K. Rowling: Magic in the Face of Adversity

J.K. Rowling's journey to becoming one of the most celebrated authors of our time didn't start with Quidditch matches and

Bertie Bott's Every Flavour Beans. It began with a single parent, a struggling bank account, and a train ride where she dreamed up a boy wizard destined for greatness.

Her manuscript for *Harry Potter and the Philosopher's Stone* was rejected a dozen times before a small publisher took a chance. The lesson here? Don't let the rejections get you down—Rowling didn't, and now her name is synonymous with literary magic.

**What You Can Learn:**

- Believe in your story, even when others don't.
- Use life's challenges as fuel for creativity.
- Keep submitting your work—success might be just around the corner (or the next rejection email).

**Spyder Robinson: From Short Stories to Stardom**

Spyder Robinson began his career writing short stories for science fiction magazines. His tales were quirky, witty, and filled with heart, and they resonated with readers who couldn't get enough of his imagined worlds. Robinson's leap from short fiction to full-length novels is proof that even modest beginnings can lead to a prolific career.

**What You Can Learn:**

- Short stories are a great way to hone your craft and build a readership.
- Don't underestimate the power of niche audiences—science fiction geeks, we're looking at you!
- Persistence pays off: every story you write brings you closer to mastering your voice.

## Ron Schulz: Turning Personal History into Legacy

From the draft you provided, Ron Schulz is a shining example of how sharing personal experiences can leave a lasting impact. His reflections on life during the 1960s and '70s aren't just a trip down memory lane—they're a bridge to future generations who might not otherwise grasp the nuances of that transformative era.

**What You Can Learn:**

- Everyone's life is a story waiting to be told—yours included.
- Write for the people you'll never meet; your work could outlive you and inspire others.
- Draw from personal history to create narratives that resonate universally.

## S.A. Baker: Building a Fictional Universe

S.A. Baker's *Winterbourne* series is a testament to sticking with your fictional world until it grows into something unmissable. Baker didn't just write a book—he created an entire universe, complete with characters, plots, and twists that keep readers hooked.

**What You Can Learn:**

- Dedication to a single project can yield massive rewards over time.
- World-building isn't just for fantasy—it's the cornerstone of any great story.
- Engaging with fans and expanding your universe can transform a book into a career.

**Lessons from the Trailblazers**

So, what ties all these writers together (besides their books being excellent company on a rainy day)? They didn't let fear, rejections, or slow starts hold them back. They sat down, wrote their stories, and kept pushing forward.

Writing isn't about overnight success—it's about showing up every day, even when you'd rather binge-watch another season of *Schitt's Creek*.

**What You Can Learn from Them All:**

- Writing is a marathon, not a sprint. Expect ups, downs, and a few caffeine-fuelled all-nighters.
- Success looks different for everyone. Whether you sell one copy or a million, every story is a victory.
- Rejections? Pfft. Every famous writer has a stack of them. Build your pile—it's a badge of honour.

**Your Turn: Make It Count**

Right now, you're at the start—or maybe the middle—of your own writing journey. Maybe you're penning your first chapter, or perhaps you're polishing the ending of your tenth book. Wherever you are, remember this: every step forward is a win.

Be inspired by the perseverance of Rowling, the wit of Robinson, the heart of Schulz, and the world-building brilliance of Baker. Your story matters, and someone out there is waiting to read it.

So, grab your laptop or your notebook, and keep going. You're in excellent company—and who knows? Someday, another aspiring writer might look to your journey for inspiration.

# Chapter 20
# **Marketing Tips and Tricks**

**Understanding Your Audience**

Marketing your book without understanding your audience is like trying to sell snowshoes in the desert—it's just not going to land. Knowing your readers is the key to crafting marketing strategies that hit the mark. Let's break this down into actionable steps to help you connect with your target audience.

**Why Knowing Your Audience is Critical to Effective Marketing**

Your readers are the lifeblood of your book's success. If you know who they are, what they like, and where they hang out, you'll spend less time throwing spaghetti at the wall and more time building genuine connections. This understanding helps you:

- Create book covers and blurbs that attract your ideal readers.
- Tailor your promotional content to meet their preferences.
- Avoid wasting time marketing in spaces where your audience doesn't exist (spoiler: not every reader is on Twitter).

### Define Your Ideal Reader Persona

Creating a reader persona is like building your ideal guest list for a dinner party. Who do you want to show up and devour your story? Think about:

1. **Demographics**: What's their age, gender, location, and occupation? For example, romance readers might skew heavily toward women aged 25–45.
2. **Preferences**: Are they drawn to fast-paced thrillers or slow-burn mysteries? Knowing this helps you highlight the right aspects of your book.
3. **Reading Habits**: Do they devour eBooks on their Kindle, prefer audiobooks, or haunt the local library for paperbacks?

**Pro Tip**: Use tools like reader surveys or casual polls on social media to gather insights. Even a simple question like, "What's your favourite book trope?" can spark great feedback.

### Explore Where Your Readers Hang Out Online

Knowing where your audience spends their time is half the marketing battle. For instance:

- **Goodreads**: The mecca of book lovers. Join groups related to your genre and participate in discussions.
- **Twitter (X)**: Use hashtags like #WritingCommunity or #AmReading to find readers who might be interested in your work.
- **Instagram**: A hotbed for Bookstagrammers who love showcasing gorgeous book covers.
- **Facebook**: Ideal for joining genre-specific groups and hosting virtual events.
- **TikTok**: Thanks to BookTok, this platform is a game-changer for reaching younger readers.

**Pro Tip**: Don't try to master every platform at once. Start with one or two that resonate with your audience and expand from there.

### Use Book Reviews and Forums to Understand Reader Expectations

Want to know what readers are looking for in your genre? The answers are often hiding in plain sight:

1. **Read Reviews**: Go through reviews of books similar to yours. Look for trends—what do readers love, and what drives them up the wall?
2. **Join Forums**: Platforms like Reddit have thriving communities for every genre imaginable. Check out subreddits like r/Fantasy, r/RomanceBooks, or r/Books for insights.
3. **Study the Competition**: Browse the bestseller lists in your category and study the blurbs, covers, and author bios. What makes these books stand out?

**Pro Tip**: Keep a notebook handy to jot down repeated reader complaints or praise. These nuggets can help you fine-tune your messaging.

## Tailor Your Messaging to Resonate with Your Audience's Interests

Generic marketing is a waste of time. Instead, speak directly to your readers' desires:

- If your audience loves thrillers, emphasize the twists and high stakes in your book's description.
- Writing a feel-good romance? Use warm, engaging language that makes readers swoon before they've even hit Chapter 1.
- Non-fiction authors can highlight how their book solves specific problems or fulfils a need.

Customizing your messaging ensures your book feels like the perfect fit for your audience.

**Pro Tip**: Experiment with different styles of social media posts or ad copy. Analytics can show you what's working and what's not.

## Collect Feedback to Refine Your Approach

Marketing isn't a one-and-done process—it's a learning curve. Collecting feedback allows you to pivot and improve:

1. **Beta Readers**: Early readers can offer insights into what resonates with your audience.
2. **Social Media Interaction**: Pay attention to which posts get the most engagement.

3. **Post-Launch Surveys**: Ask readers what drew them to your book and what they'd like to see next.

**Pro Tip**: Treat all feedback—good and bad—as valuable data. Even a critique can lead to a more focused strategy.

By understanding your audience, you'll transform your marketing efforts from aimless shouting into meaningful conversations. And when readers feel seen and understood, they're much more likely to grab your book off the (digital or physical) shelf. Happy connecting!

## Sites That Offer Reviews on Goodreads and Amazon

Getting reviews on platforms like Goodreads and Amazon is vital for your book's success. But where do you start? Fortunately, several websites can help connect authors with reviewers. Each has its quirks, pros, and cons, so let's dive in to find the best fit for your book-baby's needs.

### 1. NetGalley

**Overview:**

NetGalley is one of the most popular platforms for getting advanced reviews. You upload your manuscript, and the site connects you with avid readers and industry professionals eager to provide feedback.

**Cost:** Paid. Plans start around $50/month, with higher tiers offering additional promotional features.

**How It Works:**

- Authors and publishers upload their books.

- Reviewers (from book bloggers to librarians) request access.
- You approve requests and wait for the reviews to roll in.

**Pros:**

- Access to a large and diverse pool of professional reviewers.
- Perfect for generating pre-launch buzz.
- Reviews are often cross-posted to Goodreads and Amazon.

**Cons:**

- It's pricey, making it more suited for authors with a marketing budget.
- Not every reviewer leaves feedback, despite requesting the book.

**Pro Tip:** Use NetGalley sparingly if you're on a tight budget—focus on big releases or books you want to push extra hard.

### 2. BookSirens

**Overview:**

BookSirens connects indie authors with reviewers who are likely to enjoy their genre. It's a simpler, more budget-friendly alternative to NetGalley.

**Cost:** Pay-per-book, around $10 per reviewer, plus an initial setup fee (~$50).

**How It Works:**

- Authors upload their manuscript.
- BookSirens matches it with reviewers based on genre preferences.

**Pros:**

- Affordable for indie authors.
- Reviews are often shared on Goodreads, Amazon, and personal blogs.
- You can track reviewer performance (e.g., how often they deliver reviews).

**Cons:**

- Smaller reviewer pool compared to NetGalley.
- Reviews may not always appear on Amazon.

**Pro Tip:** Choose BookSirens if you're looking for a cost-effective way to build a steady stream of reviews.

### 3. LibraryThing Early Reviewers

**Overview:**

LibraryThing offers a program called Early Reviewers, where authors can submit their books for feedback from the site's community of book lovers.

**Cost:** Free, but authors must provide copies of the book to reviewers (digital or physical).

**How It Works:**

- You offer a set number of copies for free.
- Readers request your book, and LibraryThing matches them based on their preferences.

**Pros:**

- No upfront cost beyond providing review copies.
- Reviews often appear on Goodreads and sometimes on Amazon.
- Great for engaging a dedicated reader community.

**Cons:**

- You have to ship physical copies if you choose print.
- Review quality can vary widely.

**Pro Tip:** Opt for digital ARCs to save on shipping costs if you're using this platform.

### 4. The Reading Deals Review Club

**Overview:**

This site connects authors with readers who commit to leaving reviews.

**Cost:** Paid, starting at around $50 per campaign.

**How It Works:**

- You submit your book.
- Readers sign up, download, and agree to post a review on Amazon and Goodreads.

**Pros:**

- Reliable review commitment from participants.
- Easy-to-use platform.

**Cons:**

- Reviews can feel generic and lack depth.
- Limited to English-speaking markets.

**Pro Tip:** Use this service for boosting your review numbers early in your book's life cycle.

### 5. Goodreads Giveaways

**Overview:**

Goodreads Giveaways allow you to host contests where winners receive a copy of your book in exchange for an honest review.

**Cost:** Paid, with fees starting at $119 per giveaway.

**How It Works:**

- Set up a giveaway on Goodreads.
- Readers enter for a chance to win your book.
- Winners are encouraged (but not required) to leave a review.

**Pros:**

- Generates buzz and increases visibility on Goodreads.
- Reviews often trickle into Amazon as well.

**Cons:**

- No guarantee of reviews.
- Can be costly, especially for print book giveaways.

**Pro Tip:** Offer digital copies for giveaways to avoid shipping costs and reach a broader audience.

### 6. BookFunnel

**Overview:**

BookFunnel is a versatile tool for delivering ARCs and building your email list. While its main purpose isn't reviews, it can help you find reviewers if used strategically.

**Cost:** Paid, starting at $20/month.

**How It Works:**

- Upload your book.
- Share a link with potential reviewers or use it as part of a newsletter campaign.

**Pros:**

- Helps you control who gets your ARC.
- Easy for readers to download and access the book in their preferred format.

**Cons:**

- No built-in review system—you need to handle follow-ups yourself.

**Pro Tip:** Combine BookFunnel with social media outreach or mailing lists to build a strong pool of reviewers.

### 7. ARCreviewers.com

**Overview:**

A dedicated platform for connecting authors with ARC readers.

**Cost:** At the time of this writing - Free.

**How It Works:**

- Authors submit their books.
- The site matches your book with readers interested in your genre.

**Pros:**

- Focused exclusively on ARCs, ensuring reviewers are ready to provide feedback.
- Reviewers must review on Goodreads. They ask reviewers to add reviews on Amazon.
- They stop readers from downloading another novel until they post a review on the last one they downloaded.

**Cons:**

- The reviews are unverified purchase reviews on Amazon.

**Pro Tip:** Use ARCreviewers.com to build a dedicated reviewer base for your future books as well.

## Best Practices for Using These Sites

1. **Follow Up Politely**: A gentle nudge via email or social media can remind readers to leave their reviews.
2. **Provide Clear Instructions**: Include a note in your ARC with direct links to review pages.
3. **Respect Reader Opinions**: Not all reviews will be five stars—use critical feedback to grow as an author.
4. **Track Your Campaigns**: Keep a spreadsheet of who has received your book and whether they've posted reviews.

Building reviews takes time and effort, but these platforms can make the process less daunting. With persistence and a touch of marketing savvy, your book can gain the traction it deserves!

## Getting Amazon Reviews

Amazon reviews are like gold stars for your book. They boost your book's visibility, increase credibility, and help convince readers to hit that glorious "Buy Now" button. But how do you actually get those reviews rolling in? Here's a breakdown of practical strategies and tips for collecting honest feedback while keeping things above board (because nobody wants to tangle with Amazon's rules).

## 1. Start with Your Inner Circle

Your friends, family, and colleagues can be your first reviewers. But—and this is a big but—make sure they follow Amazon's guidelines. Reviews from people with obvious personal connections (like your mum writing "This is the BEST book ever!") might be flagged and removed.

**How to Do It Right:**

- Ask them to be objective and transparent.
- Remind them to focus on the book itself rather than their relationship with you.
- Encourage them to highlight specific things they liked (or didn't) in the story to add credibility.

**Pro Tip:** Avoid overloading your book with glowing 5-star reviews from friends—it can look suspicious. A mix of ratings makes your book seem more genuine.

### 2. Leverage Advance Review Copies (ARCs)

ARCs are a fantastic way to generate early buzz and reviews. These pre-publication copies go out to readers who agree to leave honest reviews in return.

**How to Distribute ARCs:**

- Use platforms like NetGalley, BookSirens, or ARCreviewers.com to connect with willing reviewers.
- Reach out to bloggers, BookTubers, and social media influencers in your genre.
- Offer ARCs to members of your mailing list or your social media followers.

**Pro Tip:** Be clear in your communication—ask for honest reviews but never pressure readers to leave a glowing endorsement.

### 3. Build Your Email List

Your email subscribers are some of your most loyal fans. Use this direct connection to ask for reviews after they've read your book.

**How to Ask Nicely:**

- Send a post-launch email thanking them for their support.
- Include a polite request to leave a review, along with a link to your book's Amazon page.
- Emphasize that their honest feedback—good, bad, or neutral—helps you grow as a writer.

**Pro Tip:** Include a clickable "Leave a Review" button in your email to make the process seamless.

### 4. Use Amazon's Follow-Up Tools

If you're selling physical books through Amazon, their "Request a Review" button is a handy tool.

**How It Works:**

- After a purchase, Amazon allows you to send a polite follow-up email asking the buyer to leave a review.
- The request is generic and automated but effective in nudging readers to share their thoughts.

**Pro Tip:** Use this feature sparingly to avoid annoying your readers—it's best for books that already have a few solid reviews.

### 5. Engage with the Goodreads Community

Goodreads reviewers often cross-post their feedback to Amazon. Building relationships on this platform can naturally lead to reviews.

**How to Connect:**

- Join Goodreads groups specific to your genre and participate in discussions.
- Host a giveaway or ask for volunteers to read and review your book.
- Respect community rules—don't spam forums with review requests.

**Pro Tip:** When reaching out to Goodreads users, personalize your message. A generic "Hey, review my book!" won't win anyone over.

### 6. Run a Kindle Countdown Deal or Free Promotion

Promotional deals can attract new readers and, hopefully, reviewers.

**How It Works:**

- Enrol in KDP Select to access promotional tools like Kindle Countdown Deals or Free Book Promotions.
- Once readers have downloaded your book, follow up (via email or social media) to ask for a review.

**Pro Tip:** Use the promotional period to drive traffic to your book through social media ads or email campaigns. More downloads = more potential reviewers.

### 7. Don't Forget Social Media

Your followers are your cheerleaders—don't be shy about asking them for reviews.

**How to Approach It:**

- Post a thank-you message after your book's release, with a link encouraging readers to leave a review.
- Share snippets of existing reviews to inspire others to add their own.
- Engage with readers who comment on your book posts and gently remind them how much a review helps.

**Pro Tip:** Use Instagram Stories or polls to interact with readers in a fun, casual way.

### 8. Run Contests and Giveaways

People love freebies, and a contest is a great way to generate excitement—and reviews.

**How to Do It:**

- Offer free books or swag (like bookmarks or tote bags) as prizes.
- Ask winners to leave an honest review on Amazon as part of the entry process.

Douglas Owen

**Pro Tip:** Check Amazon's rules—never condition giveaway prizes on leaving a positive review. The request should always be for honest feedback.

### 9. Follow Up Without Being Pushy

Timing is everything when it comes to requesting reviews.

**Best Practices:**

- Wait at least a week after someone has received or downloaded your book.
- Send a polite reminder, thanking them for their support and encouraging them to leave a review.

**Pro Tip:** Make it clear that reviews don't have to be long—a few sentences about what they liked (or didn't) are enough.

### The Golden Rule: Stay Honest and Authentic

Amazon takes fake reviews seriously, and so should you. Never pay for reviews or ask for falsified ratings. Stick to ethical methods, and your reviews will hold more weight with readers.

With the right strategies and a touch of persistence, building your review count can be an exciting part of your book marketing journey. Reviews are more than numbers—they're a reflection of your connection with readers. So, go ahead and start gathering those gold stars!

### Reviews Versus Verified Reviews on Amazon

When it comes to Amazon, not all reviews are created equal. The platform divides reviews into two categories: **regular reviews** and **verified reviews.** Understanding the difference between the two is essential for authors looking to boost their book's credibility and sales. Let's dive into the details and uncover why these distinctions matter.

**What Are Regular Reviews?**

**Regular reviews** are written by anyone who has an opinion about your book. The reviewer might have read your book through a library, borrowed it from a friend, or received it as a gift. These reviews still show up on your book's page and contribute to the overall star rating, but they lack the little "Verified Purchase" tag that Amazon adds for extra legitimacy.

**What Are Verified Reviews?**

**Verified reviews** are like the VIPs of the review world. They come from readers who purchased your book directly through Amazon, either as an eBook, paperback, or audiobook. Amazon adds the coveted "Verified Purchase" badge to these reviews, signalling to other potential buyers that the reviewer actually bought the book and isn't just raving about it because you're besties.

**Why Verified Reviews Matter**

- **Increased Credibility:** Readers are more likely to trust reviews with the "Verified Purchase" tag. It signals that the person reviewing the book is a paying customer, not someone with a hidden agenda.
- **Algorithm Influence:** Verified reviews carry more weight with Amazon's algorithms. More verified reviews can help boost your book's visibility and ranking, leading to increased sales.
- **Professional Appearance:** A mix of verified and regular reviews shows your book is being read by a

diverse audience, but too many unverified reviews can look suspicious.

## Why Regular Reviews Still Count

Don't discount regular reviews—they play an important role too. For instance:

- **Volume Matters:** Amazon's algorithms consider the total number of reviews, verified or not.
- **Feedback Variety:** Regular reviews can provide valuable insights and diverse perspectives.
- **Reader Trust:** Even without the "Verified Purchase" tag, thoughtful and detailed reviews can help sway potential readers.

## How to Encourage Verified Reviews

- **Sell Directly Through Amazon:** The more sales you make via Amazon, the higher the likelihood of verified reviews.
- **Offer Discounts or Promotions:** Run a Kindle Countdown Deal or make your book free for a limited time to encourage purchases and reviews.
- **Remind Your Readers:** Politely ask your audience (via newsletters, social media, or at events) to leave reviews after purchasing on Amazon.

## Pro Tip: Balance Is Key

While it's great to aim for verified reviews, a healthy mix of both verified and regular reviews gives your book authenticity. Don't fret over controlling who buys your book and who doesn't—focus on getting your story into readers' hands.

Both regular and verified reviews have their place in an author's journey to success on Amazon. Understanding how they work and their importance can help you create a well-rounded review strategy. Remember, every review, verified or not, is a little nudge for the next reader to take a chance on your book!

## Using Testimonials to Your Advantage

Testimonials are the sparkling jewels of the marketing world. They provide social proof, build trust, and can be the ultimate "yes" factor for readers deciding whether to invest their time (and money) in your book. When used strategically, testimonials can elevate your marketing game and make your book irresistible. Let's explore how to collect and leverage these golden nuggets of praise.

## Why Testimonials Matter

- **Instant Credibility:** A glowing endorsement from a respected name or a trusted reader can do wonders for your book's reputation.
- **Decision-Maker:** Testimonials can nudge potential readers who are teetering on the edge of buying your book into hitting that "Add to Cart" button.
- **Marketing Gold:** A well-placed testimonial can enhance book covers, Amazon descriptions, and social media promotions.

Think of testimonials as your book's cheerleaders—they hype up your work so you don't have to do all the shouting yourself.

## How to Collect Testimonials

1. **Ask Early Readers:** Beta readers and ARC (Advance Review Copy) recipients are excellent sources for testimonials. They've read your book and (hopefully) loved it.
2. **Reach Out to Influencers:** If a fellow author or industry professional reads and enjoys your book, don't hesitate to ask for a few kind words.
3. **Leverage Fan Feedback:** If readers are singing your praises in reviews or social media comments, ask for permission to use their words as testimonials.
4. **Seek Experts:** If your book is non-fiction, endorsements from field experts add extra weight. For fiction, another author in your genre works wonders.
5. **Keep It Specific:** When requesting testimonials, guide readers by asking them to focus on particular elements like the story's impact, the writing style, or memorable characters.

## Where to Use Testimonials

- **Book Cover:** A glowing testimonial from an established author or critic right on the cover can be a game-changer.
- **Amazon Description:** Start your book's blurb with a killer quote to grab attention.
- **Social Media:** Sprinkle testimonials into your posts for an ongoing confidence boost to your followers.
- **Website:** Create a dedicated page for praise or feature testimonials on your homepage.

- **Newsletter:** Share reader feedback with your email subscribers to reinforce your book's value.

## Best Practices for Using Testimonials

- **Keep It Short:** Aim for one to two sentences. Readers don't have time to wade through paragraphs of praise.
- **Highlight Names and Titles:** If the testimonial comes from a well-known author or industry figure, make sure their name and credentials are prominently displayed.
- **Refresh Regularly:** As new testimonials roll in, update your marketing materials to keep them fresh and relevant.
- **Use Visuals:** Pair quotes with professional graphics or book covers to make testimonials pop on social media.

## Pro Tips

- **Don't Fake It:** Made-up testimonials are a big no-no. Readers can spot inauthenticity a mile away.
- **Ask for Permission:** Always get explicit permission to use someone's words and name in your marketing materials.
- **Rotate Testimonials:** Feature different testimonials across platforms to keep your marketing content varied and engaging.

Testimonials are powerful tools that can help your book stand out in a sea of options. With genuine endorsements, you'll add credibility to your work, attract new readers, and build a loyal fan base. So, don't be shy—ask for those kind words, and let your book shine through the voices of those who love it!

## Facebook Ads Versus Amazon Ads

When it comes to advertising your book, two of the most popular platforms are Facebook and Amazon. But which one deserves your precious marketing dollars? Each has its strengths and quirks, so let's break it down to help you choose the right platform—or decide if you need both.

### Facebook Ads: The Social Butterfly

Facebook is a bustling hub where billions of people connect, share, and scroll endlessly through baby pictures and cat memes. Here's how it works for authors:

### Pros of Facebook Ads

1. **Wide Reach:**
   - Facebook's audience is massive. You can target potential readers based on demographics, interests, and behaviours. Want to reach fans of fantasy novels or thriller junkies? Facebook can help.
2. **Visual Appeal:**
   - Eye-catching images or videos can grab attention as readers scroll through their feed. Your book cover could be their next stop!
3. **Engagement Opportunities:**
   - Ads can spark comments, likes, and shares, letting you interact directly with your audience.
4. **Budget-Friendly Starting Point:**

○ You can start with as little as $5 a day to test the waters.

**Cons of Facebook Ads**

1. **No Guarantees:**
   ○ Facebook will happily spend every penny of your daily or weekly budget—even if it's not converting into sales. Be ready to track performance and tweak your ads.
2. **Distraction Central:**
   ○ Readers on Facebook aren't necessarily in "buying mode." They're often more interested in socialising than shopping.
3. **Steep Learning Curve:**
   ○ Facebook's ad manager is a complex beast, with endless options for targeting and customisation. Get ready to learn as you go.

**Amazon Ads: The Storefront Advantage**

Amazon is the world's largest marketplace—and the go-to site for buying books. Here's why it's a favourite for authors:

**Pros of Amazon Ads**

1. **Audience Intent:**
   ○ Unlike Facebook, people on Amazon are already in shopping mode. They're actively searching for books, making them more likely to buy.
2. **Precise Targeting:**
   ○ Amazon ads let you target by genre, similar books, or specific keywords. If someone is searching for a

bestseller in your genre, your book could appear right alongside it.

3. **Pay for Clicks, Not Views:**
   - With Amazon ads, you only pay when someone clicks on your ad. This means you're not wasting money on people who aren't interested.

4. **Data-Driven:**
   - Amazon provides detailed reports on ad performance, so you can see what's working and what's not.

## Cons of Amazon Ads

1. **More Competitive:**
   - With so many authors using Amazon ads, it can be challenging (and costly) to stand out—especially for popular keywords.

2. **Learning Curve:**
   - While it's less intimidating than Facebook's platform, Amazon ads still require time to learn and optimise for maximum results.

3. **No Social Engagement:**
   - Unlike Facebook, Amazon ads don't allow for likes, shares, or comments, so you miss out on direct interaction with your audience.

## Head-to-Head Comparison

| Feature | Facebook Ads | Amazon Ads |
|---|---|---|
| Audience | Broad, interest-based targeting | Shopping-focused readers |
| Cost | Spends your full budget daily | Pay-per-click model |
| Ease of Use | Complex learning curve | Moderate learning curve |
| Intent | Social engagement | Purchase intent |
| Metrics | Engagement and reach stats | Sales and click-through rates |

## Pro Tips for Choosing Your Platform

- **Start Small:** Test both platforms with a modest budget to see which one delivers better results for your book.
- **Match Your Goals:** Use Facebook for visibility and audience building, and Amazon for driving direct sales.
- **Keep an Eye on ROI:** Regularly analyse your ad performance to ensure your dollars are working hard for you.

## The Verdict

If you want to build your brand and engage with readers, Facebook ads can be a great tool—but be prepared to monitor your budget closely, as Facebook loves to burn through your funds. For direct sales, Amazon ads often offer better results, especially if you're targeting readers already in buying mode.

Ultimately, the best strategy might be a combination of both: use Facebook ads to build buzz and Amazon ads to close the deal. Whatever route you choose, keep experimenting and refining—your next bestseller deserves the spotlight!

**Publishing Your Book: A Strategic Plan**

Publishing a book involves more than just uploading a file and hoping for the best. By taking a strategic approach to your publishing platforms, you can maximize your book's visibility, reach, and sales. Let's dive into a practical guide for publishing on Amazon, IngramSpark, and beyond—because a little strategy goes a long way in the competitive world of publishing.

**Step 1: Publish on Amazon (e-Books and Print)**

Amazon is the go-to platform for most authors, thanks to its dominance in the eBook market and print-on-demand capabilities. Here's how to make the most of it:

**Why Amazon?**

- Massive customer base.
- User-friendly publishing tools.
- Advertising options tailored to authors.

**Key Moves for Success**

1. **eBooks and Print Versions:**
    - Publish both formats on Amazon, but don't check the *expanded distribution* box. Why? It will list your book as "distributed by Amazon" in Ingram's system, which could put off bookstores or libraries that avoid purchasing through Amazon.
2. **KDP Select for eBooks:**
    - Enrol your eBook in KDP Select for the first three months. This program gives Amazon exclusive rights to your eBook but comes with perks:

- o Access to Kindle Unlimited readers.
- o Promotional tools like free days or countdown deals.
- o Increased visibility through Amazon's algorithm.

**Pro Tip:**

Use KDP Select's advertising options to run campaigns that boost your book's visibility and gather reviews early. Reviews are gold for any book launch.

### Step 2: Publish on IngramSpark (Print Version Only)

While Amazon dominates eBooks, IngramSpark is the reigning champ for print distribution.

### Why IngramSpark?

- High-quality print options.
- Access to bookstores and libraries that shy away from Amazon.
- No exclusivity, so you can use it alongside other platforms.

### What to Avoid

- **eBook Distribution on IngramSpark:**
- Resist the temptation to distribute your eBook through Ingram. Subscription-based distributors may push your book through their portals, paying you only pennies. Plus, your focus should remain on Amazon eBook sales during the first three months.

**Pro Tip:**

Set your book's print discount strategically on IngramSpark—bookstores typically prefer a 55% discount, but make sure it works for your budget. Since bookstores will order in your book if asked by a customer, you can drop the discount to the lowest option.

**Pro Tip:**

Unless you have deep pockets, make your book unreturnable (no return or destroy). This means a bookstore cannot order and then return the book three months later, making you pay for the printing of the book. If you mark return, then Ingram will courier the returned books at your expense (yes, charging your credit card immediately). If you have destroy, then you pay for the printing and the bookstore (hopefully) will destroy the books. Have you seen those books in the closeout bin with a black marker across the top of the pages? That's what bookstores call destroyed, and they sell them to the closeout store,

### Step 3: Expand eBook Distribution After Three Months

Once your KDP Select exclusivity period ends, it's time to broaden your eBook's reach. Think of it as graduating from a cozy starter apartment to a swanky penthouse with panoramic views (of more markets, naturally).

### Where to Distribute Next

1. **Google Play Books:**
   - Great for Android users.
   - Offers a unique audience that doesn't rely on Amazon.
2. **Kobo:**

- Popular in Canada, Europe, and other international markets.
- Strong presence in indie bookstores and libraries through partnerships.
- Opens up Overdrive access.

3. **Apple Books (iBooks):**
   - Access to Apple's dedicated audience of iPhone, iPad, and Mac users.
   - Known for high purchasing power.

## Step 4: Leverage Amazon Reviews for Cross-Platform Success

By now, your Amazon reviews should be stacking up like pancakes at a breakfast buffet. Use these reviews to boost sales on other platforms.

### How to Do It

- **Quotes in Marketing:** Pull snippets from your glowing Amazon reviews for your social media, website, and email campaigns.
- **Showcase Credibility:** Readers are more likely to try your book on Kobo or Apple Books if they see it's already loved on Amazon.
- **Cross-Platform Links:** In your book's "About the Author" page, direct readers to your website, where they can find links to purchase on all platforms.

### Final Thoughts

Publishing on Amazon and IngramSpark while strategically timing your eBook's release on other platforms is like setting up dominoes for the perfect chain reaction. Start with Amazon to build momentum, use KDP Select for promotional perks, and then expand your reach to Google Play, Kobo, and Apple Books.

**Pro Tip:**

Patience is key. By focusing your initial efforts on one platform, you create a foundation for long-term success across all markets. Build, expand, and let those reviews work their magic.

Your book deserves to shine on every shelf—whether it's digital or physical. Follow this plan, and you'll be well on your way to seeing it thrive.

# Thank you

For reading So You Want To Write A Novel. Please take the time to either write a review or leave a star rating of the work.

Reviews and ratings are the life blood of the Independent Author and Small Press publishers. Each 5 or 2 star rating and written review tells other readers it is worth at least looking at the work. Please feel free to leave an honest review where you purchased this work.

# About Douglas Owen

Douglas Owen is a writer of fantasy, urban fantasy, science fiction, horror, and crime fiction . His short stories have been published by Cedar Cave Books and Mash Stories.

He started writing at a young age, but only started to take his writing seriously in his late 40's. In 2013 he opened DAOwen Publications. But he still finds time to write.

Doug wrote an article series called A Written View for Self Publisher Magazine, Indyfest Magazine, and Indtale Magazine. He also spent two years as a circulation manager for Indyfest and Self Publisher Magazines. also is the Circulation Manager of IndyFest Magazine.

He is also an active member of The Writers' Communicty of York Region, and spent several years as their Special Events Coordinator. One year he ran the communities special Book Shelf event, bringing multiple authors and publishers to the forefront of the region.

Constantly saying he does not want to take any other projects on, he is willing to take time and help raise funds for multiple charities.

Doug lives in Goodwood, Ontario with his wife and three cats who make sure he does not sleep past 5:00 on any given day.

Find out more about Douglas Owen on his website - https://douglasowen.ca

Follow Doug on Facebook:

Https://facebook.com/AuthorDouglasOwen